PELICAN BOOKS

A168

THE PYRAMIDS OF EGYPT

BY I. E. S. EDWARDS

I. E. S. EDWARDS

THE PYRAMIDS
OF EGYPT

DRAWINGS BY
JOHN CRUIKSHANK ROSE

—

PENGUIN BOOKS

Penguin Books Ltd, Harmondsworth, Middlesex

U. S. A.: Penguin Books Inc., 3300 Clipper Mill Road, Baltimore 11, Md

AUSTRALIA: Penguin Books Pty Ltd, 762 Whitehorse Road,
Mitcham, Victoria

CANADA: Penguin Books (Canada)Ltd, 47 Green Street,
Saint Lambert, Montreal, P.Q.

SOUTH AFRICA: Penguin Books (S.A.) Pty Ltd, Gibraltar House,
Regents Road, Sea Point, Cape Town

—

First published 1947
Reprinted 1949, 1952, 1954, 1955

Made and printed in Great Britain by
Hazell Watson and Viney Ltd., Aylesbury and London

CONTENTS

PREFACE

THE following chapters are, in the first place, an attempt to describe some of the principal features of a number of Pyramids, nearly all of which were built over a period of about a thousand years. Only those Pyramids which illustrate most clearly the evolution and subsequent decline of that class of tomb are discussed in any detail, the remainder being merely mentioned in passing. The last chapter gives some account of the methods employed in construction and of the motives which prompted the Egyptian kings to adopt the Pyramid form.

Although I have visited, either before or during the war, most of the Pyramids described and have made use of notes which I recorded on their sites, a considerable part of the factual matter is, of necessity, taken from the published reports of the various archæologists who have surveyed or excavated these monuments in the course of the past century. My debt to these archæologists and to the publishers of their reports will be apparent to every reader. Many of the interpretations given are also based on the works of previous writers; in some cases, however, I have ventured to offer explanations of my own.

I must here express my gratitude to the friends who have helped me in different ways when writing the book and, in particular, to John Cruikshank Rose, whose line-drawings are an indispensable adjunct to the text. Some of the drawings have been adapted in points of detail by Mr. Rose, either because direct reproductions from the publications in which they first appeared would have been unsuitable for the purpose of this book or because subsequent archæological discoveries have necessitated small adjustments. The authors of the books or articles from which the drawings were made are listed at the beginning of the book. For the opportunity of consulting these works while in the Middle East, I am greatly indebted to Mr. Bernhard Grdseloff, Librarian of the Egyptological Institute of the late Dr. Ludwig Borchardt in Cairo; to Dr. I. Ben-Dor, Librarian of the Palestine Archæological Museum in Jerusalem; to Dr. Nelson Glueck, Director of the American School of Oriental Research in Jerusalem, and to Mr. Seton Lloyd, Technical Adviser to the Directorate of Antiquities in Baghdad. Mr. Guy Brunton, of the Cairo Museum, kindly enabled me to obtain the photographs of objects in that Museum which are included among the Plates. For similar assistance in securing a photograph of the group-statue reproduced in Plate 10, my thanks are due to Mr. Dows Dunham of the Museum of Fine Arts, Boston. The authorities of the Metropolitan Museum have shown great generosity in allowing me to include fig. 26 before the final report of the excavation has been published. My visits to the various Pyramid sites were greatly facilitated by Dr. Étienne Drioton, Director-General of the Service des Antiquités, and by local officials of the Service.

In forming my conclusions on several problems touched upon in the course of the book, I have received valuable help from discussion with Lieut.-Colonel W. B. Emery, to whose excavations references appear in the text; with Professor J. Černý of London University; with Mr. Bernhard Grdseloff; with Mr. H. W. Fairman, Director of the Egypt Exploration Society's excavations in the two years before the war, and with Lieut.-Colonel R. D. H. Jones of the Royal Engineers. My special thanks are due to Professor A. M. Blackman of Liverpool University, and to Professor S. R. K. Glanville of Cambridge University, both of whom read my entire typescript before it went to press and whose suggestions have resulted in the introduction of several improvements; also to

Dr. Sidney Smith, Keeper of the Department of Egyptian and Assyrian Antiquities in the British Museum, who read the last chapter and contributed many helpful comments. Finally, I owe a particular debt of gratitude to my wife, who not only typed the whole of my manuscript, but helped to improve the wording of many passages in the text.

London, 1946   I. E. S. EDWARDS

PLATES

DRAWINGS

INTRODUCTION

ONE of the first questions which occur to the mind of anyone looking at an ancient monument is its date. In the case of Egyptian monuments it is often difficult, and sometimes impossible, to answer the question in terms of years before the beginning of the Christian era, because our knowledge of Egyptian chronology, especially in the early periods, is still very incomplete. We know the main sequence of events and frequently their relationship to one another, but, except in rare instances, an exact chronology will not be possible until the discovery of material of a different and more precisely datable character than anything found hitherto.

Partly for the sake of convenience and partly because a century of study has demonstrated that it is fundamentally sound, the method of grouping the kings of Egypt into thirty-one dynasties, which is first known to us from Manetho's *History of Egypt*, has been universally adopted by modern historians as a substitute for closer dating. Since the end of a dynasty did not always entail any very marked political or artistic changes, it has also been found convenient to group the dynasties into periods roughly corresponding with the most important of these changes. There are nine main periods, to which the following names and approximate dates may be given:

I and II Dynasties		Archaic Period, 3188–2815 B.C.
III — VI	„	Old Kingdom, 2815–2294 B.C.
VII — X	„	First Intermediate Period, 2294–2132 B.C.

XI — XII Dynasties		Middle Kingdom, 2132–1777 B.C.
XIII — XVII	„	Second Intermediate Period, 1777–1573 B.C.
XVIII — XX	„	New Kingdom, 1573–1090 B.C.
XXI — XXV	„	Late New Kingdom, 1090–663 B.C.
XXVI Dynasty		Saite Period, 663–525 B.C.
XXVII— XXXI Dynasties		Late Period, 525–332 B.C.

The Pyramid Age, *par excellence*, covers the second of these groups—the period beginning with the IIIrd Dynasty and ending with the VIth Dynasty. During this time the kings, with few exceptions, and many of their queens were buried in tombs having superstructures in pyramidal form. Pyramids were also built for several kings and queens of the subsequent dynasties, but they were in the nature of archaisms, lacking not only much of the architectural splendour of their predecessors, but also some of their religious significance. The total number at present known in Egypt is about eighty; many of them, it is true, are reduced to little more than sand and rubble, but they are still recognisable to the archæologist as having once been Pyramids.

Those Pyramids which belong to the Pyramid Age were built on the west bank of the Nile in the neighbourhood of Memphis, between Meidum in the south and Abu Roash in the north. If later tradition is to be believed, Memphis was built on ground which had been reclaimed by Menes, the first dynastic ruler of Egypt, by dyking the Nile so that it flowed through a channel to the east of its original course. Whether or not this tradition is true in detail, there can be little doubt that it was Menes who founded Memphis, for the archæological remains in its immediate vicinity dating from

MEDITERRANEAN SEA

XVII
BUTO XII
SAIS XVI TANIS
V ES-SIMBELLAWEIN
BUSIRIS XIX XIV
IX XI XX
III IV XVIII BUBASTIS
X ATHRIBIS VIII

LETOPOLIS II XIII
ABU ROASH HELIOPOLIS
GIZA TURA (TROJA)
ABU SIR ZAWIYET EL-ARYAN
SAKKARA MEMPHIS
DAHSHUR MAZGHUNA
LAKE MOERIS LISHT XXI
EL-FAIYUM MEIDUM XXII
HAWARA
ILLAHUN
HERAKLEOPOLIS MAGNA
XX

XIX XVIII

XVII

EASTERN

XVI BENI HASAN
EL-ESHMUNEIN DESERT
XV EL-BERSHEH
EL-AMARNA
CUSAE XIV
XII
ASYUT
XIII XI BADARI
X

IX
BEIT KHALLAF
VIII VII VI
ABYDOS
DENDEREH COPTOS
NAGADA (OMBOS) KARNAK
DEIR EL-BAHRI THEBES (LUXOR)
DEIR EL-MEDINA
ARMANT IV
GEBELEIN
III
KHARGA EL-KAB
OASIS HIERAKONPOLIS
EDFU
II

BAHRIA
OASIS

RED SEA

MILES
0 50 100

I ASWAN

FIG. 1.—*Sketch-map of Egypt.*

17

the time of the Ist Dynasty are plentiful, whereas nothing has yet been found there which can be ascribed to an earlier period. The discovery of a considerable number of pre-dynastic settlements near the Mukattam hills, on the opposite bank of the river, only emphasises the complete absence of any corresponding settlements at Memphis itself.

Hitherto, it has not been possible to determine with certainty whether Memphis was designed by Menes to be the capital of Egypt or whether it was originally built simply as a fortress-city and became the seat of government at some later date, perhaps at the beginning of the IIIrd Dynasty. The circumstances surrounding the accession of Menes to the throne would undoubtedly favour the choice of just such a place for his capital. Before his reign, Egypt was composed of two separate kingdoms: the one extending from Aswan, in the south, to the neighbourhood of Memphis, and the other covering the remainder of the country northwards, which included the whole of the Delta area. The capital of the southern (Upper Egyptian) kingdom was situated at Nekhen (Hierakonpolis) and the capital of the northern (Lower Egyptian) kingdom at Pe (Buto). Menes, at first king of Upper Egypt only, overcame the northern kingdom and merged the two former kingdoms into one, establishing himself as ruler over the whole land. Memphis would thus have been the natural place for him to build a strongly fortified city because, being situated almost at the frontier between the two former kingdoms, it would have provided a powerful deterrent against any attempts at retaliation by the vanquished northerners if at any time they had suspected weakness in the south. It would also have been the most convenient centre for administering the newly united country.

By unifying the two kingdoms, Menes performed a military feat which may have been attempted by others before his time, but never with more than temporary success. Menes, however, both achieved the military victory necessary for uniting the two kingdoms and ensured that its effects would be lasting by following it up with an astute political policy on which the greatness of Egypt in the subsequent dynasties was founded. Nevertheless, the historical fact that Egypt had once consisted of two separate kingdoms was never entirely forgotten by its people, for down to the latest times the Pharaohs still included among their titles that of "King of Upper and Lower Egypt."

We have scarcely any detailed knowledge of the methods of political administration employed by Menes and his early successors, but it seems clear that they introduced a high degree of centralisation. Recent excavations by W. B. Emery at Sakkara, the necropolis of Memphis, have brought to light numerous tombs of courtiers and officials of the first two dynasties; many more are known to be lying under the sand awaiting excavation. It is evident from the numbers of these tombs and the titles of their owners that the king was surrounded by a large body of counsellors and executives; a complete lack of biographical detail, however, precludes any reconstruction of their personal history.

Even before the reign of Menes, Egypt was divided into districts, which we generally call *nomes* after their Greek name. Their number had probably varied from time to time, as the more powerful had absorbed the weaker or the larger had decayed internally and had disintegrated; at the time when Menes achieved his conquest there appear to have been forty-two, twenty-two being in Upper Egypt and twenty in Lower Egypt. Menes allowed the *nomes* to continue as separate units, but placed at the head of each a governor, who was responsible for directing its social and religious affairs. At first these governors, or nomarchs as they are generally called, held office for only a limited period, but by degrees the office became the hereditary right of certain families. Thus there grew up a provincial ruling class which gradually threatened the authority of the king until, at the end of the VIth Dynasty, it played an important part in the collapse of the monarchy.

We know little about the political constitution of the *nomes* or their relations with the capital—though doubtless each *nome* was required to contribute to the royal exchequer, but it seems clear that they were permitted a very high degree of religious independence. Every *nome* possessed its own local deity or deities, usually represented in animal form or in human form with an animal head: Wepwawet, the wolf-god of the Asyut *nome*; Bastet, the cat-goddess of Bubastis, and Harsaphes, the ram-headed god of Herakleopolis, are examples. Some local gods, however, were always represented entirely anthropomorphically, Ptah of Memphis, Min of Coptos and Osiris being three of the best known.

Within a single *nome* many different deities might be worshipped, their relative importance naturally varying according to the number of their adherents and the wealth of their temples. In the Memphite *nome*, for example, there were, besides the principal god Ptah, also Sekhmet, a lioness-headed goddess, Nefertum, an anthropomorphic god with a lotus-flower headdress, and Sokar, a falcon-headed god who dwelt in the desert west of Memphis. Each of these deities originally possessed an independent sanctuary, but, in the course of time, Ptah, Sekhmet and Nefertum came to be considered as a single family and were worshipped in one sanctuary. There were similar triads elsewhere—Osiris, Isis and Horus forming the most famous.

In permitting complete religious independence to the different *nomes*, the early kings can hardly be accused of having allowed their conduct of affairs to be dictated by reasons of political expediency; in an age when polytheism was the universally accepted philosophy, no alteration in the established religious order would have seemed to them either necessary or desirable. With the possible exception of a few gods connected with the elements, who appear to have gained wider recognition at a very early date, most of the deities were regarded as having authority mainly within fixed geographical limits. It is certainly useless to speculate on the effect which a less liberal policy would have had on the subsequent development of Egyptian religion. But it is of importance to realise that the different elements which determined the character of that religion, as it is known to us, were chiefly local in origin. Herein lies the reason for many of the divergent, and sometimes even contradictory, beliefs held by the Egyptians in dynastic times.

The development of an official religion began in the Pyramid Age. It was derived from the cult of a temple with a powerful priesthood, situated a little to the north of Memphis at the city which the Greeks later called Heliopolis, known to the ancient Egyptians as On and so named in the Book of Genesis, where Potipherah is described as a priest of On. In very ancient times the cult of this temple was symbolised by a fetish in the form of a pillar, but by the beginning of the dynastic age it had become the centre of the sun religion. The most sacred object within the temple was the *benben*, a pyramid-shaped stone on which the Sun-god was believed to have revealed himself in the form of a phœnix.

By historical times the priests of Heliopolis had evolved a cosmogony which affirmed that Ra-Atum, the Sun-god, had generated himself out of Nun, the primordial ocean. Ra-Atum's offspring were Shu, the god of the air, and Tefnut, goddess of moisture, who in turn had given birth to Geb, the Earth-god, and Nut, the Sky-goddess. From Geb and Nut had sprung Osiris, Isis, Seth and Nephthys. These nine deities were known as the Great Ennead of Heliopolis. There was also a Little Ennead, composed of a group of lesser gods under the leadership of Horus.

Ra-Atum was not, however, the only form in which the Sun-god was worshipped at Heliopolis: Horakhti—meaning Horus of the horizon—and Khepri, in the form of a scarab, were also venerated there. Some attempt was made by the Heliopolitan priesthood to differentiate between these forms, Khepri being regarded as the morning sun and Ra-Atum as the evening sun, but the distinction was never very strictly observed. The Egyptians of the Pyramid Age clearly found little difficulty in regarding their Sun-god not as a single indivisible being but rather as a composite deity whose various attributes were derived from local solar deities, originally separate and subsequently united, without proper co-ordination, with Ra of Heliopolis. It is not surprising, therefore, that the sun-cult contains many inconsistencies as it is presented in the earliest body of religious texts in our possession, namely the texts carved on the walls of the chambers and corridors of Pyramids in the Vth and VIth Dynasties.

In order to illustrate the divergent beliefs which might exist simultaneously, it is only necessary to cite the various explanations offered to account for the daily passage of the sun across the earth. According to the view most commonly accepted, Ra, accompanied by his retinue, traversed the sky each day in a boat. The moon and the stars were likewise believed to journey across the sky in ships. No method of transport would seem more natural to the ancient Egyptian than a ship, for both he and his ancestors from time immemorial had used the Nile to travel from place to place, and it was only logical that the heavenly bodies should be conveyed on their celestial journey by similar means.

According to another school of thought, the sun was carried through the firmament on wings like a bird. This belief was particularly associated with the Sun-god in the form of Horakhti, who, since the earliest times, had been regarded as a falcon. Inasmuch as no visible object could support itself for long in the air unless it had wings, it must have seemed only reasonable that the sun should be subject to the same fundamental laws as other bodies. The falcon was chosen because it excelled all other birds known to the Egyptians in its ability to fly at a very great height.

Possibly the most picturesque of all the different ideas concerning the passage of the sun across the sky was that which ascribed to the Sun-god the form of a scarab-beetle; this conception was especially connected with him in his name of Khepri. The ancient Egyptian was familiar with the spectacle of the scarab-beetle pushing a ball of dung along the ground until it found a suitable crevice in which to deposit it. From this ball, he believed, the young scarab, by a process of self-generation, subsequently emerged. In view of an imagined resemblance between the sun, regarded as the source of all life, and the ball of dung from which the young scarab was thought to emerge, it is not surprising that the force which propelled the sun across the sky, namely the Sun-god, should have been pictured as an enormous beetle, which pushed the sun as its earthly counterpart pushed the ball of dung. In this connection it is immaterial that modern entomologists have shown that the ball of dung rolled along by the beetle is simply a reserve food-supply, while the one which contains the egg is not spherical but pear-shaped, and is kept in a hole by the mother-insect until ready to hatch.

The nocturnal course of the sun also gave rise to different theories. There was the natural explanation that it spent the hours of darkness passing by ship through the Underworld, called the Dat, before reappearing above ground each day at sunrise. A more fanciful solution, however, postulated that the sky was formed by the body of the goddess Nut, spanning the earth like an enormous arch, with her head on a level with the western horizon, her groin on the eastern horizon and her arms and legs extended beneath the horizon. The sun was consumed by this goddess every evening at sunset and traversed her body during the night, to be reborn at sunrise. It was an explanation which never lost its appeal to the Egyptians and which, until the latest times, continued side by side with that of the sun's nocturnal passage through the Dat.

The solar cult of Heliopolis, while exercising a predominant influence on the religion of the Pyramid builders, was compelled to recognise, and in time to incorporate within its theology, a cult which was certainly not solar in origin, namely that of the god Osiris. This cult, in the form in which we know it, suffers from almost as many inconsistencies as that of the sun, and from a similar necessity to embody beliefs derived from originally unrelated local gods into the cult of the principal god with whom they had become assimilated.

In remote antiquity, before the union of Upper and Lower Egypt under Menes, Osiris had been probably first the king and then the local god of the ninth Lower Egyptian *nome*, with its capital at Busiris. Subsequently his influence spread until he became the chief god of a group of *nomes* in the eastern Delta. At some time during this development he was identified with a local god named Anjeti and assumed his insignia—the shepherd's crook and the flail. Horus, later regarded as the son of Osiris, was at this time a completely independent god, ruling a group of *nomes* in the western Delta. Isis, who figures in Pyramid times as the wife of Osiris, seems also to have been a Delta goddess, but nothing is known with certainty about her origin.

After the cult of Osiris had become linked with that of the neighbouring god Horus, the two deities being regarded as father and son, its influence began to extend southwards until, by Pyramid times, Osiris had become identified with Sokar, the god of the Memphite necropolis, Wepwawet, the wolf-god of Asyut, Khentiamentiu, the jackal-god of Abydos, and

24

possibly others. The most important of these associations was undoubtedly that with Khentiamentiu, for, with the advance of time, Osiris came to be connected primarily with Abydos, while Busiris, his original home, gradually lost its significance.

Egyptian religious texts, though containing innumerable references to the legend on which the cult of Osiris was based, nowhere give a full and connected account of it. The reason for this omission is not far to seek, for the legend must have been so well known in ancient times that a detailed record was unnecessary. The earliest complete version known at present is that of Plutarch in his work *De Iside et Osiride*, which, though differing in detail, agrees in all important respects with the allusions in the Egyptian texts and must therefore represent substantially the standard account of all time. The following are the main features of the narrative as preserved in Plutarch and the Egyptian texts:

Osiris, the eldest son of the Earth-god Geb and the Sky-goddess Nut, ruled as a just and benevolent king over the whole earth, instructing mankind in the various arts and crafts and converting them from barbarism to a state of civilisation. In time, however, his brother Seth, prompted by jealousy, murdered him. Plutarch states that the murder was committed by a cunningly conceived trick: Seth, having prepared a banquet ostensibly in honour of his brother's return to Egypt from a foreign land, invited seventy-two of his friends to attend as guests. In the course of the meal a chest of clever workmanship was carried into the room and offered by Seth as a present to anyone who, when lying down inside it, fitted it exactly. By a prearranged plan, a number of the other guests first tried the chest, but were not of the right size. Osiris then entered it and, owing to his unusual dimensions, fitted it exactly. While he was still inside the chest, however, some of the accomplices closed it and carried it to the Nile. After ferrying it downstream to the Tanite mouth, they cast it adrift in the sea, which at length washed it ashore at Byblos.

Isis, when she discovered that Osiris had been murdered, set out on a long and eventful search for his corpse, which she ultimately found and brought back to Egypt from Byblos. For a time she remained at Khemmis, in the marshes of the Delta, keeping watch over the coffin of Osiris and awaiting the birth of her child Horus, who appears to have been conceived after his father's death. Seth, however, when out hunting, discovered the coffin and removed the body, which he cut up into fourteen or sixteen pieces, scattering them over different parts of Egypt. Isis again went in search of the body, and buried each piece in the place where she found it—the head at Abydos, the neck at Heliopolis, the left thigh at Bigeh, and other parts elsewhere. The only part missing was the virile member, which had been thrown by Seth into the river and devoured by the fish of Oxyrhynchus.

Another version of the story states that, after Isis had found the body, Ra ordered Anubis to embalm it; Isis then fluttered her wings over it and restored it to life. It is an important variant, because the process of embalmment, as we know it from the Egyptian mummies, was certainly connected closely with the Osirian legend. After being restored to life, Osiris became king of the region of the dead and thus assumed the rôle in which he figures throughout historical times.

The remainder of this legend, which is recorded on an excellently preserved papyrus dating from the New Kingdom, concerns the long and furious struggle between Seth and Horus, who resolved to slay his uncle and thus avenge his father's death. In the course of the struggle Seth plucked out one of his nephew's eyes, but Horus triumphed in the end and succeeded to the throne of Osiris. His missing eye was restored by the god Thoth and his title to his father's throne was endorsed by the verdict of a tribunal of the gods of Heliopolis.

As a result of this episode, Horus became for all time a model of filial devotion, while the eye which he lost in the struggle was henceforth regarded as a symbol for every form of sacrifice.

The sun-cult and the cult of Osiris were certainly not connected either in origin or in their main theological conception. Ra was primarily a god of the living, with whom certain privileged persons might be associated after death, while Osiris was essentially the god of the blessed dead and of the region of the dead. Both gods, however, shared one most important feature in common: they provided a divine example of survival after death. Osiris, though murdered by Seth, had been restored to life by the magic of Isis, and Ra, whose daily disappearance beneath the western horizon was considered as his death, was reborn each morning at sunrise. In the experiences of these gods, the ancient Egyptian found reason to hope for his own survival. But a continuance of life after physical death did not follow as a normal and natural consequence: it was something which could only be assured by observing the proper ritual and by supplying the dead with all the material assistance which had been required by the gods for their own survival. Herein lay the need for providing the dead with a tomb, whether Pyramid or otherwise, and with a burial which would conform in all the essential elements with an accepted pattern.

In spite of their meticulous attention to detail in practical matters, the Egyptians of the Pyramid Age never evolved a clear and precise conception of the After-life. That conservatism so noticeable in Egyptian art is even more emphasised in matters of religion; elements which had once been admitted into the canon continued side by side with later innovations, even though they were logically superfluous and sometimes irreconcilable. The impression made on the modern mind is that of a people searching in the dark for a key to truth and, having found not one but many keys resembling the pattern of the lock, retaining all lest perchance the appropriate one should be discarded.

Even in very early times, before the Osirian and solar cults had gained any considerable following, the Egyptians believed that man was composed of body and spirit. They also believed that the spirit could remain alive after physical death if the body were preserved and provided with the necessary sustenance. Where the After-life of the spirit took place is not known, but it may have been in a kind of Underworld to which access was gained, it was thought, through the pit of the tomb.

This simple conception of an After-life closely associated with the tomb and dependent on the preservation of the body was never entirely supplanted by other ideas, with the result that, in later times, we find Egyptian tombs provided with every imaginable article for the use of the dead. The tomb of Tutankhamen with its magnificent equipment, which included even chariots and regal accoutrements, is but a single instance of the persistence of this creed in a highly developed form more than two thousand years after its earliest appearance.

Simultaneously there grew up a more advanced eschatology—that of the cult of Osiris. Recent archæological discoveries have shown that this cult had its adherents at least as early as the Ist Dynasty, but the absence of any documentary evidence of its beliefs and tenets until a much later date renders any reconstruction of the creed in its early form very hazardous. Even in early times, however, the Osirian Hereafter was probably regarded as a kind of idealised version of this world, situated below the western horizon and presided over by Osiris. This region, called by the Egyptians the Fields of Reeds and subsequently known to the Greeks as the Elysian Fields, was represented in later times as a group of isles reached by a magic boat, where those who had been accepted by the god could dwell in perpetual spring. As was only fitting to the kingdom of the god of fertility, the ground yielded fabulous harvests, with corn growing to a height of nine cubits. The cultivation of these crops provided the fortunate dwellers of the Elysian Fields with their main occupation.

Abydos assumed a position of unique importance in the Osirian creed, and early supplanted Busiris as the chief centre of the cult. Temples equal in magnificence to any in Egypt were built there and dedicated to the god. It was at Abydos, according to one tradition, that Isis had found and buried the head of Osiris; another tradition alleged that she had buried there the whole of the body with the exception of the virile member. Every year it was the scene of a solemn festival, including a Passion Play in which the principal events in the life and death of Osiris were re-enacted. The thousands of potsherds still lying on the ground testify to the number of offerings presented to the god by pilgrims.

It was inconceivable to the ancient Egyptian, who regarded the After-life as a kind of mirror of this world, that an event of such importance in his earthly life as the annual festival at Abydos should not have its counterpart in the life to come. From the end of the Old Kingdom, therefore, many tombs were equipped with boats to enable their owners to make the journey to Abydos. By the Middle Kingdom, and possibly very much earlier, those who could afford the cost of a second tomb might even build a cenotaph at Abydos; their spirits could thus dwell at will near Osiris and participate in his annual festival while still maintaining through their real tombs the link with their native towns. For instance, Senusret III, one of the greatest kings of the Middle Kingdom, caused a rock cenotaph to be hewn for himself at Abydos, while his body was buried in his Pyramid at Dahshur. Those who could not afford a cenotaph would often set up, near the supposed shrine of Osiris, a stone slab carved with figures in relief and bearing an inscription, generally of a formal character, in order to ensure that their names would remain perpetually in the presence of the god.

In all matters concerning their religion, the Egyptians placed considerable reliance on the magic power of the written word. They believed that, by using the correct formulas, they could impose their will upon the gods. The spells inscribed on the walls of the chambers and corridors of the late Vth and VIth Dynasty Pyramids are the best example of this form of magic in the Pyramid Age. A remarkable instance, however, is also provided by the Osirian practice of placing the name of Osiris as a title before the name of the dead, with the object of transforming him into the god himself. The explanation of this universal deification may be that it was an extension of a privilege originally intended for the king alone. During his earthly life he was considered as the embodiment of Horus, the son of Osiris; it was only natural, therefore, that he should be regarded as Osiris when he had died and his son, the next embodiment of Horus, had succeeded him on the throne. In time, the privilege of becoming an Osiris was extended, first to other members of the royal family, then to a few chosen people not of royal blood, and finally it became a right claimed by all. We cannot actually trace these successive stages in the democratisation of the Osirian cult, but comparison with the course followed by other religious and funerary practices enables its development to be conjectured with a measure of probability.

In the solar cult also the After-life was originally considered as a royal prerogative. This After-life, however, was not to be spent either in the west or in the Underworld, but in a celestial region in the east. To reach it, the dead king must cross a lake, called the "Lily Lake," which extended from the northern horizon to that of the south. An austere figure ideas to be modified, even in fundamental respects, according to their different doctrines of the human make-up.

Whatever may have been the true function of the *ka* in relation to its owner during his earthly life, it is certain that the expectation of close association with it in the Next World provided him with one of his most cherished hopes of the After-life. The dead king and his *ka* are often mentioned in the Pyramid texts as being together, sometimes in the kingdom of the Sun-god where the *ka* acts as his guide, even introducing him to the god or providing him with the food necessary for his subsistence, and sometimes in the tomb, where the *ka* shares its benefits with the owner. Indeed, one of the Egyptian names for a tomb was the "house of the *ka*," and the priests responsible for its maintenance were called the "servants of the *ka*." It is hardly surprising therefore that the Egyptian texts occasionally refer to the dead as those " who have gone to their *kas*," so important an element in a blissful After-life was the union considered.

named "He-who-looks-behind"—a name resulting from the belief that he performed his duties facing backwards—ferried him across the lake, but only after he had been convinced that the king was entitled to enter the "Fields where the gods were begotten, over which the gods rejoice on their New Year's Days," as the eastern side was called. In order to convince the ferryman, the king could resort to a number of different stratagems: he could try to persuade him that he was bringing the Sun-god something which he needed; he could pretend that the Sun-god required him to perform some function, or he might have recourse to magic and take with him a jar containing a substance which would render the ferryman impotent to resist his demands. If other means failed, the king could entreat the Sun-god himself to instruct the ferryman to grant him a passage.

Having crossed the lake, the king stood at the gates of the Other World. Heralds were standing in readiness to announce the news of his arrival and the gods immediately gathered to greet him. One of the Pyramid texts describes the scene in the following words: "This king Pepi found the gods standing, wrapped in their garments, their white sandals on their feet. They cast off their white sandals to the earth; they threw off their garments. 'Our heart was not glad until thy coming,' they say" (Spell 518).

Once he had been admitted into this Other World, how was the king to employ his time? The Egyptian texts are very inconsistent on this point. In one of the earliest Pyramid texts it is asserted that he becomes the Sun-god's secretary and his duties are thus described: "King Unas sits before him [Ra]; King Unas opens his chest [of papers]; King Unas breaks open his edicts; King Unas signs his decrees; King Unas dispatches his messengers who weary not; King Unas does what he [Ra] says to King Unas" (Spell 309). Yet other texts present a picture of the king ruling in all the splendour which had accompanied his earthly sovereignty: courtiers surround his throne while his subjects prostrate themselves before him and kiss the ground at his feet. He even sits in judgment and issues edicts as he used to do on earth.

Every day the king would accompany the Sun-god on his voyage across the skies. Sometimes he is described as a rower in the barque, for example: "King Pepi receives to himself his oar; he takes his seat; he sits in the bow of the ship . . . he rows Ra to the West" (Spell 469). Elsewhere he is promoted to the position of captain of the barque. At night the voyage would be performed in the reverse direction, through the Under-world, thereby giving light to ordinary deceased mortals who were thought to dwell there.

With the advance of time, the dead king became even more closely associated with the Sun-god until, by the VIth Dynasty, he had become completely identified with him. One of the texts in the Pyramid of Teti expresses the relationship in the following terms: "O Ra . . . thou art Teti and Teti is thou . . . thou shinest as Teti and Teti shines as thou" (Spell 405). An even more striking instance occurs in the Pyramid texts of King Pepi, where the king is addressed thus: "Thou embarkest therein [the Sun's barque] like Ra; thou sittest down on the throne of Ra that thou mayest command the gods; for thou art Ra who came forth from Nut, who brings forth Ra every day" (Spell 606).

Closely connected with the problem of the location of the After-life and its occupations was the question of the form which the king would assume when entering upon it. The physical body was probably at all times thought to dwell in or near the tomb, while the immaterial element was believed to become at death a separate entity termed the *ba*. In early hiero-glyphic writings the *ba* was represented by a stork with a tuft of feathers on the front of its neck; later the sign was changed to a bearded human-headed bird preceded by a lamp. Possibly the

later sign was a relic of an ancient belief that the stars were simply innumerable *bas* lit up by their lamps. Although the physical and spiritual elements were thus separated, they were still interdependent; for the well-being of the *ba* could only be ensured, it was believed, if the body were preserved intact and able to receive it. Herein lay a further reason for the elaborate care taken to protect the body from disturbance and decay.

Another entity which played an important part in the for-tunes of the king was his *ka*. In Egyptian symbolism the *ka* was represented sometimes as a bearded human figure with a crown composed of two upraised arms bent at the elbow, and sometimes as the two arms in the same position but without the human figure. It came into existence at the time of the king's birth and remained with him after death. Two famous groups of reliefs in the temples of Deir-el-Bahri and Luxor, which date from the XVIIIth Dynasty, show the god Khnum creating at the same time both the royal child and his *ka* by moulding them on a potter's wheel.

The precise nature of the *ka* is far from clear. Four differ-ent explanations have been suggested: Gaston Maspero, one of the greatest of French Egyptologists, regarded it as a ... or double of its owner, made of the same substance coeval with him; Adolf Erman thought it was the embod... of the life force—that mysterious element which disting... the living from the dead; J. H. Breasted believed it... protecting genius comparable with the Christian con... of a guardian angel; Kees detects in it the personific... those abstract qualities, such as might, prosperity, r... splendour, which were essential for a continuance o... All four explanations can be justified in different con... none will fit the requirements of every instance. P... ancient Egyptians themselves did not always en... single and unalterable conception of the *ka*, but al...

CHAPTER I

MASTABAS

By far the greater part of the rich collections of Egyptian antiquities now in the museums of Egypt, Europe and America has been obtained from tombs—a fact which is attributable to the simple explanation that, whereas tombs of nearly every period during the three thousand years of Egypt's dynastic history have been found in considerable numbers, few of the houses in which the people lived or of the buildings in which they worked have survived. Even capitals of the importance and size of Memphis and Thebes have disappeared, leaving hardly any trace. Nothing remains of the palaces of those kings whose Pyramids have been from ancient times among the most famous monuments in the world; it is not even known whether they were built in Memphis itself or somewhere nearer to the actual sites of the Pyramids. So complete a disappearance can only be due to the nature of the materials and to the methods employed in construction. Houses and palaces were almost certainly composed mainly of mud-brick, wood and gesso; they were built, moreover, above ground. Tombs, on the other hand, lay partly below the ground, and those elements which stood above ground were, after the early dynasties, generally made of stone. Although the total number which has survived to the present day is large, it is but a fraction of those originally built; successive generations inhabiting the country have drawn liberally on the edifices of their predecessors when building for their own requirements.

In a land where stone of excellent quality could be obtained in abundance, it may seem strange that the rulers and governing classes should have been content to spend their lives in buildings of inferior quality to their tombs. The ancient Egyptian, however, took a different view: his house or palace was built to last for only a limited number of years and could be renewed or replaced whenever necessary, but his tomb, which he called his "castle of eternity," was designed to last *for ever*. Its construction was normally finished during his lifetime. In the event of death befalling him before the completion of his tomb, it sometimes happened that the original plan was modified in detail and the building brought to an abrupt finish, either in order that he might occupy it with the minimum delay or possibly so that his relatives might save themselves the expense necessary for further work on it. Equally, if he lived to see his tomb well advanced towards completion, he might enlarge it and provide himself with a bigger and more imposing resting-place than that which he had originally contemplated.

The motive which prompted the ancient Egyptian to devote such labour to the construction of his tomb was his belief that the attainment of the After-life which he desired was dependent on the fulfilment of two primary conditions: his body must be preserved from disturbance or destruction, and the material needs of both himself and his *ka* must be supplied. This motive remained constant throughout the whole course of Egyptian history. Changes in the form of the tomb occurred not infrequently as a result of experience gained or of new religious developments, but the fundamental purpose of the tomb continued unaffected.

In pre-dynastic times the dead were buried in rectangular or oval pits dug in the sand. The body, laid on its side in a contracted posture, was wrapped in a reed mat, around which were placed a few personal belongings, such as necklaces, bangles, hunting implements and pots containing food and drink. Sometimes these graves were lined with wooden boards lashed together by thongs at the corners, forming a kind of coffin around the body. No examples of their super-structures have been preserved, but it is unlikely that they consisted of anything more substantial than a heap of sand supported at the sides by a wooden frame. With the passage of time, the sand was always liable to be blown away, with the result that the body and its appurtenances would become exposed and, unless immediately reburied, must suffer des-truction. Experience doubtless taught the successors of these early Egyptians that few bodies, when once exposed, were likely to be reburied.

From the beginning of the dynastic era, the kings and nobles overcame the risk of their graves being destroyed by the elements by building over the burial-pit a superstructure composed of sun-baked mud-brick. This form of tomb has become known in modern times as a Mastaba—an Arabic word meaning a bench. It was so named because, when en-gulfed in drift-sand to nearly its full height, it resembled the low bench built outside the modern Egyptian house where the owner sits and drinks coffee with his friends.

Among the earliest known Mastabas of the Archaic Period is one found at Sakkara by W. B. Emery, which appears to have been the tomb of Aha, the second king of Upper and Lower Egypt. It consisted of a shallow rectangular pit, which was roofed with timber and divided by cross-walls into five separate compartments. The middle compartment (fig. 2, 1) probably contained the body of the king, enclosed in a wooden coffin, while some of his most intimate possessions were placed in the adjoining chambers. So far, it was only an enlarged version of the pre-dynastic tomb. Above these chambers and covering a considerably greater area was a brick superstructure, the interior of which was divided into twenty-seven cells, intended for the storage of wine-jars, food-vessels, hunting implements and other necessities of life.

The outer faces of the walls of the superstructure, which
inclined inwards from the base to the top, were built in the
form of a series of deep recesses, nine on each side and three
at each end (fig. 2, 2). The shape of the roof can only be conjectured, for no Mastaba of this period has yet been found
with its roof intact, but it may have been either convex or flat.
Two enclosure walls (fig. 2, 3 and 4), separated by a mud-
packed pavement, surrounded the building. Between the

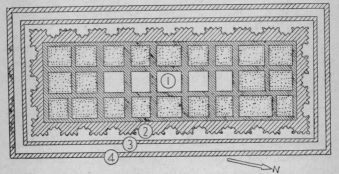

FIG. 2.—*The Mastaba of King Aha at Sakkara.*

inner wall and the eastern face of the Mastaba there may have
been an offering-place where relations could put gifts of fresh
provisions for the owner of the tomb. A coating of white
lime-stucco, parts of which may have been decorated with
coloured patterns, was laid over both the superstructure and
the enclosure walls.

Mastabas of this kind were almost certainly close copies of
the contemporary houses, thus demonstrating that the tomb
was regarded as the place where the dead were believed to
dwell. Without doubt, the arrangement of the cells was
adapted to fit the particular requirements of the tomb, but
they must have represented the various rooms in the house.

Corridors, which would have weakened the structure, were unnecessary, because it was thought that the spirit of the deceased could pass unhindered through material barriers.

By the IInd and IIIrd Dynasties the superstructures of Mastabas, while retaining the outward form of a house, had become a solid mass of rubble covered by an outer skin of brick. The recesses in the walls were often reduced to two— one near each end of the eastern wall, the southernmost of them being developed into an offering-room, built sometimes entirely within the body of the superstructure and sometimes partly outside it. In the western wall of this offering-room there was a niche which served as a false door, through which the spirit could leave and re-enter the tomb at will. The sub-structure, on the other hand, had increased in size and im-portance to such a degree that it was often composed of a kind of central hall, out of which led a number of side-chambers, intended, in the main, to store those objects which had formerly been placed in the superstructure. Among these underground apartments, hewn out of solid rock, a closet was sometimes included. The hall was entered through a door opening southwards at the bottom of a deep vertical shaft which had been driven down from the ground-level. A flight of steps or a ramp, starting from the northern end of the Mastaba, met this shaft at a point several feet above its base. It was by this ramp or staircase that the body and some of the most personal belongings were taken to the tomb. After every-thing had been placed inside the tomb, a portcullis consisting of a heavy slab of stone, which had previously been sup-ported by props, was allowed to slide down two perpen-dicular grooves flanking the doorway. The shaft and stairway were then filled up with gravel or rubble and covered with an outer layer of brick so that no visible sign remained of their existence.

To account for the transference of the storerooms from the

superstructure to the substructure, it is fair to deduce that measures to provide greater protection for the body and its belongings had become imperative. The introduction of the Mastaba had coincided with a marked elaboration in the equipment of the tomb, and, as a consequence, the risk of robbery must have been substantially increased. While this equipment was mainly stored in a brick structure above ground or in shallow pits beneath the centre of the structure, tomb-breakers would have experienced little difficulty in forcing a way to their quarry. Deeper burial, however, would certainly present the robber with a serious hindrance, but it would also complicate the task of the tomb-builder. A noticeable reduction in storage-space and a simplification in design, therefore, followed this increase in depth.

Many Mastabas of the IVth Dynasty were still built of brick, but it was the introduction into general use of stone, previously reserved for royal monuments, which marked the most significant development of this period. Even in the brick Mastabas, the offering-room and subterranean chambers were often faced with stone. The stone employed for the purpose was a fine quality limestone quarried at Tura in the Mukattam hills. This limestone was also used to face the superstructures of the stone Mastabas, while a stone of inferior quality taken from neighbouring quarries was used to build their inner cores.

In their substructures, the IVth Dynasty Mastabas, whether made of brick or of stone, present many new features. Both types often had a single room with a deep recess in one of its walls for a coffin made of wood or stone. In the south-east corner of this room the stone Mastabas sometimes had a pit, the purpose of which is not certainly known, but it was probably intended to hold the viscera which had been removed from the body of the deceased in order to help in its preservation. After the burial, the entrance to this room was blocked by a heavy limestone portcullis. The vertical shaft leading to the top of the superstructure was then filled with rubble and its mouth covered with a slab of dressed stone. The ramp adjoining the shaft, which was regularly found in the IInd and IIIrd Dynasties, was generally omitted from the stone Mastabas, though it was frequently retained in those made of brick.

The superstructures of IVth Dynasty Mastabas sometimes embodied two notable innovations which did not, however, become general until the Vth Dynasty. The first was a statue of the owner of the tomb, occasionally accompanied by statues of other members of his family, and the second was the decoration of the stone walls of the offering-rooms with scenes carved in relief and painted. The statues were placed in a chamber built within the body of the Mastaba and known in modern times as the Serdab—an Arabic word meaning a cellar. It was so called because, having no doors, windows or apertures of any kind, apart from a hole or narrow slit in one wall approximately on a level with the face of the statue, scarcely any light was admitted into the interior. Instead of a Serdab and a statue, many of the stone Mastabas at Giza contained a limestone head of the deceased owner which was mounted on blocks and placed behind the portcullis at the entrance to the tomb-chamber.

Decorated offering-rooms were only the beginning of a process of development whereby, in the Vth and VIth Dynasties, the inside of the superstructure was gradually filled with chambers and columned halls, all of which had their walls covered with reliefs. One famous Mastaba of the VIth Dynasty contained more than thirty chambers so decorated. Among the scenes most commonly carved on the walls were those which showed servants bearing offerings of food and drink to their deceased master, harvest scenes, manufacturing processes, the owner of the tomb inspecting his estates or hunting and a wide variety of other scenes closely associated with his occupations during life.

The important developments in the Mastaba from the IVth Dynasty onwards were a direct result of the realisation that the measures which had been taken to defeat the elements and the robber had also defeated their own ultimate object, namely the preservation of the body. An inevitable consequence of burying the body in a deep chamber far from the drying influence of the hot sand was that it decomposed unless some method of embalmment were employed. Many experiments in preserving the body were undoubtedly tried, but an effective process of mummification was not discovered until a later date.

Where material methods had failed, magic was introduced. In the cult of the dead, the Egyptians believed that, without depriving the deceased person of the virtues of the prototype, a model could be substituted for any article which it was not practicable to supply in actuality. For instance, in some IInd Dynasty Mastabas dummy vases were used instead of vessels filled with provisions and were thought to be equally beneficial to the owner of the tomb. Similarly, a statue or even a figure carved in relief was considered to be an effective substitute for the human body in the event of its destruction. One of the best known Mastabas of the IIIrd Dynasty was provided with figures of the deceased owner, a high official named Hesy-Ra, carved in relief on wooden panels which fitted into the recesses on the east side of the superstructure. The figures were certainly intended to enable Hesy-Ra to leave and re-enter his tomb. Outside panels of this kind were, however, very vulnerable and the Serdab was devised so as to give the figure better protection without any corresponding loss of efficacy. Even greater security was obtained by the introduction of stone figures to take the place of those made of wood.

When once the principle of substitution by means of a representation had been recognised, it was but a step to extend its scope to cover not only individual objects, such as food-vessels or statues, but also composite scenes illustrating episodes in the life of the deceased which he wanted to enjoy again in the After-life. Scenes depicting him hunting, fowling or inspecting his estates were therefore believed to provide him with the means to continue these pursuits after his death. Likewise, scenes of harvesting, slaughtering of animals, brewing and baking were thought to guarantee a constant supply of the commodities thus produced.

In order to eliminate any risk of the spirit of the deceased failing to recognise his statue, it was usually inscribed with his name and titles in hieroglyphs. Similarly, in the scenes carved in relief, short explanatory inscriptions were inserted as a kind of commentary, often giving the names of the persons represented and sometimes describing the actions which they performed. These persons were generally relatives of the deceased or his servants, who were thus assured of an After-life in the service of their master.

In spite of all the different devices for securing subsistence which were included in the equipment of the tomb, a regular supply of fresh provisions was always thought essential for the well-being of the deceased. They were laid on a low flat altar, which stood in front of the false door built into the west wall of the offering-room constructed on the east side of the superstructure. This position probably resulted from the practice of building Mastabas on the high desert west of the Nile, so that the deceased, when looking out of the false door, would be facing the valley whence the offerings were usually brought.

Possibly the first offerings were presented by a son who, in providing for his deceased father's needs, symbolised Horus, the son of Osiris. Subsequent offerings would generally be brought by mortuary priests who were engaged by written contract and paid for their services. Payment took the form of land bequeathed by the deceased to the priests. As an instance, one of the sons of Chephren, the builder of the second Pyramid at Giza, bequeathed at least twelve towns as a mortuary endowment of this kind. Such land, having become the property of the priests, would be passed on by them to their heirs, who would also inherit the accompanying obligations with respect to the tomb. Experience must, however, have shown that even the most binding contracts would not be observed for longer than a limited period and, at an early date, the so-called funerary stela was introduced into the tomb to serve as a substitute for the actual offerings. This stela contained a magic formula declaring that the deceased had received the daily offerings in abundance; above the formula there was generally a scene, carved in relief, showing him seated at a table heaped with offerings presented to him by members of his family. While not intended to dispense with the regular supply of fresh provisions, the stela, by means of the magic power of its written word, provided the deceased with a valuable method of reinsurance against starvation and neglect.

However primitive and materialistic the Egyptian conception of the After-life may seem, it must be conceded that it was responsible for the production of some of the greatest artistic masterpieces in antiquity. Without the impetus provided by a practical motive, it is doubtful whether a fraction of the statues, reliefs or inscriptions which are now so universally admired would ever have been produced.

CHAPTER II

THE STEP PYRAMID

UNTIL the end of the Archaic Period both kings and nobles were probably buried in tombs made of brick. In the IIIrd Dynasty, however, the kings began to use stone—a material which had previously been used only for isolated parts of buildings. The construction of the first tomb of this kind has always been ascribed to Imhotep, the architect of King Zoser. His name became legendary among later generations of Egyptians, who regarded him not only as an architect but as a magician, an astronomer and the father of medicine. In Saite times he was deified, being considered the son of Ptah, while the Greeks identified him with their own god of medicine, Asklepios.

The site which Imhotep selected was a stretch of high ground at Sakkara overlooking the city of Memphis. It covered an area measuring approximately 597 yards from north to south and 304 yards from east to west. A short distance to the north lay the large cemetery of Ist and IInd Dynasty Mastabas which included the one attributed to Aha. Future excavations may reveal that it also contained the tombs of other predecessors of Zoser. In contrast with these kings, Zoser was buried not in a Mastaba, but beneath a monumental building which has become known as the Step Pyramid (Plate 2). It was the central and dominating feature of a large complex of stone buildings and courtyards intended for various ceremonies connected with the After-life of the king (fig. 3). Around the perimeter of the complex was a massive stone enclosure wall. Tura limestone was used throughout for the outer facings of the buildings and local stone for their inner cores.

Although most of the subterranean parts of the Step Pyramid had been thoroughly explored during the nineteenth century, it was not until the last twenty years that anything was known about the surrounding buildings. Time and deliberate destruction had reduced everything except the Pyramid itself to ruined heaps of masonry over which lay a thick layer of sand. Scientific excavation, followed by painstaking restoration by C. M. Firth, J. E. Quibell and J.-P. Lauer, working for the Antiquities Service of the Egyptian Government, have now enabled a fairly complete picture to be formed of the whole complex as it appeared at the time of Zoser's burial.

In its final form the Step Pyramid was a massive structure rising in six unequal stages to a height of 204 feet. Its base measurements were approximately 411 feet from east to west and 358 feet from north to south. Before attaining these dimensions, however, it had undergone a number of changes of plan, some of which can be clearly detected, while the remainder are admittedly hypothetical and cannot be demonstrated without dismantling a considerable part of the building. Those alterations which can be proved lie in the places where the monument has been most severely damaged and where, in consequence, surfaces which were once covered by later layers of stone have now become exposed. It is an instance, by no means unique, of archæological knowledge being gained at the expense of artistic loss.

Zoser first built a Mastaba consisting of a core of local stone faced with an outer layer of dressed Tura limestone (figs. 4 and 5, 1). This Mastaba, which was 26 feet in height, appears to have been unique in having a square ground-plan, each side being oriented approximately to face one of the four cardinal points and measuring about 207 feet. When completed, it was extended by about 14 feet on all four sides and a second facing of dressed limestone was added (figs. 4 and 5: 2). The height of this extension, however, was about 2 feet less than that of the original Mastaba and so a step Mastaba was formed (fig. 4, 2). A third enlargement added about 28 feet to the east side only, making the tomb oblong with the longer axis running from east to west (figs. 4 and 5, 3).

Before the facing of the third enlargement had been dressed, an entirely different design was adopted. The Mastaba, which was extended by $9\frac{1}{2}$ feet on each side, became the lowest stage of a four-stepped Pyramid (figs. 4 and 5, 4). On its northern side a beginning was made with the construction of a Mortuary Temple, but before either building had been finished it was decided to extend the Pyramid further towards the north

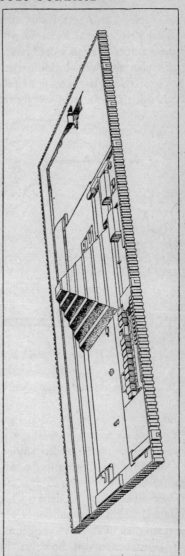

Fig. 3.—*The Step Pyramid enclosure.*

and west (figs. 4 and 5, 5). If this enlargement had been completed the height of the Pyramid would have been increased and the number of steps would have been augmented to six, but this plan also was abandoned at the level of the fourth step. The sixth and last extension of the Pyramid added a little to each side ; the six steps were completed and the whole

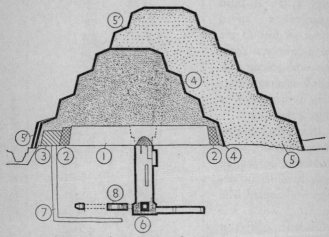

FIG. 4.—*The Step Pyramid, section looking south.*

building was cased with a final layer of dressed Tura limestone (figs. 4 and 5, 5').

The substructure of the Step Pyramid consists of a deep shaft giving access to a maze of corridors and rooms forming a hypogeum without parallel among the other Pyramids of the Old Kingdom. Owing to the fact that the construction of some of these subterranean apartments was never finished, it is not always easy to detect which were part of Zoser's design and which were additions by later explorers or robbers. The main plan of Zoser's hypogeum and the successive stages of its construction can, however, be determined with certainty (fig. 5). First, a shaft, approximately 23 feet square, was sunk to a depth of about 28 feet into the limestone substratum. A tunnel, with its ceiling 23 feet below the surface of the ground, was then driven northwards from the shaft for a

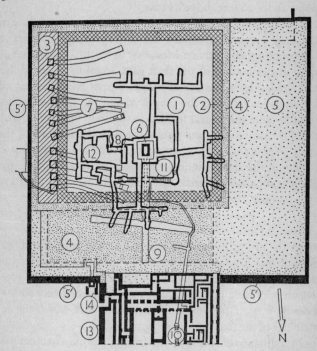

FIG. 5.—*The Step Pyramid, substructure and ground-plan.*

distance of about 66 feet. At that point, having passed the northern limit of the Mastaba which Zoser at that time intended to build, the tunnel was continued for a further 70 feet in the form of an open trench, its floor sloping gradually upwards until it reached ground-level (fig. 5, 9). Work on the shaft was then resumed until it had reached a total depth of

92 feet (fig. 5, 6). Concurrently with the deepening of the shaft, the floor of the tunnel was lowered so that it became a ramp with a progressively steeper gradient. The floor was not, however, lowered to the full depth of the shaft, but only to a point about 40 feet above its base.

In design, the vertical shaft and ramp of the substructure of the Step Pyramid resembled the corresponding elements of the contemporary private Mastabas. In the latter, however, a door at the bottom of the shaft gave access to a central hall surrounded by a number of rooms, one of which contained the body, whereas in the Step Pyramid the tomb-chamber itself became the central feature. It was built entirely of pink granite from Aswan and was situated at the bottom of the shaft (figs. 4 and 5, 6). At its northern end a hole was bored in one of the slabs spanning the roof, in order to admit the body at the time of burial. After the body had been placed in the chamber, the hole was filled with a granite plug, measuring about 6 feet in length and weighing approximately 3 tons. Above this tomb-chamber there was a room entered by a door from the ramp; it was here that the granite plug was stored until it was lowered into position. Nothing remains of this room, but it was probably built of limestone blocks. Its roof, which may have been corbelled, must have been very strong, because it bore the weight of the rubble with which the remainder of the shaft was subsequently filled.

At a distance of about 70 feet from the tomb-chamber and roughly parallel with its sides, four long galleries were hollowed out of the native rock. Flights of steps leading down from doors in the east and west walls of the ramp gave access to passages which connected the galleries one with another (fig. 5, 11). Some of these passages and galleries were never finished, but it is likely that the original intention was to cover many of their walls with panels of small blue-glazed tiles, so arranged as to resemble the reed mats which hung on the walls of Zoser's palace. Tiled panels of this kind were found in the east gallery (fig. 5, 12), which was only discovered in 1928, and in two rooms near the south-east corner of the tomb-chamber (figs. 4 and 5, 8). The panelling on the west wall of the east gallery was interrupted in three places by limestone reliefs of the king performing religious ceremonies (Plate 3A). Around the outer edge of the recesses containing these reliefs there were inscriptions giving the king's name and his titles. Similar inscriptions also flanked a doorway separating the two blue-tiled rooms near the south-east corner of the tomb-chamber. Both this doorway and some of the tiles were taken to the Berlin Museum in 1843 by the German Egyptologist, Richard Lepsius.

It is probable that, when Zoser's original Mastaba was planned, the substructure was intended to consist only of the two chambers at the bottom of the shaft, the four surrounding galleries and the connecting passages, but, after the super-structure had been enlarged for the first time, eleven vertical shafts were sunk into the ground on its east side to a depth of about 108 feet. At the bottom of each shaft a corridor was directed westwards under the superstructure (figs. 4 and 5, 7). Two fine alabaster coffins, one of which contained the remains of a child, were found at the far end of the fifth corridor from the north, while limestone pedestals for similar coffins remained in some of the other corridors. It is clear therefore that these shafts and corridors were tombs, almost certainly those of members of the royal family. Possibly each tomb was origin-ally intended to have its independent superstructure, but ultimately they were all buried under the third extension ot the monument, and the only means of access to them was by a long stairway leading to the northernmost tomb.

Until the fifth extension of the superstructure, the subter-ranean chambers and corridors were reached by descending the open trench and ramp from the north side (fig. 5, 9). The open trench, however, was blocked with rubble when the superstructure was extended northwards, and it became necessary to dig a new tunnel in its place. Beginning with a flight of steps situated some distance to the north of the final superstructure (fig. 5, 10), the tunnel followed a line to the west of the former trench and curved eastwards to join the original ramp near its upper end. Its course seems unnecessarily circuitous, and it is difficult to understand the motives which prompted such an expenditure of labour.

With the exception of the Mortuary Temple and the Serdab, the buildings surrounding the Step Pyramid are without any known precedent or parallel. Even the Mortuary Temple (fig. 5, 13) can only be compared with the offering-room of the Mastaba in so far as it was the scene of the funerary cult. Architecturally it was entirely different from its simple counterpart in the contemporary Mastaba. It was a large rectangular building attached to the lowest step on the north side of the Pyramid. This orientation was exceptional, almost every similar edifice in subsequent Pyramids being situated, like the offering-room of the Mastaba, east of the tomb. It was entered through a doorway in its eastern wall. No doors were fitted into this entrance, but an imitation of an open door was carved in the stone wall adjoining the northern jamb. Many other buildings in the complex were fitted with similar imitation doors, often carved to fit the exact measurements of the doorway. Beyond the entrance a long corridor with numerous turns led to two open courts, from one of which the staircase descended towards the substructure of the Pyramid. At the southern end of each court there were three gangways opening into a wide gallery. Short walls, flanked on the north side by fluted engaged columns, formed the divisions between the gangways. Engaged columns with various decorations constituted, like the imitation doors, one of the most characteristic features in the architecture of this complex. Their design was invariably suggested either by the single stem of some plant or by a bundle of stems bound together. Two rooms on the west side of the open courts, each with a stone basin in its floor, and a sanctuary with two recesses sunk into the face of the Pyramid, complete the few elements of this temple which are sufficiently preserved to be recognisable.

It is impossible to divine with any certainty the archetype by which Imhotep was guided when designing this Mortuary Temple, but it is tempting to regard it as a stone representation of the royal palace at Memphis. This explanation would be in keeping with the generally accepted opinion that most of the other buildings in the complex were copies of constructions in the palace compound. Whatever may be the true explanation, it is noticeable that most of the principal architectural features (e.g. courts, ablution-rooms and the recesses in the sanctuary) occur in pairs, suggesting that the temple was designed for the celebration of some ritual which had to be repeated. Such a ritual would have been performed for the king once as ruler of Upper Egypt and a second time as ruler of Lower Egypt.

The Serdab was situated a short distance to the east of the entrance to the Mortuary Temple (fig. 5, 14). It was built entirely of dressed Tura limestone, its front wall inclining inwards at an angle of 16° from the perpendicular to correspond with the angle of the lowest step of the Pyramid, which provided its back wall. Inside was a limestone statue of the king seated on a chair (Plate 3B). He was dressed in a long robe, which left only his hands, his feet and the tops of his shoulders exposed. On his head was a long wig covered by a linen headdress. His eyes, probably made of rock-crystal set in copper sockets, and part of the artificial beard attached to his chin—a symbol of royalty—have now disappeared. Two holes were cut in the front wall of the Serdab opposite the face, either to allow the smoke of incense to reach the statue or to enable the statue to look out.

Outside the Serdab was a small enclosure with two entrances, a narrow one at the south-east corner and the main one on the north. Sculptured representations of wooden doors were carved on the walls at each side of the main entrance, giving the impression of doors swung open so that the Serdab could be seen from the large open court outside the enclosure.

Two large rectangular buildings with curved roofs dominated the whole area lying east both of the Serdab court and of the Pyramid. Each was composed of a solid core of masonry overlaid with dressed Tura limestone. The southern face was decorated with four engaged columns which, together with a broad pilaster at each side, supported a cornice following the curve of the roof. In the more northern of the two buildings vertical flutings were carved on both the engaged columns and the pilasters. In the southern the engaged columns were similarly fluted, but the pilasters were ribbed. The capitals of the engaged columns resembled two large pendent leaves, a design found only in this complex. Near the top of the engaged columns were two square holes into which brackets supporting insignia may have been fitted.

Situated asymmetrically near the middle of the southern face of each building was an entrance giving access to a narrow passage which led, by way of two right-angled turns, to a small cruciform sanctuary. Three niches, intended either for offerings or for statuettes, were sunk into the walls of the sanctuary. In the northern building there were also two niches in the wall at the end of the passage. The stone ceilings of the passages were carved to resemble the log rafters with which similar corridors were roofed in buildings composed of wood and mud-brick. West of the entrance, concealed from view behind the stone facing, there was a second passage leading to a small chamber which, to judge from its resemblance to the walled-up Serdab, may once have contained a statue.

In front of the two buildings were open courts, the southern being considerably the larger. Surrounding the courts was an enclosure wall, in the east side of which, near the corner of each building, there was a broad recess. In the northern court this recess was decorated with three engaged columns, each representing a single papyrus stem and flower (fig. 6). The recess in the southern court contained only one engaged column, which appears to have represented a lotus.

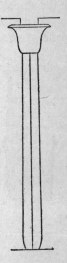

The precise purpose which these buildings were intended to serve in Zoser's After-life has never been satisfactorily explained. At one time they were believed to be the tombs of two of his daughters, Intkaes and Hetephernebti, whose names were carved on some stelæ found nearby, but recent excavation has failed to reveal anything of a funerary character in their composition and a different explanation must be sought. The decoration of the recesses in the courts seems to provide a clue, for it is known that the lotus and the papyrus were the emblems of Upper and Lower Egypt respectively. Possibly, therefore, the southern building represented the pre-dynastic national sanctuary of Upper

FIG. 6.—*Engaged papyrus column.*

Egypt, which was situated at Hierakonpolis, while the northern building represented the corresponding sanctuary of Lower Egypt at Buto. The presence of an altar, shaped like a horse's hoof, in the court of the southern building would certainly imply that the buildings fulfilled a religious rather than a secular function.

South of the enclosure wall of the southern building lay another oblong court, the east and west sides of which were occupied by a series of dummy chapels composed of solid masonry (fig. 3). In front of each chapel was a small court provided with an imitation open door. A projection from the middle of its south wall screened a niche sunk into the base of the chapel façade. Architecturally, the façades of ten out of the thirteen chapels on the west side bore a striking resemblance to the façades of the northern and southern buildings.

They consisted of three engaged columns, decorated with vertical flutings and supporting a curved cornice, the ends of which joined two broad pilasters. The capitals or these engaged columns, like those of the northern and southern buildings, were composed of two pendent leaves (fig. 7). A single round hole, cut between the leaves, supported a bracket holding an emblem. The façades of the remaining chapels of the west side and all those on the east seem to have been plain, except for a torus moulding at the top and sides.

FIG. 7. — *Capital composed of pendent leaves.*

This court and its surrounding buildings were designed to provide Zoser with the setting necessary for repeating in his After-life his jubilee ceremony, known in Egyptian as the *heb-sed*. Every king of Egypt was entitled to celebrate the *heb-sed* after occupying the throne for a certain number of years, the period varying from time to time. The origin of the festival is very obscure, but it seems to have been a relic from the remote past when kings reigned for only a limited period before being ceremonially put to death. Underlying this primitive custom was doubtless the belief that it was essential for the welfare of the kingdom that the physical vigour of its king should be unimpaired. The *heb-sed*, by enabling the king to regain his vigour through the exercise of magic, removed the necessity of replacing him by a younger man.

One of the most important elements in the *heb-sed* was a re-enactment of the coronation. In this ceremony a procession led by a *sem* priest would enter those of the chapels surrounding the *heb-sed* court in which were gathered the gods of the *nomes* of Upper Egypt. Having obtained from each god consent to the renewal of his kingship, the king would be conducted to the more southern of two thrones, placed on a dais beneath a canopy, in order to be crowned with the white crown of Upper Egypt. A similar ceremony would be repeated in the chapels of the gods of the Lower Egyptian *nomes* before the king ascended the northern throne to receive the red crown of Lower Egypt. The unification of the two kingdoms would be symbolised at a later stage by lacing lotus and papyrus flowers around a stake driven into the ground.

The significance of another ceremony in the *heb-sed* is not so apparent. The king, carrying a flail, would run a fixed course, accompanied by "the priest of the souls of Nekhen."[1] One of the reliefs discovered in the Step Pyramid seems to show Zoser performing this rite (Plate 3A). It may have been derived from a primitive belief that the fertility of the fields depended in some way on the physical agility of the king.

In addition to the chapels already described, the *heb-sed* court of the Step Pyramid still preserves at its southern end the coronation dais. The façades of the second and third chapels on the west side near the dais contained recesses approached by flights of steps. Possibly they were intended for statues of the king, the more southern statue as King of Upper Egypt and the more northern as King of Lower Egypt. The proximity of these recesses to the dais suggests that the buildings to which they belonged represented the pavilions where the king remained while the priests performed the ceremonies preceding the double coronation.

[1] The "souls of Nekhen" were the prehistoric kings of Upper Egypt whose capital was at Nekhen (Hierakonpolis).

A passage leading from the south-west corner of the *heb-sed* court connected it with a smaller court in which stood a building of medium size. Its outer walls, built with a slight batter,

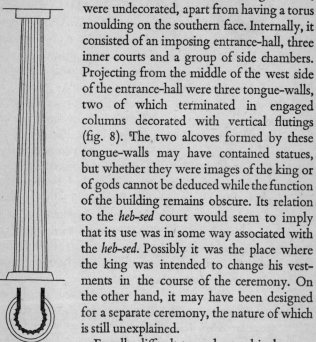

FIG. 8.—*Engaged fluted column.*

were undecorated, apart from having a torus moulding on the southern face. Internally, it consisted of an imposing entrance-hall, three inner courts and a group of side chambers. Projecting from the middle of the west side of the entrance-hall were three tongue-walls, two of which terminated in engaged columns decorated with vertical flutings (fig. 8). The two alcoves formed by these tongue-walls may have contained statues, but whether they were images of the king or of gods cannot be deduced while the function of the building remains obscure. Its relation to the *heb-sed* court would seem to imply that its use was in some way associated with the *heb-sed*. Possibly it was the place where the king was intended to change his vestments in the course of the ceremony. On the other hand, it may have been designed for a separate ceremony, the nature of which is still unexplained.

Equally difficult to understand is the purpose of a maze of corridors and chambers which led out of the *heb-sed* court at the south-east corner. In the absence of any distinctive architectural features, it has been conjectured that they too had some connection with the *heb-sed*.

A corridor linked the *heb-sed* court with the eastern end of a colonnade, close to a gateway in the enclosure wall which provided the only entrance into the complex. This colonnade consisted of a long narrow passage running westwards between a series of alcoves formed by tongue-walls which projected from each side (Plate 4). These tongue-walls, of which there were forty, terminated in engaged columns with a ribbed decoration, the ribs varying in number from seventeen to nineteen (fig. 9). Within the alcoves there may have been statues of the king, those on the south side representing him as King of Upper Egypt and those on the north side as King of Lower Egypt. Since, however, the alcoves so nearly correspond in number with the forty-two *nomes*, it has been suggested that each contained a double statue of the king and a *nome-god*, but, although groups of this kind are known in the IVth Dynasty, excavation has revealed no trace of such sculpture in this colonnade. The whole building was covered with a flat stone roof, carved on the underside to imitate rounded logs of wood. Slits cut at an oblique angle in the side walls near the roof admitted beams of light which may have been directed on the sculpture in the alcoves.

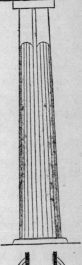

Attached to the western end of the colonnade was a small transverse vestibule. Its roof, which resembled in pattern that of the colonnade, was supported by eight

Fig. 9.—*Engaged ribbed column.*

ribbed columns joined in pairs by cross-walls. In its west wall was a reproduction in stone of an open door giving access to a large open court which occupied the whole area from the south face of the Step Pyramid to the enclosure wall. The side walls of the court were made of dressed limestone, decorated with recessed panelling. At its northern end, near the Pyramid, was an altar approached by a ramp. There were also two constructions, each in the form of a pair of hooves, south of the altar. Possibly they marked the limits of some ceremonial procession, but no evidence of its nature has hitherto come to light.

In the south-west corner of the southern court adjoining the enclosure was a rectangular building composed almost entirely of solid masonry. Its outer walls of dressed limestone were decorated at the top with a frieze of cobras. Inside, it contained only two elongated chambers set at right angles to each other. Unless this building was connected in some way with the ceremonies of the southern court, it must have served as the offering-room for a large Mastaba, the superstructure of which, with its longer axis running exceptionally from east to west, was mainly concealed within the body of the enclosure wall. Its position on the north side of the Mastaba would correspond with the orientation of the Mortuary Temple in its relation to the Step Pyramid.

The substructure of this south Mastaba shares many features in common with the Step Pyramid. A tomb-chamber, made of blocks of pink granite, was built at the bottom of the vertical shaft. Its flat roof contained a hole (which was subsequently stopped with a granite plug) to admit the body. Immediately above the tomb-chamber was a second room, intended for storing the plug before the burial, its roof supporting the rubble-filling of the shaft. The side-ramp, however, instead of entering this room like its counterpart in the Step Pyramid, skirted it on the south side and gave access directly to the galleries, all of which were situated east of the tomb-chamber. In one gallery there were three separate reliefs of the king engaged in the performance of religious ceremonies. In a parallel gallery, a short distance to the west, the backs of three doors were carved in the limestone facing of the wall. Their position, approximately behind the reliefs, suggests that the panels containing the reliefs were regarded as false doors through which the king was in the act of emerging. The walls of several of these galleries were covered with the blue-glazed tiles imitating mural hangings made of reeds (Plate 5).

Since Zoser was almost certainly buried under the Step Pyramid, it is difficult to account for the construction within the same complex of a second tomb having every appearance of being intended for him. We know that the kings of Egypt did sometimes build more than one tomb—Seneferu, the first king of the IVth Dynasty, for instance, had one Pyramid at Meidum and a second at Dahshur—and the reliefs on the false doors of the south Mastaba are strong evidence that Zoser intended the tomb for his own use. The granite tomb-chamber, however, measured only 5 feet 3 inches square, which would not have contained the body of a person of normal stature unless in a contracted position—a manner of burial which is unlikely to have been used for a royal person in the IIIrd Dynasty. It has therefore been suggested that the tomb was either a dummy, designed for use in the symbolic sacrifice of the king during the *heb-sed*, or the actual burial-place of his entrails, which were removed from the body to aid its preservation.

Two parallel structures of solid masonry covered nearly the whole of the west side of the complex. The outer wall of the first structure, where it faced the south court, was decorated with recessed panelling, which gave it a uniform appearance with the walls on the south and east sides of the court. The second structure, which was higher than the first, had a curved roof resembling the roof of the south Mastaba. It may therefore have been the superstructure of a row of tombs belonging to Zoser's attendants, but, owing to the friable nature of the underlying rock, complete excavation has hitherto been impossible. Beyond these two structures was the thick enclosure wall.

The area between the Mortuary Temple and the northern

enclosure wall may never have been finished, its only recognisable features being a large terrace with courts and a platform, measuring approximately 50 feet square, cut out of the native rock. This platform, which was faced with dressed limestone, was nearly in line with the north-south axis of the Pyramid, and it is very possible that it served as an altar. The body of the enclosure wall on this side was built in the form of cells with dividing walls of stone. Since no trace of any object which might have been placed in these cells was discovered during excavation, it is unlikely that they were ever used for the purpose of storing funerary equipment. Beneath them, however, were subterranean chambers containing bread, fruit and other means of subsistence for life in the Next World.

The enclosure wall of the Step Pyramid complex measured approximately 33 feet in height, and had a peripheral length of more than a mile (fig. 3). It was composed of a thick inner core of masonry faced, partly inside and entirely outside, with dressed Tura limestone. On the outside, at intervals of $13\frac{1}{2}$ feet, there were rectangular bastions, all of uniform size apart from fourteen which were larger. On each of these larger bastions, which were spaced irregularly around the wall, an imitation was carved of closed double doors, giving the bastions the appearance of towered gateways. The only actual doorway was near the southern corner of the east side, where two towers flanked a narrow passage leading to the entrance colonnade. Similar imitations of double doors, but in an open position, were carved on the walls inside the towers. The whole outer face of the wall was panelled, and its upper half was decorated with small inset rectangles arranged vertically in rows of eight.

Walls composed of alternating projections and recesses are found in Egyptian tombs dating from the earliest dynastic times. The brick Mastaba, not far from the Step Pyramid, which has been attributed to Aha is only one of the many examples known. In that Mastaba, however, the enclosure walls were not crenellated, but plain (fig. 2). The presence of the fourteen bastions and gateways in Zoser's wall strongly suggests that it was not intended to be a mere representation of his palace wall, but a stone copy of the famous "White Walls" built around Memphis by Menes. The "White Walls," it must be supposed, were made of mud-brick overlaid with white gesso.

To review the Step Pyramid as a whole: it is certainly not an exaggeration to describe it as one of the most remarkable architectural works produced by the ancient Egyptians. That later generations regarded it with exceptional esteem is clear, not only from the veneration which they accorded to Imhotep, but also from hieratic graffiti on the passage walls of the southern building, which record the admiration felt by some Egyptians who visited the monument more than a thousand years after it was built. No other known Pyramid was surrounded with such an array of imposing buildings to supply the needs of the king in his After-life. In their place the kings who ruled two dynasties later were content with pictorial representations carved in relief. As an example, the Pyramid complex of Sahura, the second king of the Vth Dynasty, contains only reliefs of the *heb-sed*; it has no court with buildings specially designed for use in the ceremony.

Doubts have sometimes been entertained whether so high a degree of architectural perfection could have been achieved without having been preceded by a long process of development. There is, however, no evidence that stone had been employed in any earlier building, except for the construction of isolated parts. Moreover, the Step Pyramid displays many features which suggest that its builders lacked experience in the use of stone. Small blocks which could be easily handled were used instead of the massive slabs found in later buildings, showing that the technique of quarrying and manipulating heavy pieces of stone had not then been mastered. Again, engaged columns were probably not the outcome of artistic preference, but of doubt regarding the strength of the free-standing pillar. In decoration too the patterns chosen were copied from the wood, reed or brick elements of earlier buildings; independent forms suited to stone had not yet been evolved.

Size and architectural design were not the only respects in which Zoser's Pyramid excelled the tombs of his predecessors. It was also equipped on a scale never attempted before. In spite of being subjected to plundering over a period of at least four thousand years, it has yielded during recent excavations thousands of beautifully shaped vases and dishes made of alabaster, schist, porphyry, breccia, quartz crystal, serpentine and many other stones. Considerable quantities still await removal from the tombs of the royal family, where they may be seen lying in heaps reaching from the floor to the ceiling. No food or other commodity was placed in most of these vessels; their very presence, possibly in conjunction with the recitation of a magic formula by the priest, was enough to ensure a constant supply of their appropriate contents for the king.

Before its destruction, the enclosure must have contained a considerable number of statues. Only the seated figure of Zoser in the Serdab has been preserved substantially intact, but fragments of other statues have also been found. At the northern end of the *heb-sed* court there is a limestone pedestal on the top of which are carved eight human feet; it must therefore have supported a group of four statues, possibly those of the king, queen and two princesses. In the same court there were found three large monolithic figures, only one of which had been finished. At first sight these figures resemble caryatides, but it is highly unlikely that they were

designed to stand as independent columns; they were probably intended to be built into niches. Fragments of other
statues, including at least one of the king, were discovered
outside the enclosure wall and in a recess in the south wall of
the entrance colonnade. All these statues, and possibly several
more which have now disappeared without trace, were made
not to commemorate the persons whom they represented, but
to provide their spirits with a substitute for their bodies during
the various ceremonies performed within the Pyramid enclosure. Since only two royal statues dating from an earlier
period—both representing a predecessor of Zoser, Khasekhem
—have hitherto been discovered, it is highly probable that
Zoser's reign marked a big advance in the production of
sculpture in the round. The figure in the Serdab, if it may be
regarded as typical, suggests that the collection of statues once
contained in the enclosure was of a quality comparable with
the finest masterpieces of the succeeding dynasties.

Before the recent excavations nothing remained visible of
Zoser's monumental works except the Pyramid itself, stripped
almost entirely of its outer casing; inside also the Pyramid
had suffered grievously. All the rubble-filling of the central
shaft and part of the blocking built into the side-ramp after
the burial were systematically removed by ancient plunderers,
so that to-day it is possible to stand on the granite roof of the
tomb-chamber and, with the aid of a powerful electric torch,
to see the underside of the lowest layer of stones which
covered the mouth of the shaft when the first Mastaba was
built. Beneath these stones the plunderers, when removing the
rubble-filling, had constructed a stout wooden platform, only
a few fragments of which now remain. That the stones, lacking the support of either the filling or the platform, have not
collapsed into the shaft is little short of miraculous.

Apart from the stone vessels, nothing has been preserved
of Zoser's tomb furniture. In the tomb-chamber, however,

some human remains were found; although there is no proof that they belonged to Zoser, the method of their burial would have been consistent with the practice of his time. The eleven tombs of the royal family were similarly plundered, leaving only the two alabaster coffins already described. One of these coffins—that containing the skeleton of a child—was lined with six layers of wood, each less than a quarter of an inch in thickness. They were laid with their grains running alternately in vertical and horizontal directions, and were held together by small wooden pegs. Some gold rivets, found in the innermost layer, suggest that this wooden lining was originally overlaid with gold.

It is impossible to estimate with any accuracy when the plundering of the Step Pyramid was begun. The graffiti in the southern building suggest that the surrounding structures were substantially intact during the New Kingdom, but it does not follow that the tomb itself had not been robbed of its most valuable furniture by that time. The three reliefs of Zoser in the eastern gallery may provide evidence that access could be gained to the subterranean chambers and corridors during the Saite Period. Each relief has been divided by ink lines into squares, indicating that a scale reproduction of it was planned. Since the Saites are known to have modelled some of their sculpture on the works of the Old Kingdom, it is not unlikely that they were the artists who drew these grids over the reliefs. Other intruders were guided by baser motives, and a steady process of denudation probably continued without hindrance until the present century.

Recently the Service des Antiquités, under the direction of J.-P. Lauer, has done a considerable amount of restoration work within the enclosure. The entrance colonnade, the south-east corner of the enclosure wall and isolated parts of several other buildings have been reassembled.

CHAPTER III

THE TRANSITION
TO THE TRUE PYRAMID

BEFORE the first geometrically true Pyramid was built, at least four pyramidal tombs, besides that of Zoser, had been planned. Two of these tombs were situated at Zawiyet-el-Aryan, a few miles south of Giza. The older, generally known as the Layer Pyramid, seems to have had a stepped superstructure, but so little of it has been preserved that its original shape cannot be determined with any certainty. Work on the second, which was probably also planned as a step Pyramid, may have been abandoned before it had progressed beyond the lowest courses of the superstructure; the substructure, however, had been completely excavated and the construction of the tomb-chamber begun. A rectangular shaft, measuring 82 feet in length and 46 feet in width, was sunk in the substratum of rock to a depth of nearly 85 feet. Adjoining the north side of this shaft was a wide, open corridor leading steeply up to ground-level. Two parallel flights of steps, separated by a broad raised ramp and bounded on each side by similar ramps, were cut in the rock floor of this corridor for part of its length. Down these ramps were lowered, with the aid of ropes, the large foundation blocks of limestone laid at the bottom of the shaft and the slabs of red Aswan granite used for the partly constructed tomb-chamber. By the same method also an oval granite sarcophagus, found in the tomb-chamber, must have been lowered into the shaft.

Some of the foundation blocks in the Unfinished Pyramid were found to bear the name Neb-ka, written on them by quarrymen. Since the pattern of the substructure resembles the work of the IIIrd Dynasty, it has been supposed that the tomb was intended for a king, Neb-ka (or Neb-ka-Ra), who belonged to that dynasty, but of whom nothing beyond his name is known.

The builder of the Layer Pyramid is equally obscure. Some bowls discovered in a Mastaba nearby were inscribed with the royal name Kha-bau, and the Pyramid has therefore been tentatively assigned to him. The American archæologist, G. A. Reisner, who conducted extensive investigations on the sites of both these Pyramids some years after they had first been excavated by Alessandro Barsanti, ascribed the Layer Pyramid to the IInd Dynasty. If this view were correct, it would follow that Zoser was not the first king to build his tomb entirely of stone; but the evidence, based on considerations of style alone, is certainly not conclusive.

The next Pyramid was built at Dahshur. Although it may have been planned as a true Pyramid, it was not completed as such; at a point somewhat above half its height the angle of its incline decreases abruptly (figs. 10 and 11). It has, therefore, been variously named the "Bent," "False," "Rhomboidal" and "Blunted" Pyramid. Rising at an angle of 54° 14' in the lower portion, its sides are continued to the apex at an angle of 42° 59'. Unless the change of angle was deliberate, the only apparent explanation of it is that first suggested more than a century ago by Sir J. Gardner Wilkinson, who believed that the Pyramid had been finished in a hurry, and that its height had accordingly been reduced. Confirming this view, J. S. Perring, who examined the composition of the superstructure in 1837, observed that the stones in the upper part were laid with less care than those below.

Built on a square ground-plan, each side of the Bent Pyramid measures approximately 620 feet at the base; its vertical height, when complete, would have been nearly 320 feet. It is oriented roughly on the four cardinal points, but Sir Flinders Petrie, when making his survey in 1887, found that the error from true north and south in its orientation was greater than that of either the Great Pyramid or the Pyramid of Chephren at Giza. Externally, it is the best preserved of all the surviving Pyramids; no other has retained so much of its outer casing of Tura limestone. A contributory cause of its preservation may have been the technique employed in building the casing: the stones are not laid in flat courses, but, like those of the Step Pyramid, incline inwards, thus giving the superstructure greater solidity. This method of laying rectangular blocks also had the advantage of reducing the amount of trimming necessary to bring their exterior surface into alignment with the slope of the Pyramid.

Internally, the Bent Pyramid is unique in having two separate entrances (figs. 10 and 11, 1 and 4). An aperture approximately in the middle of the northern face gives access to a narrow low-roofed corridor, which descends at a steep gradient, first through the core of the Pyramid and then through the subterranean rock (fig. 10, 1). At a distance of 257 feet from the entrance, the corridor becomes level for a further 2 feet 8 inches, where a corbelled roof suddenly rises to a height of nearly 41 feet and a kind of lofty, narrow vestibule is formed. Immediately beyond lies the lower of two chambers, measuring 20 feet 6 inches from east to west and 16 feet 2 inches from north to south, with a height of about 80 feet (fig. 10, 2). The most remarkable feature of this chamber is its corbelled roof, which is made by stepping a few inches inwards each of the fifteen upper courses of all four limestone walls, leaving at the top a span of only 1 foot in width. In the south wall of he chamber, opposite the entrance, there is a passage 10 feet in length leading to the base of a blind shaft which rises perpendicularly to a height of 42 feet 6 inches; a second passage, vertically above the first, runs from the roof of the chamber to a point higher up in the shaft. The floor of the chamber was built up to a height of several feet with small blocks of stone, some of which have been removed and piled up in the vestibule.

A second corridor leads from a point near the middle of the west face of the Pyramid to the upper chamber (fig. 11, 4). It is the only known instance during the Old Kingdom of such a corridor running from any direction except the north. After descending through the core of the superstructure for a distance of 222 feet, it reaches ground-level and then continues horizontally for a further 66 feet to join the chamber (figs. 10 and 11, 3). This chamber is not built immediately above the one connected with the northern entrance, but lies to the south-east. It has a corbelled roof, and its floor, like that of the lower chamber, was built up to a height of several feet by layers of small blocks of stone.

Access to the upper chamber cannot now be gained by way of the corridor, which has remained, since the burial, partly blocked with stones, while its entrance is still sealed with the outer casing of the Pyramid. The only means of approach is through a roughly hewn passage running from a hole in the south side of the roof of the lower chamber to a point in the horizontal section of the upper corridor. It is therefore inaccessible without the aid of a long ladder, which cannot now be introduced. Perring, who made this difficult ascent, describes a pair of portcullises which he saw in the upper corridor, one on each side of the mouth of the passage leading from the lower chamber.[1] They were not constructed in the normal way to drop perpendicularly, but were designed to slide horizontally from recesses in the side-walls. Only the outermost of the two portcullises, however, had been closed; the one nearer to the chamber still remained in its recess. Since the closed portcullis was plastered on both its inner and

[1] Vyse and Perring, *The Pyramids of Gizeh*, Vol. III, p. 67.

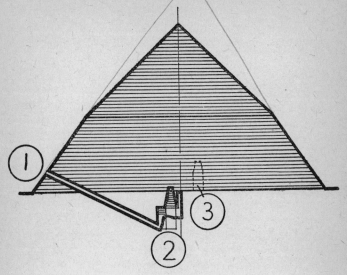

FIG. 10.—*The Bent Pyramid, section looking east.*

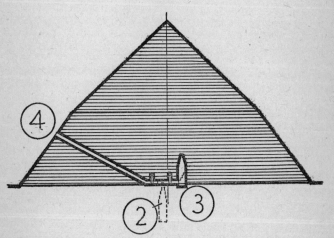

FIG. 11.—*The Bent Pyramid, section looking north.*

outer sides, Perring concluded, very logically, that it must have been closed at a time when the passage leading to the lower chamber was open; otherwise the workmen who laid the plaster would have been trapped within the Pyramid. If Perring's observations were correct, it would seem to follow that the construction of the passage connecting the two chambers dated from at least as early as the time of the burial, and was not the work of later robbers, as the roughness of its fashioning would at first suggest. It would not be the only example of such a passage being hurriedly hewn through the masonry of a Pyramid; the Great Pyramid offers a striking parallel, which will be considered in the next chapter.

Apart from some "cordage and ancient baskets" of uncertain date which Perring claims to have found in one of the corridors, no objects or tomb furniture have been recovered from the Bent Pyramid; it is not even possible to determine in which of the two chambers the coffin was placed. Tentatively, the Pyramid has been ascribed to Huni, the last king of the IIIrd Dynasty, who, according to later records, reigned for twenty-four years.[1] If this attribution is correct, the corbelled roofs in its chambers are the earliest known examples in stone of this type of vaulting, although brick corbelling had already been used in Mastabas of the IInd Dynasty.

Above ground scarcely any trace remains of the buildings which once completed the Bent Pyramid complex. Few of the architectural details will be known until the complex has been fully excavated. Some of its main features, however, have recently been ascertained by Gustave Jéquier, the Swiss Egyptologist, who examined the site on behalf of the Service des Antiquités.

At a distance of about 60 yards to the south of the Pyramid there was a second and much smaller Pyramid, the ruined superstructure of which now lies buried beneath the sand, so

[1] See, however, the postscript on p. 242.

that it is not possible to determine whether it was a true Pyramid. Internally it consisted of a sloping corridor, a short horizontal passage with a portcullis and an ascending passage opening westwards into a small corbel-roofed chamber. Subsidiary Pyramids of this kind, varying in number, are regularly found within the main Pyramid enclosures. It has generally been supposed that they were built for the queens. Some may have been used for that purpose, but others could not possibly have been tombs.

Two thick walls, a few feet apart, formed a rectangular enclosure around the Pyramid. Between the inner wall and the east side of the Pyramid there was probably a small Mortuary Temple, but no trace of it is now visible. Adjoining the east corner of the northern outer wall was the end of a Causeway, which described a wide curve as it approached the enclosure from the east—the direction of the valley. On top of the Causeway ran a passage, bounded at the sides by stone walls, which linked the enclosure with a building erected on the edge of the valley, nothing of which has yet been discovered.

The Bent Pyramid, if it has been correctly dated, provides the first example of what subsequently became the standard design for an Old Kingdom Pyramid complex, the essential elements of which were always the Pyramid itself standing on high ground within an enclosure, the Mortuary Temple, the sloping Causeway and the building on the western limit of the cultivation, usually called—somewhat erroneously—the Valley Temple or the Portal. A canal was dug from the river to the Valley Building in order to enable the funeral procession of boats to reach the complex without a long journey overland.

The last of the precursors of the true Pyramid was built at Meidum, about twenty-eight miles south of Dahshur. Its superstructure, which is still covered to about a third of its

height with sand, has been so badly destroyed that it now
resembles a high rectangular tower rather than a Pyramid
(Plate 6A). This shape is not entirely accidental, but is partly due
to the method of its construction, the main features of which
became known through Sir Flinders Petrie's excavations in
1891. Subsequent investigations, conducted at different times

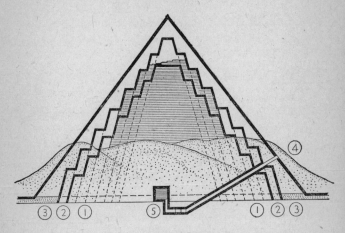

FIG. 12.—*The Pyramid of Meidum, section looking west.*

by G. A. Wainwright, Ludwig Borchardt and Alan Rowe,
have added many important details to Petrie's discoveries.

Like Zoser's Pyramid, the Pyramid of Meidum underwent
a number of transformations before attaining its final form.
It may have begun as a Mastaba or possibly as a small step
Pyramid, the superstructure of which would now be concealed
within the surviving core; its shape cannot therefore be determined with certainty. Some blocks recovered in the course
of excavation bore drawings scratched by quarrymen which
showed Pyramids with two, three and four steps, possibly
representing successive enlargements of the original design.

The first ascertainable form of the superstructure is that of a seven-stepped Pyramid (fig. 12, 1). This form was achieved by increasing the height of the earlier construction and making the tower-like building so produced furnish both the nucleus and the top step of the Pyramid. Six thick coatings of masonry, diminishing in height from the centre outwards, were then built against the four sides of this nucleus, their upper portions supplying the six remaining steps. Each of the coatings, which inclined inwards at an angle of about 75°, consisted of a core of local stone cased from top to bottom with Tura limestone. They were not bonded together, but depended on their angle of incline for cohesion. Only those parts of the casing which covered the steps were dressed, the remainder being left in the rough.

When the seven-stepped Pyramid had been completed, a considerable enlargement of the superstructure was undertaken. The top step was raised by about 45 feet and each successive step was built up to a level somewhat higher than the one above it in the previous design; a new step was added to the base (fig. 12, 2). Again the material used was local stone cased with Tura limestone, which was dressed where it was exposed.

The superstructure now visible is composed of parts of the third and fourth steps of the seven-stepped Pyramid, the whole of the fifth and sixth steps of the eight-stepped Pyramid and a small part of the seventh step (fig. 12, hatching). If the coatings which were built around the nucleus had been bonded together, the ruined superstructure would doubtless have assumed a very different appearance from that which it presents to-day. In the course of its destruction, systematic stripping of the sides, coating by coating, would have been impossible, and the Pyramid would probably have been reduced to a shapeless heap of stones.

This Pyramid was not, however, destined to remain as a

step Pyramid, although it is evident that both the seven- and the eight-stepped designs were, in their turn, intended to be final. For reasons which cannot readily be explained, the steps were filled in with a packing of local stone, and the whole structure was overlaid with a smooth facing of Tura lime-stone. By this means, the monument was transformed into a geometrically true Pyramid (fig. 12, 3). Substantial portions of the lower half of the ultimate form still remain intact, but are now almost completely covered by accumulations of sand.

The entrance to the Pyramid at each stage of its develop-ment was in the northern face (fig. 12, 4). From a point in the outermost casing, situated a little above the lowest step of the penultimate design, a corridor leads downwards at an angle of about 28°, first through the core of the superstructure and then into the substratum of rock. At a distance of about 190 feet from the entrance, the gradient ceases and the corridor continues on an even plane for a further 31 feet. Near the bottom of the gradient there is a pit in the floor, but its pur-pose is not apparent. Beyond the pit there may have been a wooden door, the frame of which would have fitted into grooves cut in the walls, roof and floor of the corridor. Two recesses, each about $8\frac{1}{2}$ feet in width and 4 feet in depth, open out of the sides of the level section of the corridor, the first on the east and the second on the west. The purpose of these recesses too is obscure, but it is tempting to think that they were intended for storing, during the construction of the Pyramid, stone plug-blocks which would have been too large to be lowered down the corridor after the burial. The area of both recesses would have been sufficient for manœuvring blocks of considerable size, and the space left vacant when they had been moved into position could have been filled with masonry. Some limestone blocks found in the recesses may actually have been used for this purpose. Such a method of sealing the passages to the tomb-chamber would be only a simplification of the side portcullises found in the western corridor of the Bent Pyramid.

At the end of the corridor a vertical shaft leads upwards, emerging in the floor of the tomb-chamber at its north-east corner (fig. 12, 5). Built partly in the rock substratum and partly in the core of the superstructure, it measures $19\frac{1}{2}$ feet from north to south and $8\frac{1}{2}$ feet from east to west. It is entirely composed of limestone, its roof consisting of overlapping layers in the form of a corbel vault. The floor also is paved with slabs of limestone, some of which have now disappeared. In the south wall there is a hole made by robbers in search of hidden treasure. Both in the shaft and in the chamber there are wooden baulks which may have been used for some purpose by the builders or, alternatively, may have been required for moving heavy funerary equipment, such as a stone sarcophagus. No trace of such a sarcophagus was, however, found in 1881 by Sir Gaston Maspero, the first archæologist to enter the Pyramid in modern times.

The buildings belonging to this Pyramid were arranged according to the same general plan as those of the Bent Pyramid complex. A wide mud-plaster pavement, bounded by a stone wall, surrounded the Pyramid. Between the south face and the wall lay a subsidiary Pyramid, now reduced to a few stones covering the substructure. Within the enclosure on the north side was a large Mastaba—an unusual feature in such a position—which has completely disappeared. Built against the middle of the east face of the Pyramid, and still almost intact, is a small Mortuary Temple composed entirely of Tura limestone. It is a very simple building, covering an area of little more than 34 feet square and rising to a maximum height of 9 feet. A door in the southern corner of its front wall opens into a passage set at right angles to the door (fig. 13, 1); beyond lies a single chamber running parallel with the passage (fig. 13, 2) and an open court which backs directly on to the Pyramid. No carvings of any kind decorate the walls of the passage or the chamber, neither of which has any opening for light except the door. In the middle of the court, opposite the door leading from the chamber, there is a low

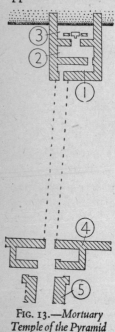

limestone altar intended for the daily offerings of food and drink for the dead king (fig. 13, 3). Two tall monolithic slabs of limestone with rounded tops, mounted on low rectangular bases of similar material, stand one on each side of the altar. Although no inscriptions have been carved on these slabs, it is clear from their shape that they were designed as funerary stelæ which might have been expected to bear the various names and titles of the king and also a formal text promising him sustenance for the After-life. The absence of such an inscription, together with the fact that the stones forming the lowest courses of the temple walls have been left undressed, would strongly suggest that the building was never finished. Possibly this explanation also accounts for the lack of a false door, which would normally have

FIG. 13.—*Mortuary Temple of the Pyramid of Meidum.*

been constructed against the east face of the Pyramid in order to allow the king to leave his tomb and partake of the offerings placed on the altar. It would, however, have been more natural to store the stones required for such a door inside the court before the walls were erected; a more probable explanation for their absence may therefore be that they were blocks of granite which, being of greater value than limestone, were removed by later despoilers without leaving any trace.

An expanse of mud-plaster paving 80 feet in width separated the Mortuary Temple from the eastern enclosure wall (fig. 13, 4). At a point in the wall nearly opposite the Temple entrance, a narrow opening gave access to the Causeway which, like its counterpart in the Bent Pyramid complex, connected the Pyramid area with a small building situated on the edge of the valley. A shallow depression in the sand is the only indication of this Causeway now visible. Past excavation, however, has shown that, when intact, it measured 235 yards in length. Its floor of mud-plaster was laid on a bed, 10 feet in width, hewn out of the rock substratum. Bounding each side was a stone wall 7 feet in height, which decreased in thickness from 5 feet at the base to 4 feet at the top (fig. 13, 5). The only break in these walls was near the upper end, where two doors allowed the Causeway to be entered from the sides. Two deep recesses at the junction of the Causeway and the enclosure wall may once have contained statues of the king, the southern as King of Upper Egypt and the northern as King of Lower Egypt; on the other hand, they may have been used for the performance of some ritual during the funeral ceremony. At the lower end of the Causeway, close to where it joined the Valley Building, there was a double door, the pivots of which fitted into two sockets cut in the rock beneath the mud-plaster floor. It is difficult to account for the presence of a door in such a position, but it may be surmised that it was intended to debar those not entitled by their office to proceed further than the Valley Building.

Excavation of the Valley Building has so far proved impracticable owing to the sodden condition of the ground, caused by a rise in the level of the Nile bed since the days when this Pyramid complex was built. The simplicity and modest dimensions of the Mortuary Temple would certainly suggest that the Valley Building was also unpretentious.

No contemporary inscriptions giving the name of the

builder of this Pyramid have been found at Meidum. In the passage and chamber of the Mortuary Temple, however, there are a number of graffiti, scribbled on the walls by visitors during the XVIIIth Dynasty, which show that the Pyramid was at that time considered to be the work of Seneferu, the first king of the IVth Dynasty. As an example, one of these graffiti may be translated as follows: "On the twelfth day of the fourth month of summer in the forty-first year of the reign of Thutmose III, the Scribe Aa-Kheper-Ra-senb, son of Amenmesu [the Scribe and Ritualist of the deceased King Thutmose I], came to see the beautiful temple of King Seneferu. He found it as though heaven were within it and the sun rising in it. Then he said: 'May heaven rain with fresh myrrh, may it drip with incense upon the roof of the temple of King Seneferu.'" Other graffiti in the Temple dating as early even as the VIth Dynasty mention the name of Seneferu, but do not state explicitly that the Temple belonged to him.

The evidence of the graffiti alone would be considered sufficient to enable the Pyramid of Meidum to be attributed to Seneferu if no other Pyramid with a comparable claim were known. At Dahshur, however, there is a Pyramid close to which, in 1894–95, J. de Morgan discovered Mastabas belonging not only to members of Seneferu's family and his functionaries, but also to priests who officiated in his Mortuary Temple.[1] Such Mastabas were usually situated near the tomb of the king to whom their owners were related or in whose service they were employed; it would therefore follow that this Pyramid too must have a claim to be regarded as the tomb of Seneferu. Fortunately, the problem is not so insoluble as it might appear, because inscriptions dating from the Old Kingdom reveal that Seneferu actually built two Pyramids, one of which was called the "Southern Pyramid." Among these inscriptions is a decree, issued by Pepi I of the VIth

[1] See postscript on p. 242.

Dynasty, exempting the inhabitants of the "two Pyramid towns of Seneferu" from certain duties. It was located by Borchardt near the Pyramid of Dahshur; this provenance is a further indication that Dahshur was one of Seneferu's two "Pyramid towns." Possibly additional evidence will be forthcoming when the complex has been excavated. Although there is no proof that the Pyramid of Meidum was the "Southern Pyramid," its geographical position in relation to Dahshur and the evidence of the graffiti create a strong presumption in its favour.

Seneferu was clearly not the only king who built more than one tomb for himself. Aha, the second king of the Ist Dynasty, seems to have had one Mastaba at Sakkara and a second at Abydos. Zoser certainly built both his Step Pyramid and a Mastaba at Sakkara, and may possibly have constructed another Mastaba at Beit Khallaf. Senusret III and Amenemhat III, both kings of the XIIth Dynasty, built Pyramids at Dahshur and second tombs elsewhere. Manifestly, however, only one tomb in each instance could have been the burial-place, while the other was, by inference, a cenotaph, the purpose of which remains conjectural. Opinion regarding Seneferu's burial-place is evenly divided. Petrie favoured the Pyramid of Meidum, basing his views on the discovery within the Pyramid of some fragments of a wooden coffin, the style of which resembled known contemporary coffins. Borchardt, on the other hand, considered the Pyramid of Dahshur the more likely sepulchre, pointing out that, whereas the tombs of mortuary priests were found at that Pyramid, none were found at Meidum. Furthermore, not only was the Mortuary Temple at the latter site left unfinished, but also a number of the surrounding Mastabas were incomplete and appear never to have been occupied. In these unfinished buildings Borchardt believed that he detected a change in an original plan to make the Pyramid of Meidum the burial-place, and the substitution for it of the Pyramid of Dahshur. Alan Rowe, in an attempt to reconcile Petrie's discovery of the coffin fragments at Meidum with Borchardt's very cogent arguments in favour of the Dahshur Pyramid, has suggested that the Dahshur Pyramid was not completed at the time of Seneferu's death and that his body was therefore placed first in the Pyramid of Meidum and later transferred to Dahshur when that Pyramid had been finished. The question is certainly not one which can be finally answered with the evidence hitherto available.

Seneferu's Pyramid at Dahshur, situated a short distance to the north of the Bent Pyramid, is the earliest tomb known to have been designed and executed as a true Pyramid.[1] Externally, its most noticeable feature is its very flat angle of inclination. Instead of rising at the normal angle of about 52°, the sides of this Pyramid incline at an angle of only 43° 36', approximating very closely in this respect to the upper portion of the Bent Pyramid. An aperture in the northern face, several feet above ground-level, gives access to the sloping corridor which descends at an angle of about 27° through the masonry core of the superstructure. At the end of the corridor there are three chambers,[2] one beyond another, the second being placed directly under the apex of the Pyramid. The first two chambers are almost identical in size and shape, each measuring about 31 feet from north to south and nearly 12 feet from east to west. Both these chambers, which are founded on the rock substratum, have high corbel-vaulted

[1] Possibly the subsidiary Pyramids belonging to the Bent Pyramid and the Pyramid of Meidum were true Pyramids, but it still remains to be proved that they were tombs.

[2] Owing to the considerable accumulations of sand and rubble which to-day encumber the lower part of the sloping corridor, the first two chambers can be entered only with difficulty. The third, probably the burial-chamber, is completely inaccessible without the aid of tackle, which cannot be introduced until the corridor has been cleared. Perring, however, reached this chamber, and the following description is based on his account.

roofs. The third chamber is reached by a short passage opening out of the south wall of the middle chamber at a height of about 25 feet above the floor. It is the largest of the three, measuring $13\frac{1}{2}$ feet from north to south and 31 feet from east to west; its corbel roof rises to a height of 50 feet.

Except in the number and size of its chambers, the Pyramid of Dahshur shows little technical advance on the Pyramid of Meidum. The fact that it was designed from the beginning as a true Pyramid has sometimes been thought to signify that its builders were applying the experience gained from the Pyramid of Meidum, which had only attained that form after a series of transformations. Both Pyramids, however, contain casing blocks dated in the same year of the reign of an unnamed king. It follows therefore that, if the Pyramids belonged to one king, work on their construction must at some stage have been carried on simultaneously. The exact position which the dated blocks, now fallen to the ground, once occupied in the Pyramid of Meidum cannot be accurately determined, but since the lower part of the casing is still intact they seem to have belonged to the upper portion. In the Pyramid of Dahshur, on the other hand, the dated blocks are situated in the lowest courses of the casing. It therefore seems likely that when these blocks were laid work was further advanced at Meidum than at Dahshur.

Without, for the present, enquiring into the motives which prompted Seneferu to build more than one Pyramid, it is possible to hazard a reconstruction of the main sequence of events which culminated in this development. Although his predecessor, Huni, appears to have abandoned the Step Pyramid design in favour of one which differed only in a single respect from the true Pyramid, Seneferu reverted to the step pattern when building his original tomb at Meidum. Before completing the tomb as it was first planned, he decided to build a second tomb at Dahshur designed from the beginning as a true Pyramid. Instead, however, of adhering to his original plan whereby he would have one Pyramid of each kind, he decided to transform the Meidum Pyramid into a true Pyramid. Why these changes of plan should have been necessary is a question which cannot be answered with certainty from the meagre information which we now possess of the political and religious events of this period, but a conjectural explanation which would account for the architectural facts will be offered in a later chapter.

CHAPTER IV

THE GIZA GROUP

SENEFERU's son and successor to the throne was Khufu, better known as Cheops, the Greek form of his name (Plate 7). Inspired possibly by the magnitude of his father's constructions at Meidum and Dahshur, he chose a plateau, situated on the edge of the desert about five miles west of Giza, and erected at its north-west corner a Pyramid of even vaster dimensions. Two later kings of the IVth Dynasty, Chephren and Mycerinus, followed his example by building their Pyramids on the same plateau, a short distance to the south. Together, these three Pyramids constitute possibly the most celebrated group of monuments in the world (Plate 1).

The Pyramid of Cheops, or the Great Pyramid, marks the apogee of Pyramid-building in respect of both size and quality. Estimated in terms of cubic content, the stone assembled in the two Pyramids of Seneferu was probably almost equal to that of the Great Pyramid, but individually they fell far short of its bulk. No exact computation of the amount of hewn stone contained in the Great Pyramid is possible, because the centre of its core consists of a nucleus of rock, the size of which cannot be precisely determined. It has, however, been estimated that, when complete, the core of local stone and the outer facing of Tura limestone were composed of about 2,300,000 separate blocks, each averaging some two and a half tons in weight and reaching a maximum of fifteen tons.

Many attempts have been made by writers on the Great Pyramid to illustrate its size by comparison with other famous buildings. It has, for instance, been calculated that the Houses of Parliament and St. Paul's Cathedral could be grouped inside the area of its base and still leave a considerable space unoccupied.[1] According to another estimate there would be room for the Cathedrals of Florence, Milan and St. Peter at Rome, as well as for Westminster Abbey and St. Paul's Cathedral.[2] It has also been reckoned that, if it were sawn into cubes measuring a foot in each dimension and these cubes were placed in a row, they would extend over a distance equal to two-thirds of the earth's periphery at the Equator. One computation of this kind has been attributed to Napoleon during his campaign in Egypt. When some of his Generals returned from climbing to the top of the Pyramid, Napoleon, who had declined to make the ascent himself, greeted them with the announcement that, according to his calculations, the three Pyramids on the Giza plateau contained enough stone to build a wall, measuring 10 feet in height and 1 foot in width, around the whole of France. The mathematician Monge, who was among the savants accompanying Napoleon on this campaign, is alleged to have confirmed this calculation.[3]

No monument in Egypt has been surveyed and measured so often and with so much care as the Great Pyramid. Even before the theories regarding the supposed esoteric significance of its angles and dimensions had been invented, Edmé-François Jomard, another of Napoleon's staff of savants, Colonel Howard Vyse and J. S. Perring (1837-38) and other pioneers of Egyptian archæology had measured the monument with as high a degree of accuracy as is required by most modern excavators. The first exhaustive survey of the monument was, however, conducted by Sir Flinders Petrie, who spent the greater part of two seasons (1880-82) at the task. His published results remained the standard work on the subject until

[1] Somers Clarke and R. Engelbach, *Ancient Egyptian Masonry*, Frontispiece.
[2] E. Baldwin Smith, *Egyptian Architecture as a Cultural Expression*, p. 96.
[3] J. Capart and Marcelle Werbrouck, *Memphis à l'ombre des pyramides*, p. 47.

1925, when they were partly superseded by a fresh survey undertaken with the help of more modern instruments by J. H. Cole of the Survey Department of the Egyptian Government.[1] From this survey it was ascertained that the following were the original measurements of the four sides at the base: north, 755·43 feet; south, 756·08 feet; east, 755·88 feet; west, 755·77 feet. While, therefore, no two sides were absolutely identical in length, the difference between the longest and the shortest was only 7·9 inches. Each side was oriented almost exactly in line with true north and south or east and west, the following being the estimated errors: north side, 2′28″ south of west; south side, 1′57″ south of west; east side, 5′30″ west of north; west side, 2′30″ west of north. As the accuracy of this orientation implies, the four corners were almost perfect right angles, their exact measurements being: north-east, 90°3′2″; north-west, 89°59′58″; south-east, 89°56′27″ and south-west, 90°0′33″. When complete, it rose to a height of 481·4 feet, the top 31 feet of which are now missing. Its four sides incline at an angle of about 51°52′ to the ground. The area covered by its base is 13·1 acres.

Although the Great Pyramid, when viewed from a distance, gives the impression of being preserved substantially intact, closer observation reveals that it has suffered severely at the hands of despoilers. About a dozen courses and the cap-stone, possibly made of granite, have been removed from the apex. The whole of the outer facing of Tura limestone, with the exception of a few pieces at the base, has been stripped off the sides. In the north face, a little below the original entrance, there is a large aperture roughly cut in the core. According to Moslem tradition, this aperture was made during the latter part

[1] *Survey of Egypt*, Paper No. 39: "The Determination of the Exact Size and Orientation of the Great Pyramid of Giza," Cairo 1925. The measurements in this report are given in metres and decimal fractions of a metre; they have here been translated into feet and decimal fractions of a foot for the sake of uniformity.

of the ninth century at the command of the Caliph Ma'mun, son of Harun al-Rashid of Arabian Nights fame, in the mistaken belief that the Pyramid contained hidden treasure. Until that time the Pyramid, though doubtless robbed of its former contents, had probably remained structurally intact. Subsequently it became a copious and convenient quarry, providing the stone required for bridges over irrigation canals, houses, walls and other buildings in the neighbourhood of Giza and Cairo.

The chambers and corridors of the Great Pyramid, if their arrangement is to be understood, must be considered in conjunction with its structural development. In contrast with the Pyramid of Meidum, the transformations which the Great Pyramid underwent in the course of construction were mainly, if not entirely, internal; its ultimate external shape and dimensions were probably those intended from the beginning. The entrance is in the north face at a height of about 55 feet, measured vertically, above ground-level (fig. 14, 1). It is not situated exactly midway across the face, but at a point about 24 feet east of the centre. From the entrance a corridor, measuring about 3 feet 5 inches in width and 3 feet 11 inches in height, descends at a gradient of 26° 31′ 23″ first through the core of the Pyramid and then through the rock. At a distance of about 345 feet from the original entrance, the corridor becomes level and continues horizontally for a further 29 feet before terminating in a chamber (fig. 14, 2). On the west side of the level section of the corridor, near the entrance to the chamber, there is a recess, the cutting of which was never completed. The chamber also is unfinished, its trenched floor and rough walls resembling a quarry. A square pit sunk in the floor may represent the first stage in an unfulfilled project for deepening the chamber. According to Vyse and Perring, who measured the chamber in 1838, its dimensions are: height, 11 feet 6 inches; east-west, 46 feet; north-south,

27 feet 1 inch. No check of their figures has since been possible because, in the course of their subsequent excavations, they filled the greater part of the chamber almost to the ceiling with blocks of stone which have not yet been removed.

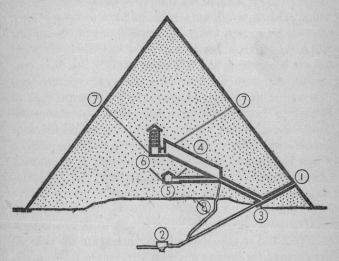

FIG. 14.—*The Great Pyramid, section looking west.*

In the south wall of the chamber, opposite the entrance, there is an opening to a blind passage, roughly hewn in the rock and obviously unfinished. The presence of this passage suggests that, if the original plan had been executed, there would have been a second chamber beyond the first and connected with it by a corridor. Such an arrangement would have as a parallel Seneferu's Pyramid at Dahshur, the main difference being that in the latter the second chamber lies directly beneath the apex and the first to the north of it, whereas in the Great Pyramid both chambers would have been situated south of a point perpendicularly under the apex.

It is of some interest to compare the half-finished rock-chamber with the brief but graphic description of the subterranean part of the Great Pyramid given to Herodotus when he visited Egypt in the middle of the fifth century B.C. Beneath the Pyramid, he was told, were vaults constructed on a kind of island, which was surrounded by water brought from the Nile by a canal. On this island the body of Cheops was said to lie. No trace, however, of either the canal or the island has yet been found, and it is most unlikely that they ever existed. Although the Pyramid had, almost certainly been opened and its contents plundered long before the time of Herodotus, it may easily have been closed again during the Saite Period, when a number of ancient monuments were restored. The story which Herodotus relates—the veracity of which he does not claim to have confirmed from his own observations—may well have been embroidered by generations of Pyramid guides extending over the greater part of two centuries.

At the time when the decision was made to alter the original project and to substitute a burial chamber in the body of the Pyramid for the one under construction in the rock, the superstructure had already been built to a height of several feet. A hole was therefore cut in the masonry-roof of the earlier Descending Corridor at a point about 60 feet from the entrance and a new Ascending Corridor was hewn upwards through the core (fig. 14, 3). The mouth of this corridor was filled, after the burial, with a slab of limestone, so that it became indistinguishable from the remainder of the roof at the upper end of the Descending Corridor. The block could not, however, have been securely fastened, because it collapsed when Ma'mun's men were boring their tunnel nearby. According to Moslem historians, it was the noise made by the fall of this block to the floor of the Descending Corridor which enabled the tunnellers to locate the Pyramid corridors, their previous operations having been directed too far to the west.

The Ascending Corridor, which is approximately 129 feet in length, corresponds in width and height with the Descending Corridor; its gradient of 26° 2′ 30″ also tallies to within a fraction of a degree. At its lower end, immediately above the gap left by the missing limestone slab, are three large plug-blocks made of granite and placed one behind another. These plugs, which completely fill the original corridor, were by-passed by Ma'mun's men, who simply cut a passage through the softer limestone of the west wall as far as a point beyond the uppermost plug. Borchardt, while making a detailed study of the walls of this corridor, observed that the stones at the lower end were laid approximately parallel with the ground, whereas nearly all those at the upper end were parallel with the gradient of the corridor. From this fact he deduced that the point at which the angle changed marked the height to which the Pyramid had already been built when it was decided to transfer the tomb-chamber to the super-structure. Borchardt also noticed that the joints of the stones at the lower end were irregular, whereas the stones at the upper end fitted closely—a feature which certainly supports his contention that the lower part of the corridor was cut through rough core-masonry already laid, while the upper part was built *pari passu* with the construction of the Pyramid. The only stones in the upper part which are not laid parallel with the gradient are the so-called "girdle-stones," a name used to describe either single stones or two stones, one above the other, through which the corridor has been hewn. These "girdle-stones," placed at regular intervals of 17 feet 2 inches, may offer a clue to the structural composition of the Great Pyramid which will be discussed in a later chapter.

When the Ascending Corridor was being constructed, the builders probably intended the burial-chamber to occupy a position in the centre of the superstructure and at no great height above ground-level. Such a chamber was actually built at the end of a passage leading from the top of the Ascending Corridor (fig. 14, 5). Called by the Arabs the "Queen's Chamber"—a misnomer which it has retained—this chamber lies exactly midway between the north and south sides of the Pyramid. Its measurements are 18 feet 10 inches from east to west and 17 feet 2 inches from north to south. It has a pointed roof, which rises to a height of 20 feet 5 inches. In the east wall there is a niche with corbelled sides; its original depth was only 3 feet 5 inches, but the back has now been cut away by treasure-seekers. Its height is 15 feet 4 inches and the width at the base 5 feet 2 inches. Presumably it was designed to contain a statue of the king, which may, however, never have been placed in position.

There are many indications that work on the Queen's Chamber was abandoned before it had been completed. The floor, for instance, is exceedingly rough; if the chamber had been finished it would probably have been paved with finer stone. Again, in the north and south walls there are small rectangular apertures from which shafts run horizontally for a distance of about 6 feet 6 inches and then turn upwards at an angle of approximately 30° (fig. 14, 6). These apertures were not cut at the time when the chamber was built—an omission which can only be explained on the hypothesis that the chamber was never finished—but in 1872 by an engineer named Waynman Dixon, who had been led to suspect the existence of the shafts by their presence in the King's Chamber above. Unlike those in the King's Chamber, however, the shafts leading from the Queen's Chamber seem to have had no outlet in the outer surface of the Pyramid; the absence of such an outlet provides further evidence of an alteration in the original plan. Possibly the same explanation also accounts for the different levels in the floor of the passage which connected the Ascending Corridor with the chamber. At first the passage is only 3 feet 9 inches in height, but nearer the chamber a sudden drop in the floor increases its height to 5 feet 8 inches.

The abandonment of the Queen's Chamber led to the construction of two of the most celebrated architectural works which have survived from the Old Kingdom, namely the Grand Gallery and the King's Chamber. The Grand Gallery (fig. 14, 4) was built as a continuation of the Ascending Corridor. It is 153 feet in length and 28 feet in height. Its walls of polished limestone rise vertically to a height of 7 feet 6 inches; above that level each of the seven courses projects inwards about 3 inches beyond the course on which it rests, thus forming a corbel vault of unparalleled dimensions. The space between the uppermost course on each side, measuring 3 feet 5 inches in width, is spanned by roofing slabs, every one of which is laid at a slightly steeper angle than the gradient of the gallery. Sir Flinders Petrie, commenting on this method of laying the slabs, says that it was done "in order that the lower edge of each stone should hitch like a pawl into a ratchet cut in the top of the walls; hence no stone can press on the one below it, so as to cause a cumulative pressure all down the roof; and each stone is separately upheld by the side-walls across which it lies."[1] At the foot of each wall a flat-topped ramp, 2 feet in height and 1 foot 8 inches in width, extends along the whole length of the gallery. A passage measuring, like the roof, 3 feet 5 inches in width runs between the two ramps. At the lower end of this passage there is now a gap, caused by the removal of the stones which formerly linked the floor of the passage with that of the Ascending Corridor and also covered the mouth of the horizontal passage leading to the Queen's Chamber. In the gap, the lowest stone in the western ramp has been removed, revealing a shaft which

[1] W. M. Flinders Petrie, *The Pyramids and Temples of Gizeh*, p. 72.

descends, partly perpendicularly and partly obliquely, first through the core of the Pyramid and then through the rock, until it emerges in the west wall of the Descending Corridor (fig. 14, 8). Its apparent purpose and the significance of some other peculiar features in the Grand Gallery will be considered after the King's Chamber has been described.

A high step at the upper end of the Grand Gallery gives access to a low and narrow passage leading to the King's Chamber. About a third of the distance along its length, the passage is heightened and enlarged into a kind of antechamber, the south, east and west walls of which are composed of red granite. Four wide slots have been cut in both the east and west walls of the antechamber, three extending to the floor and one—the northernmost—stopping at the same level as the roof of the passage. The long slots were intended for three portcullises, no traces of which have survived. Stretching across the antechamber and fitting into the short slot, there still remain two blocks of granite, one resting on the other; a third block may originally have filled the space between the upper block and the ceiling. Without such a barrier, robbers could, by climbing through the gap, have passed unhindered over the first two portcullises.

The King's Chamber, built entirely of granite, measures 34 feet 4 inches from east to west, 17 feet 2 inches from north to south, and 19 feet 1 inch in height. In the north and south walls, at a height of about 3 feet above the floor, are the rectangular apertures of shafts which differ from those of the Queen's Chamber only in penetrating the core of the Pyramid to the outer surface, the northern at an angle of 31° and the southern at an angle of 45° (fig. 14, 7). The object of these shafts is not known with certainty; they may have been designed for the ventilation of the chamber or for some religious purpose which is still open to conjecture. Near the west wall stands a lidless rectangular granite sarcophagus which once contained the king's body, probably enclosed within an inner coffin of wood. In appearance it is rough, many of the scratches made by the saw when cutting it being still clearly visible. Sir Flinders Petrie discovered that the width of the sarcophagus was about an inch greater than the width of the Ascending Corridor at its mouth; he therefore concluded that it must have been placed in position while the chamber was being built.

The roof of the King's Chamber has no exact architectural parallel. Above its flat ceiling, which is composed of nine slabs weighing in aggregate about 400 tons, there are five separate compartments, the ceilings of the first four being flat and the fifth having a pointed roof. The purpose of this construction, it appears, was to eliminate any risk of the ceiling of the chamber collapsing under the weight of the superincumbent masonry. Whether such extreme precautions were required by the character of the building may be debatable; they have, however, been justified by subsequent events. Every one of the nine slabs of granite which form the ceiling of the chamber and many of those in the relieving compartments have been cracked—presumably by an earthquake—but none has yet collapsed.

Access to the lowest of the relieving compartments is gained by a passage leading from a hole at the top of the east wall of the Grand Gallery. When or by whom this passage was cut is unknown; the first European to mention it was a traveller named Davison who visited the Pyramid in 1765. The four upper compartments were not discovered until 1837-38, when Colonel Howard Vyse and J. S. Perring forced a way to them by hollowing out a shaft from below. Some of the walls in these upper compartments are composed of limestone; since they were not intended to be seen their surfaces were not dressed and, in consequence, many of the blocks still retain the red ochre markings painted on them at the quarry.

Among these quarry-marks are the only instances of the name of Cheops found in the Pyramid.

Owing to its upward slope, the blocking of the Ascending Corridor of the Great Pyramid after the funeral presented unusual difficulties. In other Pyramids the corridors either slope downwards or are approximately level, so that they could easily be packed with large plug-blocks which would have been stored outside the Pyramid until required. The Descending Corridor of the Great Pyramid could have been blocked in this way, but not the Ascending Corridor. Not only would the task of raising heavy granite plugs through the hole in the roof of the Descending Corridor have caused many mechanical difficulties, but plugs so inserted would have served no useful purpose because they could not have been firmly secured. No alternative remained, therefore, but to store the plugs somewhere in the Pyramid while it was under construction and to move them down the Ascending Corridor after the body had been put in the burial-chamber. That such a method was adopted is clear from the fact that the three plugs which still remain in position at the lower end of the Ascending Corridor are about an inch wider than its mouth and, consequently, could not have been introduced from the Descending Corridor. Two problems, however, arise from this deduction: where were the plugs stored before being lowered down the Ascending Corridor, and how did the men who must have pushed the plugs from behind escape from the Pyramid after completing their work?

Until Petrie discovered that the horizontal passage leading to the Queen's Chamber was an inch too small in both width and height to hold the plugs, it was generally supposed that they had been stored either in that passage or in the Queen's Chamber. The necessary width and height could have been found in the gap between the top of the Ascending Corridor and the lower end of the Grand Gallery passage, but the length of the gap would have been insufficient to accommodate the plugs if placed end to end. Moreover, there can be little doubt that this gap was bridged with slabs of stone at the time when the plugs were awaiting removal to their final position. Lack of height would also exclude the passage leading to the King's Chamber and, in consequence, the chamber itself. Petrie therefore concluded that the plugs were stored in the Grand Gallery passage, where all the requirements of space would have been satisfied. Such an explanation, as Petrie recognised, was open to the objection that the plugs, by blocking the passage, would have obstructed the funeral procession—which must have either climbed over the plugs or proceeded up the side-ramps—but considerations of size seemed to preclude any other solution.

Borchardt, while accepting Petrie's main thesis that the plugs were stored in the Grand Gallery, pointed out that it failed to account for the presence of twenty-eight holes cut at regular intervals in the upper surface of each side-ramp. Two other features which remained unexplained by Petrie, but which appeared to be connected with the holes, were small blocks of stone which had been inserted in the side-walls opposite the holes, each with a slot cut roughly in its surface, and a long continuous groove sunk in the lower part of the third projecting lap from the bottom of each side-wall. This groove, which is nearly an inch in depth, extends along the whole length of both sides of the gallery. Borchardt, after a careful examination of the evidence, suggested that the holes and slots were designed to hold wooden uprights supporting a platform, also made of wood, the sides of which fitted into the long grooves. The purpose of the platform would have been to store the plugs so that the funeral cortège could pass up the passage without obstruction. Its length, which would seem excessive for the storage of only three plugs, may have resulted from an original and possibly discarded plan for filling in the whole of the Ascending Corridor with plugs.

From the moment when the first plug was introduced into the upper end of the Ascending Corridor, the workmen who were charged with the task of transferring the plugs to their final position would have been unable to leave the Pyramid by the normal way. They had, however, provided themselves with a means of escape down the shaft which leads from the gap at the upper end of the Ascending Corridor to the Descending Corridor (fig. 14, 8). It is idle to speculate whether this shaft was constructed with or without the knowledge of Cheops, but the burial of living persons was certainly not practised by the Egyptians of the Pyramid Age. The shaft would have been completely concealed at the time of the funeral by the slabs of stone bridging the gap and by the lowest stone in the western ramp, which is now missing. The removal of these stones would have presented no difficulty to the workmen when the time came for making their descent. After the last of the workmen had reached the bottom of the shaft, the opening in the west wall of the Descending Corridor would have been covered with a slab of stone so that it would have been indistinguishable from the remainder of the corridor. At the same time also the mouth of the Ascending Corridor beyond the first of the plugs would have been covered with the stone which fell to the floor of the Descending Corridor when the Caliph Ma'mun was forcing a way into the Pyramid.

Some speculation regarding the method of closing the entrance to the Pyramid has been caused by a statement made by Strabo. In his *Geographica*, written at about the beginning of the Christian Era, he writes that the Great Pyramid, "a little way up one side, has a stone that may be taken out, which being raised up there is a sloping passage to the foundations." Petrie interpreted this statement as meaning that the Great Pyramid had a flap-door composed of a single slab of stone which swung on pivots near the top of each side. In support of his theory he was able to point out that, both in the northern corridor of the Bent Pyramid and in the Pyramid of Meidum, there were sockets cut in the side-walls near the entrance which were apparently intended for holding door-pivots. Owing to the loss of the outer casing, it is impossible to say whether the entrance to the Great Pyramid was provided with similar sockets. It is, however, difficult to believe that the door described by Strabo, if his words have been correctly understood, dated from the time when the Pyramid was built. Plugs and portcullises would certainly not have been used to block the corridors of Pyramids if subsequent access to the internal chambers was contemplated; a flap-door would have presupposed such access. Possibly the entrance to the Great Pyramid, like the still intact western entrance to the Bent Pyramid, was originally covered with a layer of casing stones which rendered it indistinguishable from the remainder of the outer surface. When the Pyramid was first violated—probably during the period of anarchy which followed the end of the Old Kingdom—the robbers must have forced a way through the blocks covering the entrance. How long it remained open cannot be known, but it may have been sealed and again violated on more than one occasion during the subsequent dynasties, until eventually—possibly under the Saites—a door, corresponding with the one described by Strabo, was fitted. If this highly speculative surmise be correct, it is also necessary to assume either that the existence of the door was forgotten or that the entrance was again blocked with facing stones at some time during the period between Strabo's visit and the ninth century. No other explanation would account for the inability of the Caliph Ma'mun to find the entrance until he had forced a new passage through the core of the Pyramid.

Although the buildings which once completed the Great

Pyramid complex have either entirely or partly disappeared, the surviving remnants are enough to show that the general lay-out conformed with the standard pattern. Nothing is now visible of the enclosure wall, but part of the fine limestone pavement which covered the area between the wall and the Pyramid has been preserved. Adjoining the east face of the Pyramid was the Mortuary Temple, the floor of which was made of polished basalt laid on a foundation of limestone. The walls, in part at least, were faced with granite. North and south of the temple are two large boat-shaped pits hewn in the rock; a third pit of the same kind lies on the north side of the Causeway near the temple. All the pits appear to have been roofed, but in spite of this protection nothing remains of the boats which originally filled them; their complete disappearance strongly suggests that they were made of wood, a material which is not only perishable but could also be carried away more easily than stone. Fragments of wood were actually discovered in a boat-hollow made of brick belonging to the supposed Mastaba of Aha at Sakkara. Although it is clear that these boats were intended to provide the dead king with a means of transport in his After-life, the precise region in which they were to be employed is still obscure. In the solar cult, a boat would be required for accompanying the Sun-god on his daily journey across the heavens and his nightly journey beneath the earth; it would also be needed for reaching the region beyond the eastern horizon, where the gods were thought to dwell. In the Osirian cult a boat would be necessary for travelling to Abydos and Busiris. Until more is known about the religious beliefs of the period preceding the Vth Dynasty, the full significance of the boats will remain conjectural.

At right angles to the upper end of the Causeway, on the south side, lies a row of three subsidiary Pyramids, each with a small ruined chapel adjoining its eastern face. Beside the first Pyramid there is a small boat-pit. Reisner believed that this

Pyramid belonged to Cheops' favourite queen who, in accordance with Egyptian custom, may also have been his full-blood sister. Concerning the second Pyramid, Herodotus recounts the following legend: "The wickedness of Cheops reached to such a pitch that, when he had spent all his treasures and wanted more, he sent his daughter to the stews, with orders to procure him a certain sum—how much I cannot say, for I was not told; she procured it, however, and at the same time, bent on leaving a monument which should perpetuate her own memory, she required each man to make her a present of a stone towards the works which she contemplated. With these stones she built the Pyramid which stands midmost of the three that are in front of the Great Pyramid, measuring along each side a hundred and fifty feet."[1] Happily there is no reason for supposing that the details of this story bear any relation to historical fact. The third Pyramid was ascribed in later times to Queen Henutsen, who may have been only a half-sister of the king. By the XXIst Dynasty she had been identified with the goddess Isis and had been given the name Isis-Mistress-of-the-Pyramids. At that time also the small chapel adjoining the Pyramid was enlarged in order to provide a suitable sanctuary for the goddess.

The Causeway consisted of a corridor, built either directly on the rock-bed or, in those places where the level of the rock-bed was too low, on an embankment of masonry. According to Herodotus, the construction of the Causeway and the other buildings at the foot of the Pyramid occupied ten years. Today nothing of the corridor remains intact, but some of the embankment is still standing in a small quarry, which it bridged, and again at the point where it crossed the edge of the plateau. The lower end of the Causeway and whatever may have been preserved of the Valley Building still lie unexcavated beneath the modern village of Kafr es-Samman. A

[1] *Herodotus,* II, 126 (Rawlinson's translation).

tunnel was constructed near the middle of the Causeway, so that those who wished to cross it could do so without having to make a long detour around either the Pyramid or the Valley Building.

Herodotus, in his description of the Causeway, stated that it was built of polished stone on which were carved pictures of animals. The veracity of this statement was doubted by some archæologists because no traces of carvings in relief had been found in any of the IVth Dynasty Pyramids or in their adjoining buildings, although they were certainly included in some of the contemporary private Mastabas. To account for their absence, it was necessary to suppose that the architects of the period were preoccupied with mastering the technique of using granite and with learning the art of building in megalithic masonry. Recently, however, W. Stevenson Smith, who assisted Reisner in his excavations at the Giza necropolis, has reported the discovery of some fragments of fine low reliefs among the ruins of the Mortuary Temple at the top of the Causeway. If it is once admitted, as seems necessary in the light of this discovery, that the walls of the Mortuary Temple were decorated with reliefs, a strong presumption is created in favour of the statement by Herodotus regarding the Causeway.

South of the Causeway, close to the first of the subsidiary Pyramids, Reisner found in 1925 the only undisturbed tomb-chamber of the Old Kingdom hitherto known. It lay at the bottom of a vertical shaft which had been blocked with masonry to its entire depth of 99 feet. Within this chamber were stored the fine alabaster sarcophagus and funerary equipment of Queen Hetep-heres, wife of Seneferu and mother of Cheops. Although the sarcophagus proved to be empty, the viscera, which had been removed from the body to help in its preservation, were found in an alabaster chest—the so-called Canopic chest. To explain the absence of the body, since the chamber had never been plundered, Reisner suggested that Hetep-heres was buried in a tomb at Dahshur near the Pyramid of Seneferu, but that soon after her burial robbers broke into the tomb and removed the body with its jewellery and gold ornaments. Before they were able to steal the remainder of the equipment, however, news of the violation of the tomb had reached the king. Hoping to prevent further despoilment, Cheops, who may not have been told of the disappearance of the body, decided to transfer his mother's tomb—possibly in secret—to Giza, where it would receive the same degree of protection as his own Pyramid. As an additional precaution, no superstructure was built above the new tomb, so that when the sand had accumulated over the mouth of the shaft, no trace of its presence was visible. The fact that it remained undetected until the twentieth century, when the American excavators literally swept the sand from the rock-bed, is the best testimony to the success of the stratagem.

Among the smaller objects found in this chamber were alabaster vessels, a copper ewer, three gold vessels, gold razors and knives, copper tools and a gold manicure instrument, pointed at one end for cleaning the nails and curved at the other end for pressing down the quick; a toilet-box contained eight small alabaster vases filled with unguents and kohl. Inside a jewel-case were twenty silver anklets, each inlaid with dragonflies of malachite, lapis lazuli and carnelian. The larger objects included a canopy frame made of wood cased with gold, and two armchairs and a bed which were partly cased with gold sheeting. On the foot-board of the bed was a panel of gold inlaid with a blue and black floral design. A carrying-chair, also made of wood partly cased with gold sheeting, bore an inscription, written in hieroglyphs of gold set in ebony panels and repeated four times, which read: "The mother of the King of Upper and Lower Egypt, follower of Horus, guide of the Ruler, favourite whose every word is done for her, daughter of the god [begotten] of his body, Hetep-heres."

No description can do justice to the artistic excellence and technical perfection of the equipment of Hetep-heres; in comparison with its exquisite simplicity of design, much of the tomb furniture used in the later periods appears tawdry. Only the woodwork had suffered with the passage of time; inevitably it had either become decayed or shrunk to such a degree that it could not be used when the objects were reconstructed by the experts of the Boston-Harvard expedition before being delivered, in accordance with the terms of the excavators' agreement, to the Cairo Museum. Reisner was of the opinion that at least some of the objects had been used by Hetep-heres during her lifetime. There is nothing improbable in the suggestion. Belongings of a personal kind were certainly not placed in the tomb until the time of the funeral, although vases and jars containing stores were often made expressly for the tomb and may well have been deposited there in advance. Whether the objects actually formed part of the furnishings of the queen's apartments in the palace is, however, a matter of only secondary importance. The real interest of the discovery lies in the light which it throws on the practical and artistic achievements of the IVth Dynasty and in the concrete evidence which it provides of the kind of equipment which was once to be found in other contemporary royal tombs.

Not the least significant of the various elements designed to add to the impressive effect of the Great Pyramid was its architectural setting. Other Pyramids were surrounded by the tombs of officials and relatives of their owners, but little attention seems to have been given to their lay-out. East and west of the Great Pyramid enclosure wall, however, large cemeteries of Mastabas were arranged in parallel rows several feet apart. South of the Pyramid only a single row was built, while on the north there were none. The ownership of the tombs was also carefully planned, those in the eastern cemetery being allotted to close relatives of the king and those in the western cemetery—the larger—to officials. Although most of these Mastabas have now lost their entire outer casing, it must be supposed that they were all originally faced with Tura limestone; their colour therefore would be uniform with that of the vast Pyramid rising in their midst. Hermann Junker, who excavated a part of the western cemetery, has aptly remarked that the Egyptian conception of the dead ruler continuing in the After-life to be surrounded by his relatives and loyal followers has never found so vivid an expression as in the arrangement of the tombs in this necropolis. It may be claimed, with equal truth, that the difference between the divine majesty of the ruler and his mortal subjects was never more strongly emphasised than in the contrast between the towering Pyramid and the simple flat-topped Mastabas.

Cheops' obvious wishes for the architectural setting of his tomb appear to have commanded little respect from subsequent generations. Already in the Vth and VIth Dynasties the symmetry of the original design was being destroyed by the construction of smaller Mastabas in the spaces between the rows. The owners of these tombs were either officials of the necropolis or mortuary priests who, during their lifetime, had performed the various duties deemed necessary for securing the well-being of the dead king and his associates. In later times, particularly under the Saites, burial in the vicinity of the three Giza Pyramids was believed to confer special benefits on the dead, with the result that the whole area became honeycombed with tombs and the regularity of the earliest design must have been obscured beyond recognition.

South of the Great Pyramid complex and near the Valley Building of the Second Pyramid lies the Giant Sphinx (Plate

6B). A knoll of rock, which had been left by the builders of the Great Pyramid when quarrying stone for its inner core, was fashioned in the time of Chephren into a huge recumbent lion with a human head. It was probably overlaid with a coating of plaster and painted. The length of this colossus is about 240 feet, its height 66 feet and the maximum width of the face 13 feet 8 inches. On the head is the royal headdress; other emblems of royalty are the cobra on the forehead and the beard, now largely missing, on the chin. Although the face has been severely mutilated, it still gives the impression of being a portrait of King Chephren and not merely a formalised representation. A figure, possibly of the king, was carved in front of the chest, but scarcely any trace of it now remains. Between the outstretched paws stands a large slab of red granite bearing an inscription which purports to record a dream of Thutmose IV of the XVIIIth Dynasty before he ascended the throne. According to this inscription the prince, when hunting, decided to rest at midday in the shadow of the Sphinx. During his sleep the Sphinx, which was regarded at that time as an embodiment of the Sun-god Harmachis, promised him the Double Crown of Egypt if he would clear away the sand which had nearly engulfed its body. Unfortunately, the latter part of the inscription is too badly weathered to be legible, but it may be surmised that it related how the god's wish was fulfilled and how the prince was finally rewarded with the Crown of the Two Lands. In addition to clearing away the sand, Thutmose IV may have repaired damaged portions of the body by the insertion of small blocks of limestone—an operation which was repeated in Ptolemaic or Roman times, when the sand was once more removed and an altar was erected in front of the figure. The first excavation of the Sphinx in modern times was conducted by Captain Caviglia in 1818 at a cost of £450. Sixty-eight years later it was again freed of sand by Gaston Maspero and lastly, in 1925, the Service des Antiquités undertook once more its clearance and restoration.

In Egyptian mythology the lion often figures as the guardian of sacred places. How or when this conception first arose is not known, but it probably dates back to remote antiquity. Like so many other primitive beliefs, it was incorporated by the priests of Heliopolis into their solar creed, the lion being considered as the guardian of the gates of the Underworld on the eastern and western horizons. In the form of the Sphinx, the lion retained the function of a sentinel, but was given the human features of the Sun-god Atum. An inscription, which dates from a period considerably later than the time of Chephren, puts the following words into the mouth of a Sphinx: "I protect the chapel of thy tomb. I guard thy sepulchral chamber. I ward off the intruding stranger. I hurl the foes to the ground and their weapons with them. I drive away the wicked one from the chapel of thy tomb. I destroy thine adversaries in their lurking-place, blocking it that they come forth no more." A possible reason for the identification of the Sun-god's features with those of the deceased king may be the Heliopolitan belief that the king, after his death, actually became the Sun-god. The Giant Sphinx would therefore represent Chephren as the Sun-god acting as the guardian of the Giza necropolis.

On the south-east side of the Sphinx stands a building which, at one time, was thought to be a temple connected with the Sphinx, but is now known to be the Valley Building of the Pyramid complex of King Chephren, the Greek equivalent of the Egyptian name Khaef-Ra by which the builder of the Second Pyramid is usually known. Auguste Mariette, the founder of the Cairo Museum, discovered this building in 1853, but although he cleared the whole of the inside, considerable accumulations of sand were left against the outer walls. A further clearance was made by Mariette in 1869, when the building formed one of the principal show-places to which the distinguished visitors who attended the opening of the Suez Canal were conducted. Finally, in 1909-10, the outer walls were freed of sand by the von Sieglin expedition, under the direction of Uvo Hölscher and Georg Steindorff, when excavating the whole of the Pyramid complex.

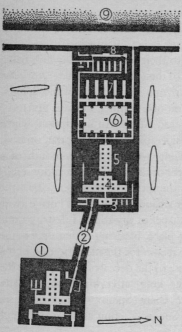

FIG. 15.—*The Valley Building and Mortuary Temple of Chephren.*

Considering the very early date of the Valley Building, its condition is truly remarkable. No other building of the IVth Dynasty, with the possible exception of the unfinished Mortuary Temple of the Meidum Pyramid, has survived in a comparable state of preservation. Built on a ground plan measuring 147 feet in each direction and rising to a height of 43 feet, its immensely thick walls are composed of coarse local limestone faced, both internally and externally, with ashlars of polished red granite from Aswan (fig. 15, 1). The four outer walls are not perpendicular, but have a pronounced batter—a regular feature in buildings of the period. Two doorways on the east side, which may originally have been flanked by Sphinxes, give entrance to the building from a terrace

cut in the rock. Around each doorway is a band of hieroglyphic inscription giving the name and titles of the
king; no other inscriptions or reliefs occur anywhere else in
the building. Short passages lead from the doorways by way
of small but lofty vestibules to a long antechamber, in the
floor of which Mariette found a deep pit containing a diorite
statue of Chephren—one of the finest examples of Old Kingdom sculpture hitherto recovered (Plate 8). Originally, this
statue, which is rather larger than life-size, was probably
placed in the T-shaped hall leading westwards out of the
antechamber; its transference to the pit, the date of which is
uncertain, may have been due to a desire to preserve it from
destruction. A total of twenty-three royal statues made of
diorite, schist and alabaster once stood against the sides of the
hall, seventeen in the stem of the T and six facing eastwards in
the cross-piece. Light entered the hall through oblique slits
cut partly in the top of the walls and partly in the underside of
the flat granite roof; the rays did not shine directly on the
statues, but were reflected from the alabaster floor and from
the massive square columns of red granite which supported
the roof. Such lighting might seem inadequate for the illumi-
nation of sculptures which, to judge from the one which has
remained intact, were artistic masterpieces. Egyptian sculptures, however, were not designed for display, but to provide
the spirit with an imperishable substitute for the human body;
dim light or even complete darkness was not thought to
hinder the efficacy of the substitute—a fact which is demonstrated by the regular practice of enclosing statues in Serdabs.

The precise use of the Valley Building in the performance of
the funerary ritual is not entirely clear. Reisner, when dis-
cussing its architectural form, expressed the opinion that it
was ultimately derived from a pavilion composed of matting
and supported by a framework of poles lashed together with
ropes. B. Grdseloff, whose recent researches have added

substantially to the amount previously known about the function of the Valley Building, has identified it with a building called in Egyptian texts *seh-nether* (Pavilion-of-the-god). In his opinion also it combined the uses of two constructions which normally stood independently when built in association with Mastabas of the Old Kingdom, namely the *Ibu* (Purification-tent) and the *Wabet* (House-of-embalmment). The purification ceremonies in the Valley Building of Chephren took place, Grdseloff suggests, in a temporary pavilion built on the roof, to which a ramp paved with alabaster gave access from a passage leading out of the north-west corner of the T-shaped hall. Round holes, which may have served as sockets for the framework of such a pavilion, are still visible in the paving of the roof. The embalming of the body, he believes, was performed in the antechamber. It has since been suggested that Grdseloff's identification should be reversed and that the purification was conducted in the antechamber and the embalmment on the roof.

Purification by washing played an important part in Egyptian ritual at all times. The king, for instance, was ceremonially washed in the sacred lake of the temple of Ra at Heliopolis before he entered the building. Similarly, before his dead body could be taken into the sacred precincts of his tomb, it was necessary that it should be purified by washing. From this purification, moreover, it was believed that the dead king was regenerated, just as the Sun-god was thought to be reborn each morning by bathing in the "Lily Lake" before embarking on his journey across the heavens. Osiris too, according to one tradition, had been revivified by the lustration of his body; the dead king therefore, when identified with Osiris, was thought to derive equal benefit from the same treatment.

After the completion of the purification ceremonies, the body of the king was taken for embalmment either to the antechamber or to the pavilion on the roof, whichever served the purposes of the *Wabet*. Elaborate mummification of the kind practised during the New Kingdom was, however, not employed in the Pyramid Age. Although there is no evidence of the use of preservatives, the discovery in the tomb of Hetepheres of a Canopic Box containing the queen's viscera proves that the most decomposable organs were removed from the body. Other Old Kingdom burials show that the bodies were carefully wrapped in linen bandages, each limb being bound separately. Pads of linen were sometimes inserted under the bandages so that the body might retain its natural form. Sometimes also the various members, such as the nose, lips, breasts and genital organs, were modelled in linen—an expedient which would have been unnecessary if a successful method of preserving the body had been devised.

A third ceremony to be performed in the Valley Building was the so-called " Opening of the Mouth." The body, purified and wrapped in bandages, was taken to the T-shaped hall where the twenty-three statues of the king had already been placed in position. Priests, at least one of whom would be a son of the dead king, would approach each of the statues in turn, sprinkle water over it, fumigate it with incense, offer sacrifices before it, touch its mouth with various implements including an adze and a chisel, rub milk on its mouth and deck it with the royal regalia. In later times these ceremonies were also performed on the dead body, but possibly this practice was not introduced until after the Old Kingdom. By their execution it was thought that the statue or mummy would be endowed with the faculties of a living person.

The performance of all three ceremonies in the Valley Building must have occupied many weeks. In the tomb of Queen Meresankh III, who may have been one of Chephren's wives, it is stated that her embalmment occupied two hundred and seventy-two days; at least as long a period would have been required for the embalmment of the king. Subsequently his body, enclosed in a wooden coffin, would have been taken out of the Valley Building by way of the passage which connected the hall with the Causeway (fig. 15, 2). On its journey through the passage the cortège would have passed the mouth of a narrow corridor leading to a small chamber built of alabaster. The purpose of this chamber is not evident, but Hölscher conjectured that a porter, whose duty it was to guard the entrance to the Causeway, lived in it; Grdseloff, however, has suggested that it was used for storing food-offerings required during the three ceremonies. He would also explain the presence of six long magazines, arranged in two storeys of three and situated at the end of a passage opening out of the south side of the hall, on the ground that they were designed for the storage of various materials and ritual instruments used in the ceremonies, a pair of magazines being allotted to each ceremony.

In order to avoid the necessity of building an embankment across a deep depression which lay directly to the east of the Mortuary Temple, the Causeway was constructed on a ridge of rock which crossed the depression obliquely from south-east to north-west. It was more than a quarter of a mile in length and about 15 feet in breadth. Nothing of its structure is now visible except part of the rock foundation and some blocks of Tura limestone from the walls and floor of its corridor. When standing, its walls rose perpendicularly on the inside, but their outer face had a marked batter. If Herodotus is correct in his statement that the Causeway of the Great Pyramid was decorated with reliefs, it must be supposed that the inner walls of the corridor of this Causeway also were decorated. It was roofed with slabs of stone laid flat. Perhaps the practice of roofing Causeways dates from the time when their corridors were first decorated with reliefs. The Causeways of the Bent Pyramid and the Pyramid of Meidum, neither of which appears to have been decorated, were certainly not roofed; possibly, therefore, the Causeway of the Great Pyramid was the first to be given a roof in order to protect the painted reliefs on its walls. Light was admitted to the corridor through horizontal slits, cut along the middle of the roof. Since rain also would enter through these slits and, unless drained, would run down into the Valley Building, a channel was sunk in the paving at the lower end of the Causeway to conduct the water through an outlet in the side wall.

When the body of the dead king was transferred to the Mortuary Temple, no one standing outside the Causeway could have witnessed the ceremony. Without doubt, such screening was intentional, although the motive which prompted it cannot be deduced with certainty. The most probable explanation seems to be that it was thought necessary to protect the dead body, after its purification in the Valley Building, from the gaze of those who were ceremonially impure. Even the fact that the body was already enclosed within a wooden coffin was apparently not considered a sufficient protection against contamination. Persons, other than priests, who were to accompany the bier to the Mortuary Temple probably underwent ritual purification before joining the cortège. Priests, as their Egyptian name *wab* ("pure") implies, were ceremonially clean at all times.

The Mortuary Temple, now reduced to ruins, was a low, rectangular building which measured about 370 feet in length and 160 feet in breadth. Its walls were composed of local stone, faced on the inside with red granite. Outside, the lowest course was also faced with granite, but the remainder of the building had a facing of Tura limestone. Five pits for boats were hewn in the rock close to the north and south walls. Two of the pits still have well-preserved roofs made of limestone slabs, but no trace of the wooden boats has been found.

Not one of the Mortuary Temples hitherto excavated has proved to be an exact replica of any other known example. They differ, however, only in arrangement and in architectural detail. From the time of Chephren until the end of the Old Kingdom, every Mortuary Temple embodied five main features: an entrance hall, an open court, five niches for statues, magazines and a sanctuary. Possibly the Mortuary Temple of the Great Pyramid followed a similar design, but, owing to its ruined condition, the details of its plan are difficult to determine.

In Chephren's temple, the Causeway did not lead directly to the entrance hall, but to a long corridor. Several chambers, perhaps intended for the storage of articles used in the temple ceremonies, opened out of the corridor. In its centre it widened into a kind of vestibule (fig. 15, 3), which was connected by a narrow passage with the entrance hall, the latter consisting of two sections, one transverse (fig. 15, 4) and the other longitudinal (fig. 15, 5). Rectangular monolithic columns of red granite, resembling those in the Valley Building, supported the roofs of both the vestibule and the entrance hall. At each end of the transverse section of the entrance hall, a long and narrow chamber penetrated deeply into the masonry core of the building. Since the end wall in each chamber was composed of a single block of granite, Hölscher conjectured that its surface was carved into a figure of the king fashioned almost in the round. If this conjecture is correct, the chambers would have been Serdabs of a kind without any known parallel in a royal Mortuary Temple.

Beyond the entrance hall lay the open court, which also had walls of red granite and a pavement of alabaster (fig. 15, 6). Traces of a drain, found in the middle of the court, suggest that an altar may have stood there, the drain being required for carrying away the blood of the animals sacrificed and the liquid of the libations offered; on the other hand, the drain may have been used simply for disposing of accumulations of rain-water. Spaced at regular intervals around the periphery of the court were statues of the king, possibly bearing the attributes of the god Osiris. Between the statues were doors leading to short passages which connected the court with a surrounding corridor. Opposite each of the five western doors, across the corridor, was a deep niche which contained a statue of the king (fig. 15, 7). The significance of the five statues—a number which does not vary in any of the subsequent Mortuary Temples—may be that each statue bore one of the five official names assumed by the king on the day of his accession.

The open court marked the limit beyond which only the priests were allowed to advance. During the temple ceremonies, secular attendants must have remained in the court while the priests proceeded, by way of the corridor in front of the statue-niches, to the sanctuary (fig. 15, 8). The main feature of the sanctuary was a false door in the west wall with a low altar at its foot. Offerings were placed on the altar daily by the priests. Since it was only the spirit of the substance provided and not the actual material which was thought to be of value to the dead, the fact that the offerings remained undisturbed until replaced would not have troubled the minds of the ancient Egyptians. Five magazines lay between the sanctuary and the five statue-niches—a coincidence in number which may not have been accidental. In construction also, the magazines shared with the niches the peculiarity of being the only parts of the temple not faced with granite and paved with alabaster. Within the magazines were stored stone vases and reserve supplies of food, which would be required by the king if the priests neglected their daily duty to provide fresh offerings.

A long ramp led from the north-west corner of the corridor surrounding the open court to the terrace on which the

Pyramid stood. The position of the entrance to the ramp implies that access to the Pyramid enclosure was permitted to persons who were not entitled to enter the innermost parts of the Mortuary Temple. At the funeral service, therefore, the whole procession may have proceeded to the Pyramid (fig. 15, 9) after the "Opening of the Mouth" ceremony had been performed on the statues in the niches. The masons and workmen who blocked up and sealed the entrance to the Pyramid must also have reached the enclosure by way of the ramp; a high wall, which surrounded the Pyramid on every side, would have prevented an approach by any more direct route.

Between the Pyramid and the surrounding wall there was a pavement about 34 feet in width on the north, east and west sides and somewhat wider on the south side, where a single subsidiary Pyramid stood approximately opposite the middle of the king's Pyramid. The Mortuary Temple was separated from the east face of the Pyramid by a paved alley-way. In other enclosures the two buildings are generally contiguous, so that there is no open space between the false door and the Pyramid. To account for this anomaly, Borchardt conjectured that a second false door stood against the east face of the Pyramid, but no trace of its existence was revealed during excavation.

The most distinctive external feature of Chephren's Pyramid, apart from its size, is the substantial portion of its outer casing which still remains intact near the apex. Some of the casing has also been preserved at the base. The stone employed is, however, different in each place, the upper remnant being composed of Tura limestone and the lower of red granite—a material which was used only as a casing for the bottommost course. Herodotus, in his description of the Pyramid, states that Chephren "used the many-coloured stone of Ethiopia for the basement,"[1] apparently in the mis-

[1] Book II, 127.

taken belief that granite was employed not merely as a casing but as a kind of platform on which the Pyramid was built. The capstone, which has now disappeared, may also have been made of granite.

Owing to its position on somewhat higher ground, Chephren's Pyramid creates the illusion of being taller than the Great Pyramid. In reality, its present height of 447½ feet falls short of that of its neighbour by 2½ feet. Originally, it rose to a height of 471 feet and was therefore about 10 feet lower than the Great Pyramid, when the latter was also undamaged. The area covered by Chephren's Pyramid to-day is approximately 690½ feet square; formerly each side measured 707¾ feet, so that the dimensions at the base were about 48 feet less in each direction than those of the Great Pyramid. The faces of the Pyramid, which slope at an angle of 52° 20′, rise more steeply than the faces of the Great Pyramid—a fact which explains the small difference in height between the two buildings when compared with the considerable inequality of their base dimensions.

Internally, Chephren's Pyramid bears little resemblance to the Great Pyramid. It has two entrances, one in the north face, at a height of nearly 50 feet, and the other directly below, hewn in the rock foundation of the surrounding pavement (fig. 16, 4 and 1). Both entrances are situated at a distance of about 41 feet to the east of the Pyramid's main north-south axis. From the upper entrance, a low and narrow corridor descends at an angle of 25° 55′ through the core of the Pyramid until it enters the rock; here it becomes horizontal and continues on a level plane to the tomb-chamber (fig. 16, 3). The roof, walls and floor of the whole of the sloping section and of a small part of the horizontal section are lined with red granite. Near the end of the granite lining vertical slots have been cut in the walls to receive a portcullis, also made of granite, the damaged remains of which are still in position.

The tomb-chamber has been hewn, with the exception of its roof, entirely out of the rock; the pointed gable roof consists of limestone slabs laid at the same angle as the faces of the

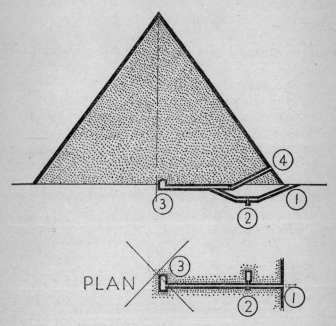

FIG. 16.—*The Pyramid of Chephren, section looking west, and plan.*

Pyramid. With its longer axis running from east to west, the chamber measures 46½ feet in length, 16½ feet in breadth and 22½ feet in height. On the west side of the chamber, a fine rectangular sarcophagus of polished granite has been let into the floor up to the level of its lid. The lid itself, which lies near by, is broken into two pieces—a condition in which it was found in 1818 by Giovanni Belzoni, the first European explorer to enter this Pyramid in modern times. No trace of Chephren's body was discovered in the sarcophagus.

The lower corridor (fig. 16, 1), at its beginning, follows a course similar to the upper corridor; it is, however, completely hewn out of the rock. After descending at a gradient of 21° 40', it becomes horizontal for a short distance and then rises steeply to emerge in the floor of the horizontal section of the upper corridor. A granite portcullis stood also in this corridor, but the walls were not lined with granite. In the east wall of the horizontal section, there is a recess opposite which a sloping passage leads down to a chamber, measuring 34 feet 3 inches in length, 10 feet 4 inches in breadth and 8 feet 5 inches in height (fig. 16, 2). There can be no doubt that this chamber, at the time of its construction, was intended to contain the royal sarcophagus; some explanation for its abandonment must therefore be sought. Two exceptional features which may offer a clue in solving the difficulty immediately strike the eye: the chamber is situated very near the entrance to the Pyramid and the entrance itself lies beyond the limits of the superstructure. In other contemporary Pyramids, the tomb-chamber is located approximately beneath the apex and the entrance is situated in the northern face. If, however, it be supposed that, when the chamber and corridor were constructed, it was planned to build the Pyramid some 200 feet further north, both the chamber and the entrance would have occupied their customary positions. A possible reason for the change in plan was the discovery of a suitable rock foundation for the Causeway concealed beneath the sand on a line south of the one originally chosen.

A problem for which it is more difficult to find a satisfactory solution is the purpose of the sloping passage which connects the lower apartments with the upper corridor. The only explanation which has been suggested is that it was used for transferring the sarcophagus from the old chamber to the new, but the process of cutting an additional passage through the rock would seem unnecessarily laborious when it would have been possible to extract the sarcophagus from the old chamber by way of the lower entrance corridor and to introduce it into the new chamber from above, before building the gable roof. The fact, however, remains that the passage was constructed and that, after serving its purpose, it was blocked with limestone boulders, many of which have never been removed. Blocking of the same kind completely fills the lower entrance corridor so that it cannot now be entered.

West of the Pyramid, outside the enclosure wall, lies a series of galleries which Sir Flinders Petrie identified as the barracks in which were housed the masons and workmen employed in building the Pyramid complex. These galleries are now almost entirely concealed beneath the sand, but Petrie, who surveyed them in 1880-82, has stated [1] that they numbered ninety-one, each measuring about 88 feet in length, $9\frac{1}{2}$ feet in width and 7 feet in height. The walls of the galleries are composed of rough pieces of limestone faced with a coating of dried mud; the floor also is overlaid with a coating of the same material. Wide pilasters of hewn limestone serve as terminals to the walls at the entrance end. The east end of each gallery is closed by a single wall running at right angles to the galleries and oriented almost exactly parallel to the west side of the Pyramid.

Considered in relation to its predecessors, Chephren's Pyramid provides the first recognisable example of a complex in which all the architectural elements of the standard pattern appear in their fully developed form. Earlier complexes, notably that of the Great Pyramid, embody many of its salient features, but they are either not in a comparable state of preservation or, like the Mortuary Temple of the Meidum Pyramid, architecturally still in embryo. In Chephren's

[1] Petrie, *The Pyramids and Temples of Gizeh*, pp. 101-3.

Pyramid complex, the Valley Building is largely intact, the foundations of the Causeway are plainly visible and enough of the Mortuary Temple remains to enable its ground-plan to be determined with certainty. Each of these structures, moreover, contains in its design all the basic elements of the subsequent Pyramid complexes; modifications in detail and substantial decorative innovations were to be introduced, but the essential skeleton was to remain unchanged.

The Third Pyramid of the Giza group stands in the southwest corner of the plateau (Plate 1). Although it had been ascribed to Mycerinus both by Herodotus and by Diodorus Siculus, who visited Egypt in the middle of the first century B.C., the identification was not confirmed until 1837-38, when Colonel Howard Vyse found the name of Mycerinus written in red ochre on the roof of the burial-chamber in the second of the three subsidiary Pyramids within the complex. Further proof was obtained by the expedition of Harvard University and the Boston Museum of Fine Arts, which excavated the site between the years 1905 and 1927 under the directorship of G. A. Reisner.

Contemporary records shed no light on the life and character of Mycerinus. In very late times he seems to have gained a reputation for piety and justice, while Cheops and Chephren were regarded as having been wicked and tyrannical kings. Herodotus, in whose writings this tradition is preserved, speaks of Mycerinus in the following terms: "This prince [i.e. Mycerinus] disapproved the conduct of his father, reopened the temples and allowed the people, who were ground down to the lowest point of misery, to return to their occupations and to resume the practice of sacrifice. His justice in the decision of causes was beyond that of all the former kings. The Egyptians praise him in this respect more highly than any of their other monarchs, declaring that he not only gave his judgments with fairness, but also, when anyone was dissatisfied with his sentence, made compensation to him out of his own purse and thus pacified his anger."[1] The gods, however, had ordained that Egypt should suffer tyrannical rulers for a hundred and fifty years. The reigns of Cheops and Chephren, according to this legend, had already accounted for a hundred and six years, so that forty-four years of affliction still awaited the Egyptians when Mycerinus ascended the throne. Not to be foiled of their purpose, the gods decided that the reign of the "just and pious" Mycerinus must be cut short, but not without warning him that this fate was impending. To quote the words of Herodotus: "An oracle reached him from the town of Buto, which said 'six years only shalt thou live upon the earth, and in the seventh thou shalt end thy days.' Mycerinus, indignant, sent an angry message to the oracle, reproaching the god with his injustice—'My father and uncle,' he said, 'though they shut up the temples, took no thought of the gods and destroyed multitudes of men, nevertheless enjoyed a long life; I, who am pious, am to die so soon!' There came in reply a second message from the oracle—'For this very reason is thy life brought so quickly to a close—thou hast not done as it behoved thee. Egypt was fated to suffer affliction one hundred and fifty years—the two kings who preceded thee upon the throne understood this—thou hast not understood it.' Mycerinus, when this answer reached him, perceiving that his doom was fixed, had lamps prepared, which he lighted every day at eventime, and feasted and enjoyed himself unceasingly both day and night, moving about in the marsh-country and the woods, and visiting all the places that he heard were agreeable sojourns. His wish was to prove the oracle false, by turning the nights into days and so living twelve years in the space of six."[2]

There is certainly no reason for believing that the legend

[1] *Herodotus*, Book II, 129 (Rawlinson's translation).
[2] *Ibid.*, 133 (Rawlinson's translation).

quoted by Herodotus is founded on historical fact, although evidence that Mycerinus met an untimely death, possibly after a reign of eighteen years, is to be seen in all the buildings of his Pyramid complex. Mycerinus must have intended to follow the example of Chephren by constructing his Valley Building and Mortuary Temple of limestone faced with ashlars of granite and his Causeway of limestone. Reisner's excavations, however, have shown that this plan was never realised and that the greater part of the work was either hastily finished in materials of inferior quality or even left incomplete. Only the foundations of the Valley Building were made of stone; the superstructure was composed almost entirely of crude brick. The Causeway consisted of an embankment of stone, upon which was built a brick corridor overlaid, both inside and outside, with white plaster and roofed with wooden logs. In the Mortuary Temple, the foundations and the inner core of some of its walls were composed of limestone. A beginning had also been made with laying floors of granite and with adding granite facings to the walls, but crude brick was again the material used for completing the greater part of the building.

Examples of tombs and monuments left unfinished by the owner, but completed by his son or successor, are not uncommon. It would therefore be only natural to suppose that Shepseskaf, who is believed to have succeeded Mycerinus, was the king who built the crude brick additions to the Pyramid complex. Proof that Shepseskaf did, in fact, contribute towards the completion of the complex is provided by an inscription, found in the ruins of the Mortuary Temple, which states that he "made it [the temple] as his monument for his father, the King of Upper and Lower Egypt [Mycerinus]." Both the Valley Building and the Mortuary Temple were, however, repaired and slightly modified in design at a later date. These repairs and alterations were attributed by

Reisner to the priests who officiated in the temple during the
Vth and VIth Dynasties. Their labours, he pointed out, might
not have been inspired by considerations of duty alone, but
also by motives of self-interest. As mortuary priests, they
would have been entitled to enjoy the fruits of the rich en-
dowments bequeathed by the dead king in return for service
in his temple; they would also have been qualified to dwell
in his Pyramid City—a residential enclosure attached to the
Valley Building, the inhabitants of which were exempt from
the payment of certain taxes. To secure these privileges,
however, it would have been necessary for them to preserve
intact the fabric of the buildings and to maintain at least some
show of performing the temple services. Architecturally and
in their internal lay-out, both the earlier and the later forms
of the buildings differed considerably from those of Chephren,
but no fundamental changes in general composition were
introduced.

During his excavations of the Valley Building and the
Mortuary Temple, Reisner discovered a large number of
statues and statuettes, most of which represented the king
either alone or as a member of a group. Among those found
in the Valley Building were some beautifully carved slate
triads composed of the goddess Hathor, the king and one of
the *nome* deities (Plate 9). There can be no doubt that
Mycerinus intended to have forty-two of these triads, each
showing him in company with a different *nome*-god or
goddess, but only four and some fragments were discovered;
possibly the remainder were never carved. Another fine piece
of sculpture, also found in the Valley Building, was a slate
group-statue of Mycerinus and Queen Khamerernebty II
(Plate 10). As works of art, these statues are worthy of comparison with the best of their kind yet known. They have all
been carved in the naturalistic style typical of the Old Kingdom, with the result that a high degree of individuality in

points of detail is evident. Of the eight representations of the king's face, no two are exactly alike, but the majority portray the features with slightly bulging eyes, a rounded nose and a protruding lower lip. In many respects the face resembles that of Chephren, as portrayed in the famous diorite statue (Plate 8), but the cheek-bones in the latter are higher and the face narrower. Fifteen statuettes of the king had been left unfinished—a fact which can be explained by the king's untimely death and the parsimony of his successor. While the abandonment of these statuettes before completion must be deplored on æsthetic grounds, they throw more light in their present condition on the technical processes employed by Egyptian sculptors than if they had been preserved as finished works. Reisner, who conducted a minute examination of the figures, was able to detect eight distinct stages of development, some of which corresponded with the different stages illustrated by unfinished statues in scenes of sculptors' workshops represented in the wall decorations of tombs.

The Pyramid of Mycerinus occupies less than half the area covered by the Great Pyramid. Each side measures 356½ feet at the base. Its vertical height is now 204 feet; when complete, it was 14 feet higher. The upper portion is cased, in the normal manner, with dressed Tura limestone, but the lower sixteen courses have an outer facing of red granite, some of which has been left in the rough. It is possible that Mycerinus intended to case the whole Pyramid with granite; the change of material may therefore indicate the stage reached at the time of his death. On the other hand, the combination of limestone and granite may have been deliberate, so that the only evidence of untimely death would be the undressed granite at the base.

Internally, at least one and probably two changes of plan are apparent. The first design consisted of a sloping corridor of the usual kind (fig. 17, 1) tunnelled through the rock and leading to a rectangular burial-chamber, the longer axis of which ran from east to west. When this design was abandoned, the floor of the burial-chamber (fig. 17, 2) was deepened and

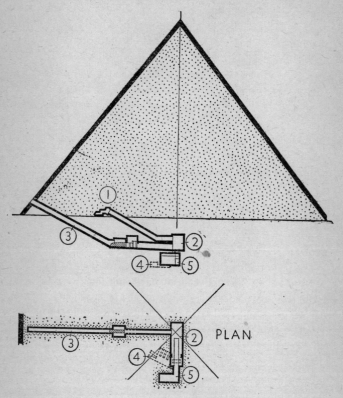

FIG. 17.—*The Pyramid of Mycerinus, section looking east, and plan.*

a second sloping corridor cut beneath the first (fig. 17, 3). The only reason for this change of plan seems to have been a decision to enlarge the superstructure of the Pyramid and the consequent necessity for constructing the corridor at a lower level in order to preserve the position of the entrance in the new north face at about the same height above the ground. As far as the point where it enters the rock, the new corridor is lined with granite. At the foot of the slope, the horizontal continuation of the corridor is enlarged into an antechamber, the rock walls of which are decorated with carved panelling. Three granite portcullises stood in the corridor between the antechamber and the burial-chamber.

The third and last design did not involve any alteration of the earlier plan, but only the addition of two chambers, the first being a magazine for storing objects which the dead king wished to have close to his body, and the second a new burial-chamber. Access to these chambers is gained by way of a ramp sloping westwards from the middle of the floor of the original burial-chamber and terminating in a short, horizontal passage. The magazine, which lies on the right side of the passage, is approached by a flight of steps (fig. 17, 4). It is a rectangular room with four deep cells in the east wall and two in the north, the entire room being hollowed out of the rock. The new burial-chamber is situated at the far end of the passage (fig. 17, 5). Its walls, floor and roof are composed entirely of granite. The underside of its pointed roof has been rounded, thus giving it the appearance of a barrel-vault. Within this chamber, Colonel Howard Vyse found a rectangular basalt sarcophagus, the outer faces of which were carved with a panel decoration. Unfortunately, this fine sarcophagus, which must originally have contained the body of Mycerinus, was lost when the ship which was transporting it to England foundered off the coast of Spain. In the original burial-chamber, Colonel Vyse had discovered some human bones and the lid of a wooden anthropoid coffin inscribed with the name of Mycerinus. This lid, which is now in the British Museum, can hardly have been made in the time of Mycerinus, for it is of a pattern not used before the Saite Period. The identity of the bones is extremely problematical; there is certainly no proof that they belonged to the king. Borchardt, possibly influenced by the dating of the lid, believed that the whole of the third design was the work of Saite restorers who, on entering the Pyramid, found the upper burial-chamber in complete disorder, and the remains of the body lying exposed. Since Borchardt expressed this view, however, excavation of the tomb of Shepseskaf has revealed that it contained both a magazine and a burial-chamber resembling in style those of this Pyramid. With this knowledge there appears to be no reason to doubt that the third design dates from the time of Mycerinus. The Saites, it must be supposed, simply placed the body in a new inner coffin and restored it to its original sarcophagus, making no structural alterations of any kind.

South of the Pyramid of Mycerinus lies a row of three subsidiary Pyramids, none of which appears to have been completed. The largest and most advanced stands at the eastern end of the row. Like the main Pyramid, it was cased, in part at least, with granite. Neither of the other two Pyramids had progressed beyond the construction of its inner core when the work was abandoned. Adjoining the east face of each Pyramid stood a small Mortuary Temple composed mainly of crude brick, and therefore probably built by Shepseskaf after the death of Mycerinus.

No evidence of their owners' identity was discovered during Reisner's excavation of these Pyramids, but the size of the first would suggest that it belonged to Khamerernebty II, the principal queen. In the second, Colonel Vyse discovered a small granite sarcophagus and some human bones, which he judged to be those of a young woman. This Pyramid may therefore have been the tomb of a younger queen or a princess. The ownership of the westernmost Pyramid in the row remains completely obscure.

Apart from the three major Pyramids at Giza and Seneferu's Pyramids at Meidum and Dahshur, only one Pyramid

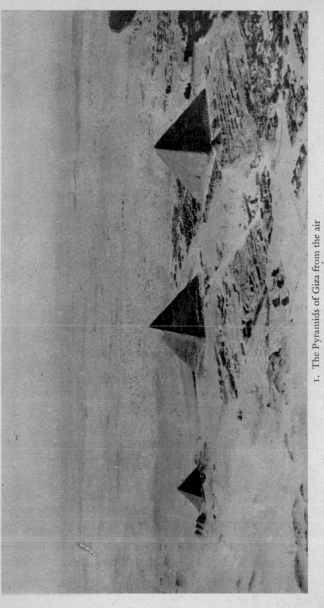

1. The Pyramids of Giza from the air

2. The Step Pyramid, south and west sides. *Sakkara*

3a. Limestone relief of Zoser performing a religious
ceremony. *Sakkara*

3b. Limestone statue of Zoser. *Cairo Museum*

4. The Step Pyramid, entrance colonnade – a reconstruction. *Sakkara*

5. Tiled panelling in the South Mastaba – a reconstruction. *Sakkara*

6a. The Pyramid of Meidum

6b. The Giant Sphinx. *Giza*

7. Ivory figure of Cheops. *Cairo Museum*

8. Diorite statue of Chephren. *Cairo Museum*

9. Slate Nome Triad: Mycerinus, Hathor and the goddess of the Jackal-nome. *Cairo Museum*

10. Slate group-statue of Mycerinus and Queen
Khamerernebty II. *Museum of Fine Arts, Boston*

11a. The Causeway of Unas. *Sakkara*

11b. Famine scene. Causeway of Unas. *Sakkara*

12. The ruined Funerary Temple of Neb-hepet-Ra Menthuhetep. *Deir-el-Bahri*

13b. Amenemhat III as a young man. *Cairo Museum*

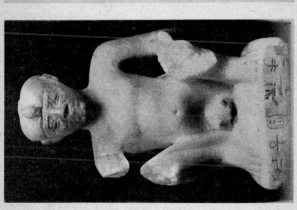

13a. Alabaster statuette of Pepi II as a child. *Cairo Museum*

14a. The Pyramids of Meroe

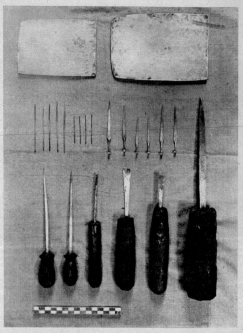

14b. Copper implements of the 1st Dynasty.
Cairo Museum

14c. Quarrymen's wedge-slots. *Aswan*

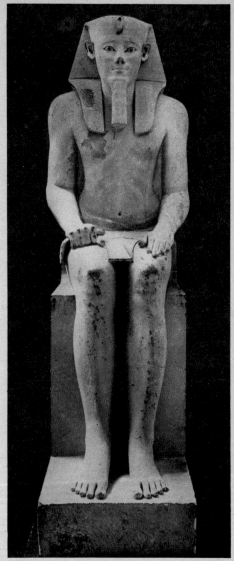

15. Limestone statue of Senusret I. *Cairo Museum*

of a IVth Dynasty king is known. Its builder, Dedefra, is believed to have reigned between Cheops and Chephren. The site which he chose was a commanding eminence at Abu Roash, some five miles to the north of the Giza plateau. Of the superstructure, so little remains that it is impossible to estimate its original dimensions or even to be certain that it was ever completed. The substructure consists of an open trench which slopes downwards to the base of a vertical shaft measuring about 30 feet in depth, 30 feet from north to south, and 70 feet from east to west. It is surprising that Dedefra should have elected to revert to the open trench and vertical shaft design of the IIIrd Dynasty, when his predecessor Cheops had succeeded in constructing the subterranean portions of his tomb by the less laborious method of tunnelling. Some difference in the quality of the rock foundation of the two Pyramids may, however, account for the change in technique. Physical considerations undoubtedly determined the line of the Causeway which, instead of running from east to west, approaches the Mortuary Temple from the north. By following this line, it was possible to utilise a ridge of rock and thus reduce the amount of building necessary for raising it to the required level. Petrie, who surveyed this Causeway, estimated that it was nearly a mile in length and, in places, 40 feet high. Nothing is now visible of the Valley Building, but enough of the Mortuary Temple, standing as usual on the east of the Pyramid, has been preserved to enable its ground-plan to be clearly traced. Its walls are made of mud-brick—a fact which strongly suggests that the building was hastily erected after the death of the king. Immediately south of the building lies a deep pit, the shape of which implies that it once contained a ceremonial boat.

Shepseskaf, who completed the Pyramid complex of Mycerinus, did not himself build a Pyramid. His tomb, which is situated at Sakkara, was examined in 1858 by Mariette, who wrongly identified its owner first as Unas, the last king of the Vth Dynasty, and subsequently as Aty, a successor of Unas. In 1924 the Service des Antiquités conducted a thorough excavation of the site under the direction of Gustave Jéquier, and the real ownership of the tomb was established. Known to the Arabs as the *Mastabat Fara‘un*, this tomb was built in the form of a huge rectangular sarcophagus resting possibly on a low platform. The sides of the sarcophagus inclined inwards at an angle of about 65°, and the square ends projected vertically above the level of the vaulted roof. Only the inner core of local stone is now visible, but originally it was cased with Tura limestone and given a skirting of granite. On the east side of the building stood a small Mortuary Temple, from the south-east corner of which a long Causeway, with walls of crude brick, led down to the Valley Building.

A queen named Khentikaues, who may have been married to Shepseskaf, built on an open space lying between the Causeways of Chephren and Mycerinus a tomb which was essentially similar to the *Mastabat Fara‘un*. At one time it was thought to be an unfinished Pyramid, but the recent excavations of Selim Bey Hassan on behalf of Cairo University have proved that, in reality, the superstructure was in the form of a sarcophagus mounted on a high, square podium. Its Mortuary Temple, which consists of only three rooms, has been hewn entirely out of the rock core of the podium, and is therefore not a separate construction. The Causeway runs first towards the east and then turns a complete right angle southwards, finishing at a Valley Building which extends along the full length of the Valley Building of Mycerinus.

Viewing the Pyramids of the IVth Dynasty as a whole, it is undeniable that they are characterised chiefly by the employment of megalithic masonry. Reisner has estimated that some of the blocks of local stone embodied in the walls of the Mortuary Temple of Mycerinus weigh as much as 220 tons, while the heaviest of the granite ashlars, all of which have been transported 500 miles from Aswan, may exceed 30 tons. The use of such massive blocks offered two main advantages: greater stability was attained and the number of joints to be fitted was reduced. Cheops, who may have been a megalomaniac, could never, during a reign of about twenty-three years, have erected a building of the size and durability of the Great Pyramid if technical advances had not enabled his masons to handle stones of very considerable weight and dimensions. How completely they had mastered this art may be gauged from Petrie's observation that the joints in the casing of the Great Pyramid measured only one-fiftieth of an inch in thickness.

A parallel development to the handling of heavy blocks was the progress made in the art of cutting hard stones. Even as early as the Ist Dynasty, there is an instance of the use of granite for paving a chamber, while the small burial-chambers in Zoser's Step Pyramid and South Mastaba are composed entirely of this material. It was, however, only in the IVth Dynasty that structures of the size of Chephren's Valley Building and Mortuary Temple were faced completely with granite. Basalt also occurs sporadically long before the IVth Dynasty, but not in the quantity employed in the pavement of Cheops' Mortuary Temple or the lost sarcophagus of Mycerinus. Petrie has even expressed the opinion that one of the subsidiary Pyramids of the Great Pyramid had arris lines of basalt extending down each corner to prevent wear and weathering.

Statuary during the IVth Dynasty made a very big advance both in quantity and in quality. Reisner, after examining all the fragments of sculpture discovered in Chephren's Valley Building and Mortuary Temple, calculated that the Second Pyramid complex alone contained between one hundred and two hundred separate statues. A similar number may well

have been made for the Great Pyramid and the Pyramid of
Mycerinus, so that the aggregate of statues in the three complexes possibly reached a figure not far short of five hundred.
The full effect of the stimulus to the sculptor's art given by the
interest of these kings only becomes apparent in the two following dynasties, when nearly every private tomb in Giza
and Sakkara included a statue of its owner. Artistically, the
relatively few specimens which have survived from the three
Giza Pyramids bear testimony of a greater experience in
portraying the human features than any earlier statues.

In marked contrast with the abundant evidence of sculpture
in the round is the almost complete absence of any trace of
reliefs in the IVth Dynasty Pyramid complexes. The only
examples revealed by excavation were found in the Mortuary
Temple of Cheops and in the chapel of the second of his
subsidiary Pyramids. Other fragments of reliefs from temples
of Cheops and Chephren, however, have been recovered
from buildings of the Middle Kingdom at Lisht whither they
had been taken and reused. All these pieces show that the art
of carving in low relief, so exquisitely illustrated in the
galleries of the Step Pyramid and South Mastaba, was not lost
during the IVth Dynasty, but unless the future holds in store
some unsuspected discovery, it must be assumed that it was
not extensively employed.

CHAPTER V

PYRAMIDS OF THE
Vth AND VIth DYNASTIES

ALTHOUGH documentary records are lacking, the character of the political events which attended the close of the IVth Dynasty may be conjectured from a number of indirect indications. The three successors of Cheops—Dedefra, Chephren (Khaef-Ra) and Mycerinus (Men-kau-Ra)—had proclaimed their recognition of the Sun-god Ra by forming their names of compounds with his name. There is some evidence also that Chephren and Mycerinus had adopted the title "Son of Ra"—a royal title which figures regularly from the Vth Dynasty onwards. It seems therefore reasonable to infer that the cult of Ra was already in the time of these kings superseding the more primitive cult of Atum in Heliopolis. At the end of the IVth Dynasty, however, Shepseskaf not only departed from the type of tomb built by his predecessors, but, so far as is known, did not follow their precedent by acknowledging unequivocally, either in name or in title, his association with Ra. Whether he was guided by motives of religious principle or political expediency cannot be deduced from the evidence available, but, in view of the caution and conservatism shown by the Egyptians at all times in matters appertaining to religion and the After-life, it is difficult to believe that Shepseskaf would have introduced such fundamental changes if he had not thought that the increasing power of the priesthood of Ra directly menaced the authority and independence of the throne. Shepseskaf's struggle, which was perhaps passive and not waged with destructive bitterness, failed to achieve any permanent success, for his death, after a reign of little more than four years, led to the accession of a line of kings who raised the cult of Ra to the position of the official state religion.

A papyrus in the Berlin Museum, known as the Papyrus Westcar, has preserved a legend concerning the origin of the Vth Dynasty which may embody a kernel of truth. The papyrus itself probably dates from the Second Intermediate Period, but it was certainly a copy of an older document. According to this legend, the first three kings of the dynasty— Userkaf, Sahura and Neferirkara—were triplets begotten of Ra and born of the wife of a priest of Ra. Userkaf may well have been sprung from a priestly stock, and it seems likely that he himself held the office of High Priest of Heliopolis before ascending the throne. His mother was Neferhetepes, who appears to have been a daughter of Dedefra. Sahura and Neferirkara were possibly brothers, the sons of Shepseskaf and Khentikaues, whose heresy, however, they made no effort to revive.

Each of these three kings and three of their successors built special Sun Temples in honour of Ra. Contemporary inscriptions mention all six temples, but only those of Niuserra and Userkaf have hitherto been found (fig. 18, 1 and 2). Incomparably the better preserved, because it was built of stone, was Niuserra's temple, excavated in 1898–1901 by Ludwig Borchardt and Heinrich Schaefer on behalf of Baron von Bissing and the Deutsche Orient-Gesellschaft (fig. 19). It was erected on the summit of a low mound situated on the edge of the desert at Abu Gurab, about a mile north of Abu Sir, where Niuserra built his Pyramid. A Causeway surmounted by a covered corridor led up to the mound from a large pavilion standing inside a spacious enclosure. At the upper end of the Causeway, and still recognisable, is a paved court 330 feet long and 250 feet broad, in which the principal feature is a rectangular podium built to support a squat obelisk, the sacred

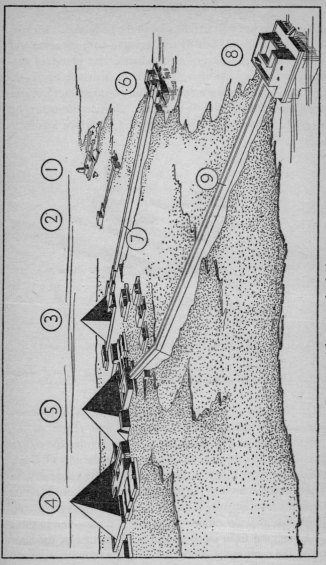

FIG. 18.—*The Pyramids of Abu Sir—a reconstruction.*

symbol of the Sun-god. At the foot of the podium stands a low
sacrificial altar composed of five massive slabs of alabaster.
Gutters cut in the pavement conducted the blood of the
animals offered on the altar to nine large alabaster basins. A
small sacrificial enclosure and a group of magazines occupy
the whole northern side of the court. Outside the court, to
the south, lie the brick foundations of a pit which formerly

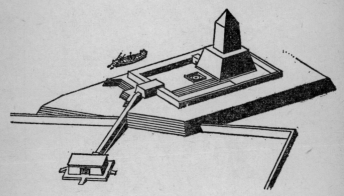

FIG. 19.—*The Sun-temple of Niuserra.*

contained a model of the boat used by the Sun-god in his daily
journey across the sky.

Temples and mortuary buildings of the Vth Dynasty
were lavishly decorated with painted wall reliefs of the
highest artistic quality. In Niuserra's Sun Temple the reliefs,
which have now been transferred to the museums of Cairo
and Berlin, were found in the corridor of the Causeway, in
its continuation around the east and south sides of the court
and in a chapel situated between the end of the corridor and
the obelisk. A wide variety of subjects is represented in these
reliefs, ranging from the flora and fauna created by the Sun-
god to the ceremonies connected with the foundation of the

temple and the *heb-sed* of the king. The representation of the *heb-sed* implies that this temple was not built until many years —possibly thirty—after the king had ascended the throne. It is highly improbable, however, that Niuserra would have delayed the construction of a Sun Temple until so late in his life; the stone building may therefore have replaced an earlier temple of brick and have been erected for the special purpose of celebrating the *heb-sed*.

The practice of building Pyramids, discarded by Shepseskaf, was resumed by the kings of the Vth Dynasty. Both in size and in quality, however, these Pyramids were inferior to their predecessors, being composed merely of a core of small stones within a casing of Tura limestone. In consequence of their poor construction, all the Pyramids of this period have suffered severely, and some have been reduced to little more than mounds of sand and rubble.

Userkaf built his Pyramid at Sakkara, close to the northeast corner of the Step Pyramid enclosure. By the time of the Vth Dynasty, Zoser's tomb may have acquired a particular sanctity and burial in its vicinity may have been thought to confer special benefits. Such an explanation would account for Userkaf's choice of a site which in other respects seems to have been unsuitable for a Pyramid. Immediately to the east, where the Mortuary Temple would normally have been constructed, the ground rises steeply; only a small chapel was therefore built against the eastern face of the Pyramid, while the main temple stood exceptionally on the southern side. C. M. Firth's excavations on behalf of the Service des Antiquités in 1928-29 revealed that the temple had been destroyed in antiquity and that its site had been reused in the Saite Period for building tombs, the superstructures of which were actually composed of stone taken from Userkaf's temple and from the neighbouring Pyramids. So completely had the temple been destroyed that many details of its plan, which appears to have been abnormal, could not be determined with any certainty. Among the ruins, the excavators found some fragments of scenes, delicately carved in low relief, showing the king in the presence of the gods and on fowling expeditions in the marshes of the Delta. They also discovered the head of a colossal red granite statue of the king, which is of special interest as being almost the only royal head of the Vth Dynasty at present known, and the earliest instance—if the Giant Sphinx be excluded—of a work of sculpture exceeding life size.

Sahura, Neferirkara and Niuserra chose for their Pyramids a plateau on the desert edge near the modern village of Abu Sir (fig. 18, 3, 4 and 5). While conforming with the standard lay-out, the complexes of Sahura and Niuserra surpassed in artistic magnificence anything which had previously been attempted. Ludwig Borchardt, who excavated this group of Pyramids on behalf of the Deutsche Orient-Gesellschaft in 1902-8, estimated that the area of wall-surface covered by reliefs in Sahura's complex alone amounted to about 10,000 square metres. Unfortunately, later inhabitants of the neighbourhood discovered that the fine Tura limestone of the reliefs produced the best lime, with the result that of the original total only about 150 square metres, broken into innumerable fragments, survived their depredations. Niuserra's complex had suffered even more severely than that of Sahura. The complex of Neferirkara was never finished, and it is probable that the work was abandoned before many of the intended reliefs had been executed.

The Valley Building of Sahura was provided with two landing-stages, one facing towards the east and the other towards the south (fig. 18, 6; fig. 21, 1 and 2); ramps connected the landing-stages either with a canal or with the Nile, which, during its annual period of inundation, may well have spread so far beyond its normal bounds. Recessed in the east face of the building was a portico, the floor of which was composed of black polished basalt and the ceiling of limestone, painted blue to represent the sky and decorated with golden stars carved in relief; the eight monolithic columns were of granite and the walls, above a granite dado, were of limestone decorated with painted reliefs. In design, the columns were imitations of date-palms with their leaves tied vertically in a bunch to form the capitals (fig. 20). Each column bore, within a rectangular frame, the king's name and titles carved in hieroglyphs and inlaid with green paste. A similar, though less deeply recessed, portico was constructed in the south face of the building; its floor, however, was of limestone and its columns were cylindrical, lacking any form of capital. Both the porticos were connected by passages with a small T-shaped hall, the only apartment within the building. The reliefs in this hall probably showed the king, in the form of either a sphinx or a griffin, trampling underfoot Asiatics and Libyans, who were led to him bound as captives by the gods. This scene was repeated, possibly with slight variations, on the

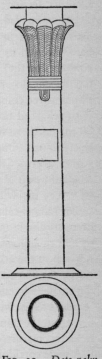

FIG. 20.—*Date-palm column.*

inner walls of the Causeway at its lower end (fig. 18, 7; fig. 21, 3).

Sahura's Mortuary Temple consisted of the five main elements already found in the Temple of Chephren—an entrance hall, an open court, five niches for statues, magazines and a sanctuary. The entrance hall (fig. 21, 4) is too badly damaged to allow all the details of its construction to be determined with certainty, but its floor was of limestone and its walls, above a granite dado, were probably of the same material decorated with painted reliefs. The open court (fig. 21, 5) was paved with polished basalt; apart from an alabaster altar standing in the north-west corner, it was completely bare. Around its four sides ran a cloister which resembled in construction the eastern portico of the Valley Building, except that its star-decorated roof was supported by only one row of palm-tree columns. The walls of the cloister were covered with reliefs of the king triumphing over his enemies, those on the northern side being Asiatics and those on the southern side Libyans. One of these reliefs, found in the south-west corner, shows Sahura in the act of slaying a captured Libyan chieftain; two of the chieftain's sons and a woman, who may be either his wife or his daughter, stand by imploringly. Other Libyan captives, some of whom are women and children, are also represented in a similar attitude. Elsewhere in the scene live animals, taken as booty, are shown; their number is given in the accompanying inscriptions as 123,440 head of cattle, 223,400 asses, 232,413 deer and 243,688 sheep, but only the smallest fraction of this vast total is actually represented. Similar scenes, which may have amounted to eleven in number, from the remainder of the cloister were too fragmentary to be reconstructed in detail.

A wide corridor, also paved with basalt and decorated with reliefs, surrounded the outside of the court. From the surviving fragments, it is evident that these reliefs were mostly different in character from those of the court or the Causeway. On the northern side were scenes of the king harpooning fish and fowling with a throw-stick. On the southern side, in a relief measuring about 30 feet in length, the king is shown hunting. Behind him stand his successor Neferirkara and a group of courtiers. In front are antelopes, gazelles, deer and other

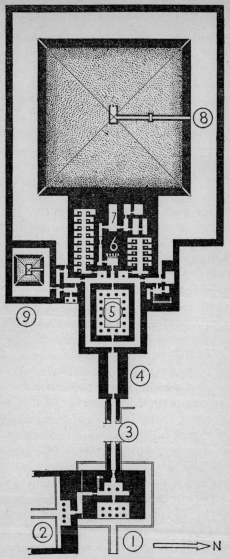

FIG. 21.—*The Pyramid complex of Sahura.*

horned animals driven by beaters into a large enclosure where
the king shoots them with arrows from his bow. Hounds seize
some of the wounded beasts by the throat and despatch them.
Here and there the sculptor has varied the regularity of the
scene with such lively touches as a jerboa and a hedgehog
about to disappear into their holes and a hyæna seizing a
wounded antelope as its private quarry. The preservation of
this remarkably fine piece of sculpture was due to the mere
chance that this part of the corridor became in later times a
sanctuary which housed a much-venerated figure of the fire-
goddess Sekhmet.

Some of the most interesting reliefs in the whole temple
were carved on the east wall of the western corridor. North of
the door leading from the open court, the king, accompanied
by his courtiers, was represented witnessing the departure of
twelve sea-going ships to a land which is not specified, but
which was probably Palestine or Syria. In the corresponding
position on the south side of the door, the king and his retinue
watched the return of the ships laden with cargo and carrying
a number of Asiatics. It is not clear whether the ships had been
engaged in a naval operation or employed on a commercial
errand; the cargo may, therefore, have been either booty or
merchandise and the Asiatics either prisoners or slaves obtained by trading. Even in the reign of Seneferu, the Egyptians had procured timber from Syria, so that this expedition
represented no fresh enterprise initiated by Sahura.

Access to every part of the complex could be gained directly
or indirectly from the western corridor. By way of a door at
the northern end, it was possible to reach either the Pyramid
enclosure or a staircase leading to the roof of the temple; a
similar door at the opposite end of the corridor also led to
the Pyramid enclosure and, in addition, to the subsidiary
Pyramid court (fig. 21, 9) and a side entrance into the complex.
In the middle of the corridor, on the west side, a passage fol-

lowed by a short flight of steps opened into a small chamber containing the five statue-niches (fig. 21, 6). A door in the southern wall of this chamber provided the only means of access to the sanctuary (fig. 21, 7) and five rooms lying beyond, of which at least two were used for the performance of some kind of ceremony in the temple ritual. The sanctuary measured about 45 feet in length and about 15 feet in breadth. Its floor may have been paved with alabaster—a material which was certainly used for the low altar standing at the foot of the granite false door in the west wall. Above a dado of granite, the north, south and east walls were composed of limestone and were decorated with reliefs of gods bringing gifts of provisions to the king.

The magazines, arranged in two rows, were approached by way of passages leading from two deep recesses in the west wall of the western corridor, seventeen from the southern recess and ten from the northern recess. Supporting the roof of each recess was a granite column, 12 feet in height and shaped like a cluster of six papyrus stems tied together, the capital being formed of their buds (fig. 22). The magazines were constructed in blocks of two storeys, each consisting of one room, and every block had its own staircase. It seems likely that the smaller group of magazines was intended for the storage of particularly valuable objects, such as decorated vases and gilded statues, used by the mortuary priests on special occasions. Some fragments of relief from the walls of one of the rooms showed the king holding an investiture; it is possible, therefore, that this room contained specimens of the gold decorations awarded by the king to his officials in recognition of distinguished service. The magazines in the larger group were probably used for storing stone vessels and provisions.

An interesting feature in Sahura's complex was its very elaborate drainage system. Rain falling on the roof escaped through stone spouts in the form of lions' heads which projected from the top of the outer walls. In the unroofed parts of the complex, the rainwater flowed through apertures at the base of the outer walls, to which it was conducted by channels cut in the paving. A different method of drainage was, however, employed for removing water and other liquids used during the temple ceremonies, some of which may have be-

come ritually impure and would therefore be dangerous to touch. Five stone basins, lined with copper and provided with lead plugs to fit the vents, stood in different parts of the inner temple, two in the rooms beyond the sanctuary, one in the sanctuary itself, another in the corridor leading to the sanctuary and the last in the smaller group of magazines. Pipes made of copper connected these basins with an underground drainage system consisting of a line of copper pipes which ran beneath the paving of the inner temple, the open court, the entrance hall and the Causeway as far as the lower end, where it terminated in an outlet in the southern side. All the metal for this piping must have been mined in Sinai or in the eastern desert; it is more than 1,000 feet in length, and the use of such a quantity of this valuable metal provides eloquent testimony of the importance attributed to its presence by Sahura.

FIG. 22.—*Papyrus-cluster column.*

Both externally and internally Sahura's Pyramid has suffered severely. When complete, its sides measured about 257 feet at the base and its vertical height was about 162 feet. Only a few fragments of the original Tura limestone casing have been preserved, but a considerable part of the rough inner core remains intact. The corridor leading to the burial chamber is almost completely choked with fallen masonry, so that it is virtually impassable. From its entrance in the north face (fig. 21, 8), at a point a little to the east of the middle and on a level with the surrounding court, it slopes downwards at an angle of 27° for a distance of about 14 feet to continue horizontally for 27 feet, where it was blocked by a granite portcullis; from there it ascended at a gentle gradient until it entered the oblong burial-chamber. Blocks of Tura limestone lined the whole corridor, with the exception of the entrance slope, a few feet on each side of the portcullis and a short section at the end, where it was lined with granite. The burial chamber was built entirely of Tura limestone; its pointed roof consisted of three superimposed layers of masonry. Perring, who was able to examine the roof, estimated that its largest blocks measured 35 feet in length, 9 feet in width and 12 feet in thickness. In spite of their size and weight, however, only two of these blocks remain unbroken.

Neferirkara, whose reign probably lasted for more than ten years, planned a Pyramid complex closely resembling that of Sahura, but on a larger scale (fig. 18, 4). He was not, however, destined to see it completed. At the time of his death, the foundations of the Valley Building may have been laid, the Causeway—but not the corridor above it—had been constructed and work on the five statue-niches and sanctuary of the inner temple had reached an advanced stage. The Pyramid, although nearer completion than the buildings in the remainder of the complex, was also unfinished; it measured 360 feet square at the base and rose to a height of 228 feet, so that it was slightly bigger than the Pyramid of Mycerinus. The few fragments surviving from the outer casing show that the lowest course at least was composed of granite, the surface of which had not been dressed. Neferefra, Neferirkara's short-lived successor, who may have started to build a Pyramid at a short distance to the south-east, and Niuserra continued the construction of both the Pyramid and the Mortuary Temple after Neferirkara's death, but they used only crude brick and modified his plans. The Valley Building and Causeway were left unfinished, and were subsequently appropriated by Niuserra. As a consequence, Neferirkara's mortuary priests, who would otherwise, no doubt, have followed the normal practice of building their Pyramid City in the vicinity of the Valley Building, grouped their houses of crude brick against the walls of the Mortuary Temple.

In order to use the Causeway of Neferirkara without any alteration, it would have been necessary for Niuserra to build his Pyramid complex immediately to the east of Neferirkara's Mortuary Temple. He chose, however, a site lying to the north-east, so that only the lower half of the Causeway could be used as it stood. The upper half was dismantled and a large part of it rebuilt at the required angle towards the north-east (fig. 18, 9). This angle was somewhat lessened by the exceptional placing of the entrance hall and cloistered court of the temple opposite the southern half of the east face of the Pyramid. Unless this position was deliberately selected with a view to shortening the distance between the temple and the older Causeway, the decision to depart from the normal practice of constructing the temple in line with the main east-west axis of the Pyramid must have been dictated either by the presence in that area of an obstruction—possibly a tomb—or by the unsuitable configuration of the ground.

Niuserra's complex differed from that of Sahura in detail only, but it provides a good illustration of the extent to which the standard plan could be adapted to fit the physical requirements of any particular site. The Valley Building (fig. 18, 8) had two porticos, the larger facing eastwards and the smaller westwards; instead, however, of the palm columns found in Sahura's Valley Building, these porticos were furnished with papyrus-cluster columns of red granite. Tura limestone, red granite and black polished basalt were again used in combination for the ceilings, walls and floors of the apartments. Basalt was also employed in the construction of a dado for the walls of the corridor of the Causeway. Above this dado the walls were faced with Tura limestone and decorated with reliefs showing various scenes, which included the representation of the king as a lion or a griffin trampling his enemies underfoot. In the Mortuary Temple, papyrus-cluster columns supported the roof of the ambulatory surrounding the cloistered court. The magazines, owing to lack of space in the inner temple, were mostly built outside the north and south walls of the entrance-hall. The sanctuary occupied its normal position due east of the burial-chamber, and therefore considerably north of the east-west axis of the temple. South-east of the main Pyramid lay the usual subsidiary Pyramid.

A successor of Niuserra, Dedkara Isesi, built his Pyramid at Sakkara. This Pyramid, known formerly by its Arabic name "Haram esh-Shauwāf"—the Pyramid of the Sentinel—was only identified as the tomb of Isesi in the autumn of 1945, when it was excavated by the Service des Antiquités under the direction of Alexandre Varille.

The last king of the dynasty, Unas, erected his Pyramid close to the south-west corner of the Step Pyramid enclosure wall and almost diagonally opposite the Pyramid of Userkaf, the founder of the dynasty. Recent excavations by the Service des Antiquités, under the direction first of Selim Bey Hassan and subsequently of Abdessalam Hussein Effendi, have revealed that a larger part of the Causeway has been preserved in this Pyramid complex than in any other known instance (Plate 11A). Although only the upper end has so far been completely cleared of sand, its course has been determined over the whole distance of about 730 yards which separates the Valley Building from the Mortuary Temple. It does not follow a straight line, but changes its direction twice in order to use the natural features to their best advantage. In spite of these adjustments, however, it was still necessary to bridge depressions in the ground, possibly 25 feet in depth and considerably greater in width. Some of the blocks employed in the bridging embankment were taken from the buildings of the Step Pyramid enclosure—a fact which proves that Zoser's famous monument was already falling into disrepair at the end of the Vth Dynasty. The sides of the embankment were built with a steep batter, which reduced its width at the top to about 22 feet. On this massive foundation the usual covered corridor was laid; its walls, possibly 12 feet in height, were about 6 feet 8 inches in thickness, and the central passage approximately 8 feet 7 inches in width. The flat roof was made of slabs measuring 1 foot 6 inches in depth which projected inwards from each side, leaving in the middle a gap of about 8 inches in width to admit light. South of the Causeway lay a boat-pit 148 feet in length and lined entirely with Tura limestone.

Scenes covering a wide range of subjects were delicately carved in low relief on the inner walls of the corridor. One group of reliefs illustrated the transport by ship from Aswan of the granite date-palm columns and architraves used in the construction of the Mortuary Temple. Another series represented craftsmen hammering gold, casting copper objects and polishing vessels made of gold and stone. Elsewhere, labourers on the royal estates were shown gathering figs, harvesting corn and collecting honey. Long trains of servants were depicted bringing provisions of every kind to the tomb. Hunting scenes included specimens of every horned animal known to the Egyptians, as well as a giraffe, a lion, leopards, wolves, hyænas, jerboas and hedgehogs. Possibly the most graphic scene of all illustrated the victims of a famine, whose bodies were so emaciated that they were reduced to little more than skin and bone (Plate 11B). Unfortunately the scene is incomplete and it is difficult to imagine its context; even the nationality of the people cannot be identified with certainty.

Since, however, tomb reliefs depicted only incidents or events which the dead owner wished to perpetuate, it must be supposed that the starving people were not Egyptians and that the missing portion contained scenes of provisions being sent to them by Unas. All these reliefs were painted in bright colours, traces of which are still clearly visible. The ceiling also was painted with golden stars carved in relief on a sky-blue background.

Unas' Mortuary Temple was partly excavated by Alessandro Barsanti on behalf of the Service des Antiquités in 1900. A second and more complete excavation was undertaken by the Service des Antiquités in 1929 under the direction of C. M. Firth. In plan and construction it resembled very closely the Mortuary Temple of Sahura, though the lay-out of the corridors and magazines in the inner temple was somewhat different. Its floors also were different, alabaster having been used as paving where basalt had been employed by Sahura. In contrast with the large number of reliefs surviving from the Causeway, only a few fragments, showing servants bearing offerings, have been preserved from the temple.

Externally, the Pyramid of Unas presents no feature of special interest. Its original base measurement of 220 feet square and its perpendicular height of 62 feet seem modest in comparison with the monuments of the IVth Dynasty. Internally, however, many innovations are apparent. The entrance, although on the north side, is not in the face of the Pyramid, but under the pavement. Three portcullises of granite formerly blocked the corridor leading from the entrance to a square vestibule (fig. 23, 1). On the east side of this vestibule lies a long, narrow room, in the east wall of which are three statue-niches (fig. 23, 2). The burial-chamber occupies a corresponding position west of the vestibule (fig. 23, 3). At the far end of the chamber stands a rectangular stone sarcophagus which, although undamaged, had been robbed of its contents long before 1881, when it was found by Sir Gaston Maspero, the first archæologist to clear a way into the Pyramid. All the apartments are built of Tura limestone, with the exception of the west wall of the burial-chamber and the western halves of its north and south walls, opposite the ends of the sarcophagus, where the limestone is replaced by alabaster on which an elaborate panel design and a false door have been carved and painted.

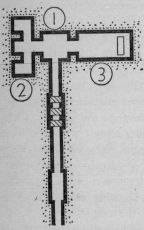

More notable, however, than the structural innovations of this Pyramid are the vertical columns of hieroglyphic inscription which entirely cover the walls of the vestibule and the limestone portions of the walls of the burial-chamber. Every hieroglyph has been filled with a blue pigment, so that it stands out clearly against the white background. These inscriptions are known as the Pyramid texts. They are found not only in this Pyramid but also in the VIth Dynasty Pyramids of Teti, Pepi I, Merenra and Pepi II, in the Pyramid of a king named Ibi, whose date is uncertain, and in the Pyramids of Pepi II's three queens. They do not form a continuous narrative, but consist of a collection of spells assembled with little regard to content and in no fixed order. Although most of the spells occur in more than one Pyramid, very few are repeated in all the Pyramids in which the texts are found; in the Pyramid of Unas, for instance, only two hundred and twenty-eight spells are included out of a known total exceeding seven hundred.

Fig. 23.—*Chambers and corridors of the Pyramid of Unas.*

The purpose of the Pyramid texts, like that of every other element in the Pyramid complex, was to secure for the king or queen a happy After-life. So powerful was the magic of the written word that its presence alone provided a sufficient guarantee that the thought expressed would be realised. Doubtless the spoken word, if delivered by a qualified person, possessed at least equal virtue, but its utterance was dependent on the goodwill or diligence of other people. A text which is generally inscribed on the north wall of the burial-chamber reproduces the ritual which the priests used to recite every day in the Mortuary Temple when laying the provisions on the altar in front of the false door. By having this ritual in writing and supplies of provisions in the magazines of his temple, the king believed that he would eliminate the risk of suffering hunger and thirst, even if the priests should neglect to perform their duties. Many of the texts describe the journey of the king to the Other World, situated in the sky beyond the eastern horizon, and his activities on arrival. It is clear that the king could count on little assistance from the gods when making this journey, but, armed with the magic power of the texts, he might expect to overcome successfully its many hazards. With their help, moreover, his association with the Sun-god in his daily voyage across the sky was assured. Among the texts were also collections of hymns to the gods and prayers on behalf of the dead king.

For the most part, the Pyramid texts were certainly not inventions of the Vth or VIth Dynasties, but had originated in extreme antiquity; it is hardly surprising, therefore, that they sometimes contain allusions to conditions which no longer prevailed at the time of Unas and his successors. As an example, Spell 662 includes the words "Cast the sand from thy face," which could only refer to the burial practices of pre-dynastic times when the king was interred in a grave dug in the sand. Another anachronism of a similar kind, but with reference to the brick Mastabas of the Archaic Period, occurs in Spell 355: "The bricks are removed for thee from the great tomb." A relic of even more ancient times is contained in a passage (Spells 273-274) which describes the dead king as a hunter who catches and devours the gods so that he may appropriate their qualities unto himself. On the other hand, many of the texts expressly mention the Pyramid and, in consequence, may not have originated before the IIIrd–IVth Dynasties; for instance, Spell 599 states: "They [the gods] are those who will cause this work to be enduring and this Pyramid to be enduring." It seems certain, in view of the constant references to the solar cult, that the texts were compiled by the priests of Heliopolis. When making the compilation, probably in the Vth Dynasty, they used old religious and funerary spells and added some incantations of a later date to meet contemporary needs.

Although the Pyramid texts were designed to help the dead king, their presence in his tomb introduced a new complication of a very serious kind. Being written in hieroglyphs, they included many images of living creatures. Such images not only possessed the value of a particular hieroglyphic sign, but also, through the power of magic, became actual embodiments of the creatures which they represented. The lion, for instance, was simultaneously both a phonogram with the value of *ru* and the living animal itself endowed with all its attributes. Images of human beings, which form some of the most common hieroglyphic signs, likewise fulfilled a dual function. To overcome the dangers to the dead king which would have resulted from the presence of a multitude of potentially hostile and destructive creatures in his close vicinity, the Egyptian priests and sculptors resorted to a number of different devices. Sometimes the dangerous signs were omitted or replaced by signs representing inanimate objects which possessed the same hieroglyphic value. Human beings were deprived of their legs and bodies so that they consisted of heads and arms alone. Animals could be rendered harmless by the simple expedient of mutilating their bodies and carving them in two separate halves. Serpents were represented intact, but the scorpion was deprived of its tail. One creature which, with a single exception, was never allowed to appear on the walls of the burial-chamber was the fish. This omission was not, however, due to any fear lest the fish should molest the owner of the tomb, but was the result of a belief that the fish, although innocuous to living people, would defile a dead body.

During the Middle Kingdom, the Pyramid texts were retained in a modified form. The custom of inscribing the texts on the walls of the chambers and corridors of the tomb was, however, abandoned. Instead, they were written on the interior surfaces of the rectangular wooden coffins used in that period—a fact which has caused them to become known as the Coffin Texts. By that time also they had ceased to be the exclusive property of royalty and had been usurped by the nobility, thus following the same course of democratisation as so many other practices which had been designed in the first instance as a royal prerogative. Under the New Kingdom, the texts, after undergoing still further modifications, were written on papyrus and were called the Book of Coming Forth by Day, better known in modern times as the Book of the Dead.

Teti, Pepi I and Merenra built their Pyramids at Sakkara, Teti choosing a site north-east of the Step Pyramid and his two successors moving southwards to sites in the neighbourhood of the Mastaba of Shepseskaf. All three complexes followed conventional lines, but the full details of their construction cannot be ascertained until they have been excavated more completely. The Pyramids themselves, though small in comparison with earlier works and now gravely dilapidated, are nevertheless of considerable importance on account of their texts, which include many spells not recorded in the Pyramid of Unas. One of the three Pyramids—that of Pepi I—has a particular claim to be remembered for its texts because they were the first examples of their kind to be found. Before their discovery by Maspero in 1881, it was supposed that the interior walls of Pyramids had at all times been left bare and uninscribed.

Pepi II, who succeeded Merenra, ascended the throne as a child (Plate 13A) and died, according to Manetho, a centenarian. Later Egyptian historical records credit him with having ruled for ninety-four years, which, if correct, would mean that his reign was by far the longest in the whole course of Egyptian history. His Pyramid complex, or what remains of it after centuries of depredation, is situated a short distance to the south of those of his two predecessors and within 300 yards of the north-west corner of Shepseskaf's Mastaba. It was excavated between the years 1926 and 1936 by Gustave Jéquier, who succeeded in recovering the whole of its ground-plan and not a little of its structure. As a result of his work, it is possible to see the plan of the standard Pyramid complex in its final and most highly developed form.

In front of the Valley Building and projecting for a considerable distance beyond its northern and southern limits, lay a broad terrace (fig. 24, 1). To reach this terrace from the level of the Valley, it was necessary to mount a short ramp at either end and continue by a longer ramp ascending at a right angle. A high limestone wall of great thickness bounded the terrace on its north, south and west sides. Narrow staircases built in the masonry at each end of the wall led up to a parapet which extended along the wall for the whole of its length. In the middle of the long west wall stood a door set in a granite frame, on which the names and titles of the king were carved in large hieroglyphs. Beyond the door was a passage running through the thickness of the walls to an elongated hypostyle hall with eight rectangular pillars, probably made of lime-stone. As in the rest of the building, only the floor and founda-tions of this hall have been preserved substantially intact, but the excavator found among the debris some fragments of delicately carved and painted low reliefs which had once adorned the walls. The scenes represented appear to have been of the conventional kind, showing the king slaying his enemies, fowling in the marshes and associating with the gods. It was undoubtedly the most important apartment in the whole building, the remainder of which consisted of maga-zines and two subsidiary chambers, apparently with bare walls. No trace of any sculptures in the round was revealed during the excavations, but it is not improbable that the building once housed a number of statues of the king.

Although in a far poorer state of preservation, the Causeway of Pepi II (fig. 24, 2) resembles that of Unas in many respects. Both Causeways change their direction twice, either in order to make the best use of available natural features or possibly to lessen the angle of their gradient. In their dimensions also the corridors surmounting the two Causeways were approxi-mately alike. In contrast, however, with the very substantial portions of relief which have been preserved in the corridor of Unas, only scattered fragments have been recovered from that of Pepi II. From these fragments it seems evident that the scenes at the lower end of the corridor were similar to those occupying a corresponding position in the corridor of Sahura: the king, represented both as a sphinx and as a griffin, was shown trampling under foot the traditional enemies of Egypt, who were led to him as captives by the gods. Accompanying this scene, as elsewhere, was another set of reliefs showing the goddess Seshat compiling a register of the victims and of the booty acquired. The scenes at the upper end of the corridor were of a purely funerary character. Long processions of servants were shown carrying produce from the royal estates

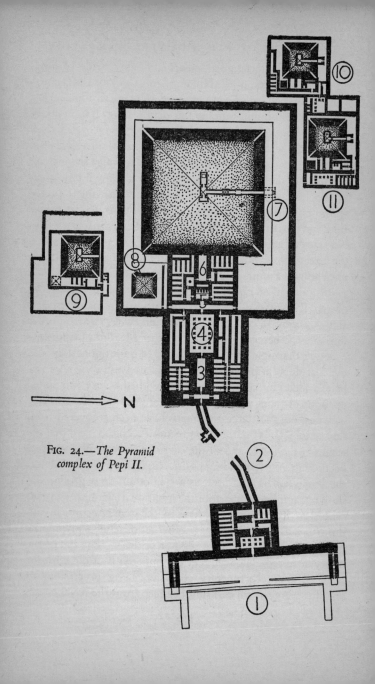

FIG. 24.—*The Pyramid complex of Pepi II.*

to the tomb. In a neighbouring scene similar processions, but composed of gods and goddesses, advanced towards the king, who was seated on his throne. Near the top of the corridor, doors in the side-walls allowed those priests who approached the complex from the north or the south to reach the Mortuary Temple without being obliged to go first to the Valley Building and then climb up the whole length of the Causeway. A porter, who was stationed in a lodge built against the wall of the corridor, guarded the southern door to prevent unauthorised persons from entering the sacred precincts. No vestiges of a similar lodge were discovered in the north side, where even the position of the door could not be accurately determined, but it must be supposed that such a building formerly existed.

The Causeway in this complex was separated from the entrance hall of the Mortuary Temple (fig. 24, 3) by a transverse corridor, which can scarcely be regarded as a new architectural element, because it appears to have been intended merely for the purpose of giving access to staircases leading to the roof from rooms at either end. In shape and size the entrance hall followed the standard pattern. Its walls were decorated with reliefs, one of which showed the king hunting hippopotami from a boat made of reeds. Immediately beyond the entrance hall lay a cloistered court which, although conforming in plan with the courts of the Vth Dynasty temples, was considerably less elaborate in its architecture (fig. 24, 4). The eighteen pillars of reddish quartzite which supported the roof of the ambulatory were not carved in imitation of date palms or papyrus clusters; they were rectangular monoliths decorated on the outer face only with figures of the king and one of the gods. Slabs of limestone took the place of the polished basalt or alabaster pavements of Sahura and Unas. No brightly coloured reliefs seem to have adorned the walls of this court, which, in comparison with many of its predecessors, must have appeared plain and even monotonous.

Beyond the cloistered court lay the central transverse corridor, which not only served to separate the inner apartments of the temple from those lying outside the enclosure wall of the Pyramid, but constituted the focal point of the whole complex. Although developed architecturally from the western section of the corridor, which in earlier temples surrounded the outer walls of the cloistered courts, it had now become an independent element and the southern, eastern and western sections of the former corridor had been discarded. Doors at the northern and southern ends of this corridor gave access to the Pyramid enclosure, in the south-east corner of which stood the subsidiary Pyramid (fig. 24, 8). East of the corridor, flanking the northern and southern sides of the cloistered court and the entrance hall, lay extensive groups of magazines. Niuserra, apparently owing to lack of space within his inner temple, had also constructed magazines on each side of the entrance hall, so that Pepi II can certainly not be credited with having introduced an architectural innovation in this respect. West of the corridor, and approached by way of a small court or hall containing the five statue-niches (fig. 24, 5), were the inner apartments and the remainder of the magazines.

Only fragments of the reliefs from the central transverse corridor have been preserved, but Jéquier's reconstructions have demonstrated that they were among the most interesting in the whole temple. At the southern end of the east wall, the king was shown in the act of smiting a captured Libyan chieftain on the head with his mace. Behind the chieftain stood his wife and two sons, begging for mercy. The scene is not merely reminiscent of that in the temple of Sahura, but is actually copied from it, even the names of the wife and the two sons being repeated. This almost exact duplication of a scene in the temples of two kings whose reigns were separated by about two centuries furnishes conclusive proof that temple reliefs did not necessarily record historical episodes from the life of the king; all the evidence indeed goes to show that they were intended to depict the ideal life which the king wished to live in the Next World. Elsewhere on the same wall the king, wearing the crown of Upper Egypt and carrying in his hands a flail and a small rectangular portfolio, was four times represented performing a ritual ceremony which involved running between some hoof-shaped boundary stones set at a distance apart. This ceremony, an earlier example of which occurs in the Step Pyramid (Plate 3A), formed part of the *heb-sed* and seems to have been designed, at least originally, to restore fertility to the ground. Another scene on the wall, which may also be connected with a fertility rite, shows the king standing near a high pole supported by four wooden stays. Two men, one above the other, were represented in the act of climbing the stays, while attendants held ropes attached both to the stays and to the pole. Replicas of this scene, which is a little suggestive of the mediæval maypole ceremonies, occur in later times on the walls of the temples of Karnak, Luxor, Denderah and Edfu; in the replicas, however, the god of fertility, Min, stands facing the king on the other side of the pole and receives his homage.

From a recess in the west wall of the central transverse corridor, a short staircase led upwards to the hall or court with five statue-niches (fig. 24, 5). Nothing now remains within the niches except one badly damaged pedestal, which serves to show that the statues were made of limestone. In accordance with the regular Egyptian custom, they were probably painted and each statue would be inscribed with at least one of the king's five titles and with his name. Double doors of wood concealed the statues from view when they were not required for ritual purposes. A second group of statues may have been permanently hidden, if a hollow space lying in the masonry of the building behind the five niches has been correctly interpreted as a Serdab.

Passages opened from each end of the statue hall, the northern leading to a small group of magazines and the southern to a narrow chamber which, in turn, was connected with a larger series of magazines and with a square vestibule situated next to the sanctuary (fig. 24, 6). Among the reliefs which decorated the walls of the narrow chamber was one of the many examples in this temple of the king vanquishing his enemies. Only a few fragments were preserved, but they provided a clue to the reconstruction of the whole scene, for Jéquier recognised that it had survived in a copy made by Amenhetep II in the temple of Karnak nearly a thousand years after the death of Pepi II. The central position in the scene was occupied by a gigantic figure of the king, who brandished a mace over the heads of a bunch of foreign captives. Behind the king was a small human figure representing his *ka*, presumably serving as his protector. Elsewhere in the scene the goddess Seshat was shown recording on a scroll the number of captives slaughtered and the amount of booty taken. The frequent occurrence of such scenes in Mortuary Temples suggests that periodic ceremonies were held to commemorate a victory gained in early times by the Egyptians over their foreign neighbours. A similar explanation may also account for the presence in both this temple and in certain of its predecessors of statues representing foreign captives in a kneeling position, with their arms bound. Of all these statues not one has been discovered intact, and the majority bear every sign of having been mutilated deliberately. Possibly, therefore, they were used during the commemoration ceremonies as substitutes for live captives, whose slaughter in cold blood would have been alien to the Egyptian mentality.

A single pillar, which may have been octagonal in shape,

supported the roof of the square vestibule. On each of its four walls, the king was shown being received by the deities of Egypt and by high ecclesiastical and secular officials, who had assembled to greet him as he entered the temple by way of the sanctuary from his tomb. The deities, who numbered about a hundred, stood erect, each carrying a sceptre in one hand and in the other the hieroglyph for "life." The officials, about forty-five in number, were bowed in an attitude of humble deference before their royal master. Butchers were shown slaughtering cattle in preparation for a feast.

The sanctuary (fig. 24, 6), which measured approximately 51 feet in length, 17 feet in width and 24 feet in height, was the largest single apartment within the inner temple. Its vaulted ceiling was decorated in the regular style with golden stars on a sky-blue background. Nothing remains of either the false door, which covered the bottom half of the west wall, or the low altar placed at its foot. The painted reliefs of the north, south and east walls, although broken into hundreds of pieces, could be substantially reconstructed. On both the longer walls, the king was shown seated at a table laden with food. Behind him stood his *ka*. In front of each table was a procession of about a hundred and twenty-five offering-bearers consisting of priests, provincial officials, courtiers and other dignitaries who, by being included in these reliefs, were assured of an After-life in the service of the king. Among the offerings brought by the bearers were ducks, geese, wine, beer, fruit, bread and vegetables. Cattle, antelopes, gazelles and goats were led by ropes attached to their necks or front legs. Pigeons and quails were carried in cages. Above these reliefs was a deep frieze composed of further quantities of provisions. This frieze was also continued on the east wall, where a scene of cattle being slaughtered took the place occupied on the north and south walls by offering-bearers.

In no other Mortuary Temple has it proved possible to

reconstruct so much of the original decoration of the sanctuary or to see how completely it was devoted to the satisfaction of the physical requirements of the dead king. Every kind of sustenance was represented in the reliefs, so that if the priests omitted to provide daily supplies of fresh provisions on the altar he would not suffer from hunger or thirst; by the mere presence of the magic formula which accompanied the reliefs, the images would assume all the properties of their material counterparts. As a further precaution, wine and dried provisions may have been stored in a group of magazines lying to the north and connected by a passage with the sanctuary.

Before its excavation by Jéquier, a tumulus rising from the desert provided the only visible evidence of Pepi II's Pyramid, which, like other Pyramids of its time, had been built of small stones bonded with a mortar of Nile mud and held together by a heavy casing of Tura limestone. This method of construction had the great disadvantage that there was nothing to hinder the swift disintegration of the whole building when once a part of the outer casing had been removed. Originally the Pyramid measured about 258 feet square at the base, and its perpendicular height was approximately 171 feet; it was somewhat larger than any of its immediate predecessors. In one respect it was unique: a square girdle composed of masonry and cased with Tura limestone had been built around its entire base, broken only on the east side where the temple joined the face of the Pyramid. This girdle, which measured about 21 feet in breadth, rose to the level of the second or perhaps the third course of the Pyramid casing. Since it was laid directly against the casing, it follows that the girdle must have been added to the Pyramid after the lower part, at least, had been completed. There is indeed every reason to believe that it was an addition to the original plan, for Jéquier discovered that the north, south and west sides of the enclosure wall had been dismantled and subsequently rebuilt further from the Pyramid, presumably in order to allow adequate space for the girdle. It is difficult to imagine why this addition was made, but it may have been necessitated by an earthquake, which had shaken the fabric of the building; the girdle would thus have been intended to increase its stability. A suggestion that the girdle might provide an explanation of the rectangular construction added to the base of the Pyramid when it is used as a hieroglyph ($\triangle$) is hardly convincing, because the girdle is without any known parallel and its introduction in this instance seems to have been an afterthought, possibly dictated by an accident. It is far more probable that the hieroglyph represents a Pyramid surrounded by its enclosure wall.

When dismantling a portion of the girdle lying outside the entrance to the Pyramid, Jéquier discovered that some of the blocks in its structure were decorated with reliefs. As a rule, reliefs embodied in the inner cores of walls or buildings prove to be relics of earlier constructions which have been re-used, often after a lapse of many centuries. These reliefs, however, were undoubtedly of the same date as those in the Mortuary Temple nearby, and the logical deduction seemed to be that they had once belonged to a building which had been pulled down when the girdle was added to the sides of the Pyramid. The character of the building could be determined fro them reliefs, which closely resembled those of the sanctuary in the inclusion of processions of officials bearing offerings to the king, seated at a table, and scenes of animals being slaughtered; the two buildings had evidently been designed for very similar purposes. An instance of an offering-chapel standing at the entrance to the tomb was known from the Pyramid of Teti, the first king of the VIth Dynasty, and other examples dating from later periods had been found elsewhere. There could be little room for doubt, therefore, that a chapel of the same kind had also been built at the entrance to this Pyramid (fig. 24, 7), but the addition of the girdle had necessitated its removal. Subsequently, it may have been replaced by an entirely new chapel, of which no trace has been preserved, or the plan may have been discarded.

All the Pyramids of the VIth Dynasty were alike in the general design and arrangement of their internal apartments. The entrance corridor descended steeply for a short distance and then continued horizontally as far as a square vestibule lying between the Serdab and the burial-chamber. At the beginning of the horizontal section, the corridor widened and also became higher, thus forming a kind of chamber. Within this chamber, in the Pyramid of Pepi II, Jéquier found some fragments of alabaster and diorite vases inscribed with the king's name and with the names of some of his predecessors. From an examination of these fragments, Jéquier concluded that the vases, which may have contained perfume, had been deliberately broken in the performance of a funerary rite at the entrance to the tomb. The Pyramid texts were carved on the walls of this chamber and on the whole of the remainder of the interior, with the exception of those parts of the corridor which were lined with granite, the Serdab and the western end of the burial-chamber in the neighbourhood of the sarcophagus, where the walls were faced with alabaster decorated with the false door and panel design. Although less well preserved than the corresponding texts in the Pyramid of Unas, they were both more numerous and more highly developed.

Outside the enclosure wall of the king's Pyramid lay three small Pyramids belonging to the queens Ujebten, Iput and Neit (fig. 24, 9, 10 and 11). A fourth queen named Ankhes-en-Pepi, whom he married in the latter part of his long reign and who survived him, was not buried in a Pyramid. Each of the three Pyramids possessed its own complex, which embodied in miniature the principal elements of the Mortuary Temple and

Pyramid enclosure of the king. The clearest example of their lay-out may be seen in the Pyramid of Neit (fig. 24, 11). A narrow entrance in the south-east corner of the limestone enclosure wall gave access to a vestibule which in turn was connected with an open court surrounded on three sides by square columns. Both the vestibule and the court were decorated with reliefs which showed the queen either presenting offerings to various goddesses or receiving the homage of her family and attendants. A corridor led from the north-west corner of the court by way of a group of five magazines to the inner temple, which consisted of a long chamber or store-room, a small court with three statue-niches and the sanctuary. Behind the long chamber and the niches lay a Serdab constructed in the masonry of the building, and in that respect not unlike the Serdab situated between the niches and the sanctuary in the king's temple.

Neit's Pyramid, which measured approximately 79 feet square at the base and rose to a height of about 70 feet, was in all essential features only a replica of the king's Pyramid on a reduced scale. In front of its entrance stood a small offering-chapel, the inner walls of which were partly adorned with reliefs showing the queen receiving provisions. An altar for the mortuary offerings rested at the foot of a false door, which formed the south wall of the chapel; since this door also covered the mouth of the Pyramid corridor, it could not have been put into position until after the funeral. Inside the Pyramid the side-walls of the corridor, beyond a single portcullis of granite, were decorated with Pyramid texts, which were continued in the burial-chamber except at its western end where the walls were faced with alabaster and ornamented with the false door and panel design. The granite sarcophagus, when round, was empty and without a lid. By its side, sunk in the floor of the chamber, was a Canopic chest of the same material, which had once held four jars containing the viscera of the queen. At the opposite end of the burial-chamber, a short passage led directly to the Serdab without the intervening vestibule of the king's Pyramid.

Perhaps the most interesting feature in each of the three complexes of the queens was the subsidiary Pyramid situated near the south-east corner of the main Pyramid. Subsidiary Pyramids of the same kind in the complexes of the Vth and VIth Dynasty kings had been regarded by some Egyptologists as tombs of the royal consorts, on account of their resemblance to the subsidiary Pyramids erected by Cheops and Mycerinus, which certainly bear every appearance of being royal tombs. This conjecture was rendered improbable, however, by the discovery that Pepi II, although incorporating the usual subsidiary Pyramid in his own complex, had also built separate Pyramids with independent complexes for his queens; it was conclusively disproved when it became known that each of the queens' complexes contained its subsidiary Pyramid. While the full explanation of these Pyramids has yet to be found, some indication of their true purpose was provided by the subsidiary Pyramid of Neit, which had been filled with vessels of alabaster and pottery. It seems therefore to have been thought that the Pyramid imparted some particular efficacy to the contents of these vessels, since they could otherwise have been stored in the magazines.

In the small court outside Neit's subsidiary Pyramid, Jéquier found sixteen wooden models of boats buried side by side in a shallow pit. Although instances of such models in Old Kingdom tombs are comparatively rare, they were often included in tombs of the Second Intermediate Period and Middle Kingdom as part of the furniture of the burial-chamber and were placed on the lid of the sarcophagus. The difference between the position allotted to the models in the two periods was probably not accidental, but was the result of an important distinction in their purpose. In the Middle Kingdom they

being probably the best—but, in spite of possessing even greater liveliness and less regularity in form, the majority show an unmistakable deterioration in their technical qualities.

In contrast with the considerable quantity of reliefs found in the royal tombs of the Vth and VIth Dynasties, very few statues of the kings for whom the reliefs were made have come to light. There is no reason, however, to doubt that originally each temple housed at least the five statues in the niches, while other statues may have stood in the open courts. Those temples of the VIth Dynasty which were provided with Serdabs seem also to have contained a number of statues hidden completely from view. The artistic quality of these lost sculptures may be conjectured, not only from the few royal survivals, such as the colossal head of Userkaf discovered in his temple at Sakkara, but from the many statues of contemporary courtiers and officials which have been preserved in Mastabas. Without doubt, the finest pieces date from the early part of the Vth Dynasty, when the lessons learnt from the sculptors who had carved the magnificent statues of Chephren and Mycerinus were still remembered. In the latter half of the Vth Dynasty and in the VIth Dynasty, the standard declined appreciably, but several pleasing specimens, including the alabaster figure of Pepi II as a child (Plate 13A), were produced.

CHAPTER VI

LATER PYRAMIDS

FOLLOWING the close of the Old Kingdom, Egypt experienced one of the darkest periods in her long history. Not only was no attention paid to the development of arts and crafts, but most of the temples and tombs of the Pyramid Age, with their artistic masterpieces and untold treasures, were systematically pillaged and destroyed. According to Manetho, two dynasties of ephemeral rulers, namely the VIIth and the VIIIth Dynasties, occupied the throne at Memphis, but their authority was only local, and complete anarchy prevailed throughout the greater part of the country. So great was the chaos that much of the land remained uncultivated; in a number of districts at least there was famine. At some time during the VIIIth Dynasty an attempt seems to have been made to restore order in the eight southernmost *nomes*, where a confederation was formed under the hegemony of the nomarch of Coptos. About forty years later, however, a nomarch of Herakleopolis Magna named Khety conquered the whole of Upper Egypt as far as the First Cataract at Aswan and became the founder of the IXth Dynasty (*c.* 2230). His kingdom extended northwards as far as Memphis, but may not have included the whole of the Delta, part of which was perhaps still under the control of Asiatic invaders.

Approximately a hundred years after Khety's conquest, Intef, the nomarch of Thebes, rebelled against the contemporary ruler in Herakleopolis and claimed for himself the title of King of Upper and Lower Egypt. A similar title was adopted by his two successors, both of whom were also named Intef, but it was an empty boast, for their dominion, although embracing the whole country as far as Aswan in the south, at no time extended beyond Abydos in the north. In spite of their limited realm, however, they were regarded in later times as the first three kings of the XIth Dynasty. The three remaining kings of this dynasty were all named Menthuhetep, the second of whom—Neb-hepet-Ra Menthuhetep—was one of Egypt's greatest kings. Early in his reign of fifty-one years he recaptured Abydos, which his predecessor had lost, and then drove northwards to overcome his weaker rival in Herakleopolis and established himself as the undisputed ruler over all Egypt. If some reliefs which once decorated a chapel built by Neb-hepet-Ra Menthuhetep at Gebelein may be regarded as a record of historical events, he also conducted successful campaigns against the Nubians, Libyans and Asiatics; evidence of such a kind, however, is not always reliable. Unlike Menes, whose achievements of a thousand years earlier he had in some degree emulated, he did not transfer his residence northwards, but continued to live at Thebes, which thus became, for the first time, the seat of government. Little exact information is available regarding his provincial administration; it seems likely, however, that the nomarchs, with perhaps a few exceptions, were again appointed by the king and that the right of hereditary succession was suppressed. The arts, after two and a half centuries of neglect, began to revive; a sculptor of the period named Iertisen has left an inscription, now in the Louvre, in which he makes the following claims: "I was an artist skilled in my art, pre-eminent in my learning . . . I knew [how to represent] the movements of the image of a man and the carriage of a woman . . . the poising of the arm to bring the hippopotamus low and the movements of the runner. . . . No one succeeds in all this [task] but only I and the eldest son of my body."

Sculpture was not the only branch of the arts which pros-

pered under Neb-hepet-Ra Menthuhetep. Architecture too
made remarkable progress, as is demonstrated by his singu-
larly impressive funerary temple, which was excavated first by
Édouard Naville and H. R. Hall on behalf of the Egypt Ex-

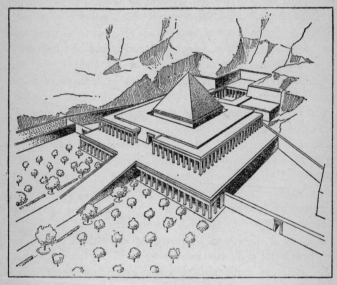

FIG. 25.—*The Funerary Temple of Neb-hepet-Ra Menthuhetep—
a reconstruction.*

ploration Fund (1903-1907) and subsequently by H. E. Winlock for the Metropolitan Museum of New York (fig. 25 and
Plate 12). Built at Thebes, in a deep bay in the cliffs on the west
bank of the river in the region known as Deir el-Bahri, this
temple embodied in its design many striking innovations.
An unroofed Causeway, nearly three-quarters of a mile in
length and bounded at the sides by stone walls, led from the
Valley Building at the edge of the cultivation across the
desert to a large forecourt, surrounded on all sides except the

west by high walls. Limestone statues of the king, represented in the mummy-form of the god Osiris, were set at intervals of about 30 feet against the inner walls of the causeway. At the west end of the forecourt, a colonnade with two rows of square columns masked the eastern revetment of a broad terrace on which the temple was built. Among the painted reliefs which decorated the revetment were battle scenes depicting a campaign against the Asiatics, processions of foreign captives, companies of Egyptian soldiers armed with bows, and a fleet of ships. In front of the colonnade, planted in pits filled to a depth of 30 feet with a mixture of black soil and river sand, were rows of trees forming a kind of grove. All the trees were tamarisks with the exception of eight, arranged in two rows of four on the fringes of the avenue leading by way of a ramp to the top of the terrace; these eight trees were sycamore figs and each shaded from the sun's rays a seated statue of the king.

The terrace, which was partly hewn out of rock and partly composed of masonry-filling, resembled an inverted T in shape, the cross-piece lying adjacent to the forecourt, and the stem being cut back into the face of the cliff. On the cross-piece stood a square building faced externally on all sides except the west by colonnades. Painted reliefs, of which only fragments have been preserved, adorned both the interior and the exterior of its four walls. Rising from its centre was a Pyramid mounted on a high rectangular podium; it was an absolutely solid structure, consisting of a rubble-core cased with dressed limestone and possessing neither corridors nor chambers. Between the podium and the walls of the building lay an ambulatory, the flat roof of which was supported by rows of octagonal columns, three rows on the north, south and east sides and two rows on the west side. Beyond the square building, on the narrow section of the terrace, were situated a cloistered court and a hypostyle hall containing eighty octagonal columns arranged in ten rows. A small chapel built inside the hypostyle hall protected a statue of either the king or a deity, placed within a niche carved out of the cliff.

Before deciding to build a funerary temple of such dimensions, Neb-hepet-Ra Menthuhetep had erected on the terrace a row of six cubical shrines made of limestone. Behind each shrine, and sunk to a considerable depth into the rock-bed, was a vertical shaft which led to a small burial-chamber lying approximately beneath the shrine. These tombs and shrines belonged to six ladies of the royal family, some of whom may have been queens and others princesses; all had died and been buried while the king still intended to confine his funerary temple to the front part of the terrace. The extension of the building westwards necessitated either the removal of the shrines—an operation which would certainly not have been undertaken without transferring the entire tombs elsewhere —or their incorporation into the new construction. The latter course was chosen and the shrines were embodied into the wall separating the square building with the Pyramid from the cloistered court, three on each side of the doorway connecting these two parts of the temple. It was not an ideal solution because most of the reliefs decorating the exterior of the shrines were covered by the new wall, but, to the minds of the Egyptians, the existence of the reliefs was the first consideration; whether they were visible or invisible was less important. No disturbance of the tombs lying beneath the shrines was entailed by the extension of the temple; they had indeed gained in security, since the mouths of four out of the six shafts were now concealed beneath the paving, walls or pillars of the cloistered court, while the two remaining shafts were also covered by a newly laid pavement. It must have been mainly due to the added protection and concealment thus afforded that all except two of these tombs had escaped being robbed more than once. Of their contents, the most valuable discoveries were undoubtedly the limestone outer sarcophagi of two of the queens named Kawit and Ashayet, both of which were decorated on their outer surfaces with beautifully carved reliefs. Among the scenes represented were incidents in the daily life of the queens, such as the performance of their toilet by a maid, drinking milk from cows which were shown accompanied by their calves, visiting a royal farm where peasants were engaged in filling the granaries with corn and preparations for a banquet. Somewhat similar scenes also were painted on the interior of Ashayet's sarcophagus, but a band of painted inscription was the only decoration inside the sarcophagus of Kawit.

Neb-hepet-Ra Menthuhetep constructed within the temple both a cenotaph and a tomb. The entrance to the cenotaph lay at the bottom of a large pit sunk in the floor of the forecourt. From this entrance, a passage had been tunnelled for a distance of 155 yards through the subterranean rock to a point directly beneath the Pyramid, where it terminated in a spacious chamber which, though it had never been opened before its excavation by Howard Carter in 1900, was found to contain nothing except the remains of offerings, a seated statue of the king wrapped in fine linen and an empty wooden coffin. Under this chamber and connected with it by a vertical shaft was another room which yielded only a few pots and three roughly made wooden boats. To account for the existence of this cenotaph, it has been conjectured that it was used for a mock burial ceremony in the course of the *heb-sed*, which the king probably celebrated in the thirty-ninth year of his reign. Such an explanation would find support not only in the presence of the seated statue instead of the body of the king, but also in the attire of this statue, which represented the king wearing the archaic dress normally worn by kings when performing the *heb-sed* ceremonies. The real tomb lay at the end of a tunnel even longer than that of the cenotaph. Starting in the cloistered court, it descended in a straight line under the hypostyle hall to a burial-chamber situated far beneath the cliff. This chamber, which was lined with granite, contained a shrine made of alabaster and granite, within which, it must be supposed, a painted wooden coffin holding the mummy of the king was placed. When it was opened by the excavators, the only objects discovered in the chamber, apart from the shrine, were two small boats, some broken sceptres, cones and bows. Neither the mummy nor the coffin was found.

No exact replica of the funerary temple of Neb-hepet-Ra Menthuhetep was ever built. His successor, Seankh-ka-Ra Menthuhetep, began to prepare a site for a similar building not far south of Deir el-Bahri, but, having ascended the throne at a ripe age, he died before the preparations for its construction had advanced beyond the initial stages, and further work was abandoned. Five hundred years later, however, a famous queen of the XVIIIth Dynasty named Hat-shepsut instructed her architect, Senmut, to build for her a Mortuary Temple embodying the chief architectural features of the temple of Neb-hepet-Ra Menthuhetep. In fulfilment of her command, Senmut designed the larger and more magnificent terraced temple which stands on the north side of the ruins of Menthuhetep's building and which has justly become one of the most celebrated monuments of Egypt.

Very soon after the death of Seankh-ka-Ra Menthuhetep, the country was once again in confusion. A fourth Menthuhetep, who bore the name Neb-tawi-Ra, occupied the throne for part of the seven years which elapsed before order was restored, but, for reasons which are still obscure, later records do not credit him with having been a legitimate ruler. His successor was his Vizier and Commander-in-Chief Amenemhat, who thus became the founder of the XIIth Dynasty—a dynasty composed of four kings named Amenemhat, three kings named Senusret and a queen named Sebek-neferu[-Ra]. It was one of the greatest dynasties in Egypt's history. The name of the founder, which means literally "Amen-is-at-the-head," shows that he was born in Thebes where the god Amen was already established; his forbears, however, may have lived in Eshmunein, the earlier home of this god. He did not follow the example of the kings of the XIth Dynasty by making Thebes his capital, but, profiting from their experience and from his knowledge of the difficulty which they had perhaps found in maintaining control over Lower Egypt from such a distance, he transferred his seat of government northwards and established it at a place called Ithet-Tawi, "She who hath captured the Two Lands." The exact location of Ithet-Tawi has not been determined with certainty, but it must have been situated in the vicinity of Lisht, where the tombs of both Amenemhat I and Senusret I, his successor, have been found.

Influenced by the funerary monuments of the Old Kingdom, some of which could be seen from Lisht, Amenemhat I constructed his tomb on a plan conforming in its main features with the standard Pyramid complex. In one respect, however, its design resembled that of the Deir el-Bahri temple of Neb-hepet-Ra Menthuhetep: it was erected on rising ground with its buildings on two different levels. On the upper terrace stood the Pyramid, surrounded by a stone wall. West of the Pyramid, also on the terrace but outside the stone wall, lay a row of tombs belonging to members of the royal family, all of which were found, when excavated in 1920 by an expedition of the Metropolitan Museum, to have been robbed in antiquity of their entire contents. On the lower and smaller terrace east of the Pyramid stood a Mortuary Temple, near which, to the north and south, were the tombs of a few particularly favoured courtiers. Both the terraces and the adjacent tombs were enclosed by a rectangular wall of brick. Outside this wall lay a cemetery containing the Mastabas of about a hundred nobles and officials.

When constructing the inner core of his Pyramid and the

walls of the Mortuary Temple, Amenemhat I employed a large number of limestone blocks taken from Old Kingdom tombs at Dahshur, Sakkara and Giza. Many of these blocks had been decorated with reliefs or inscribed with texts and, since it is likely that the buildings to which they originally belonged were already falling into ruin when the blocks were removed, their re-use has preserved a number of interesting fragments of sculpture which might otherwise have been lost. In consequence, however, of the complete desolation to which this Pyramid and its complex had been reduced by the time of their excavation, it was sometimes difficult to distinguish the re-used Old Kingdom blocks from those which had been prepared in the XIIth Dynasty for the decoration of this temple. The difference in style, which might have been expected between reliefs of the two periods, was not always very marked, because Amenemhat I deliberately reproduced some of the technical characteristics of Old Kingdom reliefs and occasionally made actual facsimiles of scenes from Old Kingdom tombs.

The entrance to this Pyramid occupied its normal position on ground-level in the middle of the north face. In front stood an offering-chapel of the kind found in the Pyramids of Teti and Pepi II with a red granite false door built into the back wall. Behind the false door lay a granite-lined corridor leading towards the burial chamber. Enormous plugs of granite were used for blocking this corridor after the king's funeral. Very little is known about the internal arrangements of the Pyramid apart from the corridor because, owing to a considerable rise in the level of the Nile bed, the burial-chamber is now permanently flooded and the seepage of water is so rapid that all efforts to reach it have hitherto failed.

Senusret I built his Pyramid at a distance of about a mile and a half to the south of the Pyramid of his predecessor. Its ownership was first determined in 1882 by Sir Gaston Maspero, who found some fragments of alabaster objects bearing the name of Senusret I inside the Pyramid. Twelve years later, J.-E. Gautier and Gustave Jéquier excavated a considerable part of the site, and the remainder, together with the surrounding cemetery, was cleared by successive expeditions of the Metropolitan Museum, working intermittently from 1906 to 1934 under the direction of A. M. Lythgoe, A. C. Mace and Ambrose Lansing. Fundamentally, it resembled closely the complex of Amenemhat I. Whereas only the general outline of the latter can be ascertained with certainty, however, the greater part of the original plan of Senusret I's complex has been established, and the extent to which its Mortuary Temple was copied from the Mortuary Temples of the VIth Dynasty, as illustrated by that of Pepi II, is clearly evident (fig. 26).

A corridor 8 feet wide, built on top of the Causeway, linked the Valley Building—scarcely a trace of which was discovered—with the entrance hall of the Mortuary Temple. Above a dado stippled red and black in imitation of granite, the limestone walls were decorated with scenes of a conventional kind. At intervals of about 33 feet on both sides of the corridor were statues of the king represented as the god Osiris, each one standing in a recess. Similar statues, six of which were discovered in a pit near the Pyramid, originally stood against the walls of the entrance hall (fig. 26, 1), thus emphasising that this apartment was essentially a continuation of the corridor on the Causeway. In the cloistered court (fig. 26, 2) there were also statues of the king, probably one against each of the twenty-four rectangular pillars supporting the roof of the ambulatory. Ten of the number, made of the finest Tura limestone, were found by Gautier and Jéquier lying side by side in a pit where they had been concealed in antiquity, like the Osiride figures, by someone who was anxious to preserve them from impending destruction. Although displaying slight differences in facial expression, they are really duplicates, each statue being a life-size representation of the king seated on his throne and wearing the customary regal

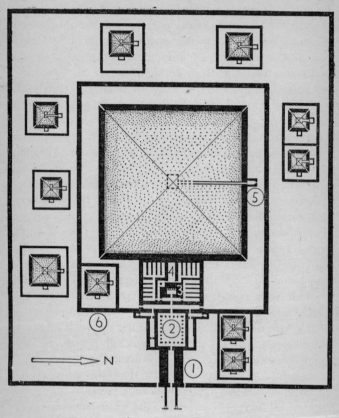

FIG. 26.—*The Pyramid complex of Senusret I.*

attire (Plate 15). Other statues, no doubt representing the king standing, were placed behind the wooden doors of the five niches within the inner temple (fig. 26, 3). The remainder of the inner temple contained only the usual magazines, antechambers and the sanctuary (fig. 26, 4); no Serdab for a further group of statues seems to have been constructed in the masonry between the niches and the sanctuary.

The arrangement of the enclosure walls in this complex was almost identical with the plan of the walls in the complex of Amenemhat I. An inner wall of stone, decorated at regular intervals with panels on which the king's names were inscribed, enclosed the Pyramid, the inner apartments of the Mortuary Temple and the subsidiary Pyramid (fig. 26, 6). Between this wall and a mud-brick outer wall lay a wide court in which were situated the cloistered court and the entrance hall of the Mortuary Temple and nine small Pyramids belonging to members of the royal family. Each of these Pyramids was provided with its own miniature Mortuary Temple, offering-chapel and enclosure wall. Beneath the floor of the offering-chapel, a shaft was sunk vertically downwards to a considerable depth. A second shaft of the same kind was constructed, usually at a short distance to the east of the first, and was connected with it by a subterranean passage. It is not easy to account for the presence of the second shaft, but it may have been intended to enable the sarcophagus to be introduced at a stage in the construction of the tomb when the small offering-chapel had already been built. The body and probably the wooden inner coffin would be lowered down the first shaft, and thence conveyed to the burial-chamber by way of a corridor which was subsequently blocked at intervals by portcullises sliding to the side.

In the burial-chamber of one of the small Pyramids lying at the western end of the southern row, the excavators of the Metropolitan Museum found a fine, but empty, quartzite sarcophagus. So closely did it fit the chamber that the ancient plunderers, when searching for hidden treasure, had been compelled to break through its sides and floor in order to reach the walls of the chamber; their destructive work, however, appears to have yielded no reward. A Canopic chest, composed of the same material as the sarcophagus and made with equal care, lay in a niche in the south-east corner of the burial-chamber. Neither the sarcophagus nor the Canopic chest bore any inscription which would enable the name or title of the royal owner to be identified.

The king's Pyramid occupied an area of approximately 352 feet square and rose to a height of about 200 feet. Its superstructure consisted of a framework of eight massive stone walls radiating from the centre outwards to the four corners and to the middle of each side. The eight compartments so formed were further divided into two sections of unequal size by walls built parallel to the sides and about half-way between them and the centre. These sixteen compartments were filled with rough pieces of limestone laid in white sand, the whole mass being held together by a heavy casing of well-cut blocks of Tura limestone. The entrance was not in the face of the superstructure, but under the paving of the offering-chapel (fig. 26, 5). From there a corridor, which measured only 3 feet 1 inch square in section, sloped downwards in the direction of the burial-chamber. For a distance of about 36 feet it was lined with slabs of dressed limestone, but beyond that point the lining was composed of granite. Although the body and the inner coffin were probably taken to the burial-chamber by way of this corridor, it seems unlikely, in view of its small dimensions, that the outer sarcophagus was similarly conveyed. Perhaps it was taken by a separate shaft which may still lie concealed beneath the ruins of the superstructure. Nothing is known about the burial-chamber, which, like its counterpart in the Pyramid of Amenemhat I, is now under water.

Three out of the four successors of Senusret I built Pyramid complexes at Dahshur, on the edge of the cultivation east of the two Pyramids built during the Old Kingdom. The earliest of these complexes, which belonged to Amenemhat II, embodied no important innovations in design or in method of construction. It acquired, however, a particular distinction at the end of the last century as the provenance of part of the so-called Dahshur treasure—a remarkable collection of jewellery and personal accoutrements discovered by J. de Morgan and now preserved in the Cairo Museum. The owners of this part of the treasure were two princesses named Khnumet and Ita, whose graves were included among a group of royal tombs lying close to the king's Pyramid on the west side. In technical skill and artistic taste the whole treasure demonstrates the work of the Egyptian goldsmith and lapidary at the highest stage of its development.

Senusret II, who succeeded Amenemhat II, discarded the most persistent of all the conventions of Pyramid architecture, namely the location of the entrance on the north side. The supposed advantages of an entrance corridor oriented towards the circumpolar stars must therefore have counted for less in his eyes than the increased security likely to result from an approach starting in a more unexpected quarter. It certainly added to the difficulties of the archæologist, for Petrie, who excavated his Pyramid—situated at Illahun on the edge of the Faiyum—worked for some months in 1887-88 without being able to find a way inside. After a considerable expenditure of time and labour in the following year, he succeeded in discovering to the south of the Pyramid a shaft which descended vertically to a passage tunnelled at a depth of 40 feet below the ground and leading by a devious course to a burial-chamber built entirely of granite. Subsequently he found, still further south, a second and larger shaft which also descended to the passage. By this shaft, as Petrie observed, the magnificent red granite sarcophagus found in the burial-chamber must have been lowered to the passage, because the first shaft was about 1 foot 7 inches narrower than the width of the sarcophagus.

Commenting on the workmanship of this sarcophagus, Petrie declared that it was one of the finest pieces of mechanical work ever executed in such hard and difficult material. The parallelism, according to his calculations, was almost perfect, and the errors in regularity amounted to no more than one hundredth of an inch in a cubit. Apart from the sarcophagus, the chamber contained an offering-table made of alabaster.

In its superstructure also, the Pyramid of Senusret II differed in many respects from its predecessors. To a height of 40 feet from the ground, the inner core consisted of a knoll of rock; above that level, in place of rock, there was a framework of retaining walls with the intervening spaces filled with mud bricks. This core was cased in the normal manner with blocks of fine limestone, the lowest course being embedded in the rock foundation to counter the outward thrust of the structure. Around the base on each side lay a shallow trench filled with sand, the purpose of which was to absorb rainwater flowing off the face of the Pyramid. Such a trench, Petrie estimated, could easily hold the volume of water resulting from the heaviest downpour likely to occur in Egypt. Two walls encompassed the Pyramid, one of stone bordering the trench and one of brick standing further back. Beyond the outer wall was a single row of trees planted in pits which had been sunk in the rock and filled with earth.

Between the two enclosure walls on the south side of the Pyramid lay four shaft-tombs made for members of the royal family. When excavating the easternmost of these tombs in 1913, Petrie and his assistant, Guy Brunton, discovered a collection of jewellery and personal possessions belonging to a princess named Sat-Hathor-Iunut, the owner of the tomb. It was a collection which rivalled in every respect that previously found at Dahshur. Among the most important pieces were a magnificent gold diadem, two gold pectorals inlaid with paste and precious stones, one bearing the name of Senusret II and the other the name of Amenemhat III, necklaces consisting of beads made of gold, amethyst, carnelian, lapis lazuli and felspar, a gold collar composed of beads in the shape of double lion heads, bead girdles of gold and precious stones, bracelets and rings. Toilet objects included razors with copper blades and gold handles, alabaster vases for unguents and cosmetics, other vases designed for the same purpose but made of polished obsidian partly overlaid with gold, and a silver mirror with a handle of obsidian and gold. The whole collection had originally been placed in three ebony caskets, at least one of which was inlaid with gold, ivory, carnelian and blue faience. All these objects, with the exception of a small number retained by the Cairo Museum, are now in the Metropolitan Museum of Art, New York.

Senusret III and Amenemhat III, whose Pyramids at Dahshur lie to the north and south respectively of the Pyramid of Amenemhat II, followed the example set by Senusret II, both in the employment of brick for the inner core of the superstructure and in the elaboration of the substructure into a kind of maze of chambers and corridors. In the same way also the entrance to the substructure was not placed on the north side, but at a point outside the body of the Pyramid, which could only be discovered either by chance or by exhaustive search, with the result that J. de Morgan, when excavating these Pyramids in 1894-95, spent many months of fruitless labour before finding a way to the burial-chamber. Ultimately he located the entrance to Senusret III's Pyramid in the court on the west side of the building, and the entrance to the Pyramid of Amenemhat III in a similar position opposite the southern corner of the east face. In spite of this subterfuge, the architects of the Pyramids had failed to defeat the ancient plunderer, and de Morgan reaped only a meagre reward for his efforts. He was, however, more fortunate when excavating the tombs of the royal family on the north side of each Pyramid, finding in the tombs of the princesses Sat-Hathor and Merit (in the enclosure of Senusret III) and in the tomb of the princess Nubhetep (in the enclosure of Amenemhat III) collections of jewellery of the same character as the treasure buried with the princesses of Amenemhat II and Senusret II. Like the earlier treasures also, this jewellery had not been laid on the mummies of the princesses, but had been concealed in a separate place within the tomb—a fact which has given rise to the theory that a different, and possibly inferior, set of jewellery was prepared specifically for each mummy, while the jewellery found consisted of the objects actually worn by the princesses in their lifetime.

Reigning for at least forty-six years, Amenemhat III ranks as one of the outstanding monarchs of Egyptian history. His fame rests not on military achievement or administrative prowess—though a more complete knowledge of the political and social conditions of his time might well reveal that in these respects also he deserved recognition from posterity—but on the works of art and monumental constructions, including two Pyramids, with which his name has been associated. Undoubtedly, the surviving portraits of this king are among the finest pieces of sculpture ever produced by the ancient Egyptians (Plate 13B); they mark the culmination of the renascence in the arts which originated in the time of Neb-hepet-Ra Menthuhetep and continued to develop without noticeable interruption until the end of the XIIth Dynasty. But long before the spade had brought to light any of these sculptural masterpieces, Amenemhat III had been immortalised by the classical historians as the constructor of Lake Moeris in the Faiyum and as the builder of a Labyrinth in the neighbourhood of the lake, which was considered to bear comparison with the older Labyrinth of Minos at Knossos in Crete. Diodorus, who visited Egypt in the middle of the first century before the Christian era, describes the lake in the following terms:

"Moeris . . . dug a lake of remarkable usefulness, though at the cost of incredible toil. Its circumference, they say, is 3,600 stades, its depth at most points fifty fathoms. Who, then, on estimating the greatness of the construction, would not reasonably ask how many tens of thousands of men must have been employed, and how many years they took to finish their work? No one can adequately commend the king's design, which brings such usefulness and advantage to all the dwellers in Egypt.

"Since the Nile kept to no definite bounds in its rising, and the fruitfulness of the country depended upon the river's regularity, the king dug the lake to accommodate the superfluous water, so that the river should neither, with its strong current, flood the land unseasonably and form swamps and fens, nor, by rising less than was advantageous, damage the crops by lack of water. Between the river and the lake he constructed a canal 80 stades in length and 300 feet in breadth. Through this canal, at times he admitted the water of the river, at other times he excluded it, thus providing the farmers with water at fitting times by opening the inlet and again closing it scientifically and at great expense. No less than 50 talents had of necessity to be expended by anyone who wished to open or shut this sluice. The lake has continued to serve the needs of the Egyptians down to our own days, and it has its name from its constructor, being still called the Lake of Moeris."[1]

Although Amenemhat III may well have undertaken some irrigation or land reclamation schemes in the neighbourhood of this lake, Diodorus and the classical writers were probably mistaken in ascribing its actual creation to him, for it was almost certainly in existence before his time, and its name was undoubtedly derived not from his pre-nomen—possibly pronounced Nemāre—which was known to the Greeks colloqui-

[1] Diodorus Siculus, *The Historical Library*, Bk. I, LI and LII (W. G. Waddell's translation).

ally as Mares, but from a town on the lake called Mi-wer (possibly identical with the modern Ghurāb) or from the canal linking the Nile with the lake, which was also called Mi-wer.

Happily, Amenemhat III's connection with the Labyrinth has been proved to be based on a firmer historical foundation, as Petrie was able to show in 1888-89 when he excavated this king's second Pyramid at Hawara and discovered that its Mortuary Temple was, in fact, designed as a kind of Laby-rinth. It was a large construction, covering an area of about 1,000 feet in length and 800 feet in breadth. In plan, it differed from every other known Mortuary Temple, consisting not of a series of courts and corridors leading to a sanctuary, but of a large number of separate courts arranged in rows. Few architectural details could, however, be recognised by Petrie, so complete had been its destruction. Some conception of its former appearance may be gained from Strabo's description, written at about the beginning of the Christian era:

"We have here [besides Lake Moeris] also the Labyrinth, a work equal to the Pyramids, and adjoining to it the tomb of the king who constructed the Labyrinth. After proceeding beyond the first entrance of the canal about 30 or 40 stadia, there is a table-shaped plain, with a village and a large palace composed of as many palaces as there were formerly *nomes*. There are an equal number of aulæ, surrounded by pillars, and contiguous to one another, all in one line and forming one building, like a long wall having the aulæ in front of it. The entrances into the aulæ are opposite to the wall. In front of the entrances there are long and numerous covered ways, with winding passages communicating with each other, so that no stranger could find his way into the aulæ or out of them with-out a guide. The [most] surprising circumstance is that the roofs of these dwellings consist of a single stone each, and that the covered ways through their whole range were roofed in the same manner with single slabs of stone of extraordinary size, without the intermixture of timber or of any other material. On ascending the roof—which is not of great height, for it consists only of a single storey—there may be seen a stone-field, thus composed of stones. Descending again and looking into the aulæ, these may be seen in a line supported by twenty-seven pillars, each consisting of a single stone. The walls also are constructed of stones not inferior in size to these.

"At the end of this building, which occupies more than a stadium, is the tomb, which is a quadrangular pyramid, each side of which is about four plethra in length and of equal height. The name of the person buried there is Imandes. They built, it is said, this number of aulæ, because it was the custom for all the *nomes* to assemble there together according to their rank, with their own priests and priestesses, for the purpose of performing sacrifices and making offerings to the gods, and of administering justice in matters of great importance. Each of the *nomes* was conducted to the aula appointed for it."[1]

The Pyramid to which Strabo refers stood on the north side of the Labyrinth. Its superstructure, in keeping with the practice of its time, was composed mainly of mud brick overlaid with a casing of limestone. In its substructure, the intricacies of design already embodied in its immediate precursors were further developed, with the result that Petrie was able to force a way into its passages only after weeks of toil extending over two seasons. From the entrance, situated about 80 feet west of the middle of the south face, a flight of steps (fig. 27, 1) descended to a small chamber (fig. 27, 2), beyond which lay a short passage leading to a dead end. Concealed in the roof of this passage, however, was a block of stone twenty tons in weight which slid sideways, thus forming a trap-door through which access could be gained to a second chamber (fig. 27, 3) and to the passages lying beyond. One of

<hr />

[1] Strabo, *Geographica*, Bk. XVII, I, 37 (Bohn's Classical Library).

these passages was intended solely to delude any plunderer who might succeed in penetrating past the first trap-door, for although it had been carefully blocked, it was blind. The other passage, which had been closed only by a wooden door, led

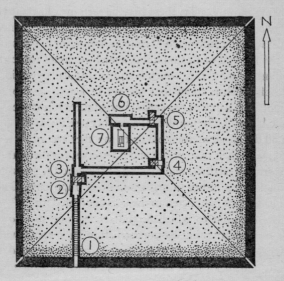

FIG. 27.—*The Pyramid of Amenemhat III at Hawara.*

by way of two right-angle turns and two further roof trap-doors (fig. 27, 4 and 5)—neither of which had been closed after the funeral—to a large antechamber (fig. 27, 6). At each end of the antechamber, a false well had been sunk into the floor and subsequently blocked with stone so that plunderers, labouring under the delusion that the entrance to the burial chamber lay beneath, might be tricked into wasting time and effort in removing the filling. Another stratagem intended for the same purpose was the blocking of the entire northern half of the antechamber, although nothing but a solid wall was concealed behind.

In order that the real way of approach to the burial-chamber (fig. 27, 7) should be intelligible, it is necessary first to describe the method by which this chamber was constructed. Before the superstructure was built, a large rectangular shaft was sunk into the rock at a point somewhat to the west of the centre of the area ultimately to be covered by the base of the Pyramid. Into this shaft, after it had been lined with stone, the burial-chamber, composed of a single block of yellow quartzite and shaped like a box without a lid, was lowered. The length and breadth of this monolith, Petrie calculated, were about 22 feet and 8 feet respectively and the height was about 6 feet; its weight must have amounted to about 110 tons. Notwith-

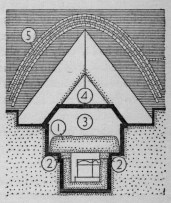

FIG. 28.—*The Burial-chamber of Amenemhat III at Hawara.*

standing the hardness of the material, it was exquisitely cut and polished, while the inner corners were so sharp that, at first sight, Petrie supposed them to be jointed. The roof of the chamber consisted of three slabs of yellow quartzite lying side by side, each measuring about 4 feet in thickness (fig. 28, 1). These slabs did not rest directly on the walls of the monolith, but were laid on a course of stone blocks placed on top of the walls in order to heighten the ceiling of the room (fig. 28, 2). Above the burial-chamber were two relieving chambers, the lower with a flat roof (fig. 28, 3), and the upper with a pointed roof composed of limestone blocks, each weighing nearly 50 tons (fig. 28, 4). Lastly, an enormous arch of brick, 3 feet thick, was built over the pointed roof to support the core of the Pyramid (fig. 28, 5).

Until the tomb had been finally closed, the roof-slab which lay nearest to the antechamber was propped up, leaving a gap between it and the course of blocks on which it was ultimately to rest. A cross-trench in the floor of the ante-chamber led directly to this gap. The king's mummy was therefore taken by way of this trench to the gap and then let down into the burial-chamber, where a large quartzite sar-cophagus had already been placed in position before the roof-slabs were lowered into the shaft. A second, smaller sarcopha-gus, made of the same material and intended for the princess Ptah-neferu, had been built into the chamber, probably at the same time. Canopic chests, also made of quartzite, were in-cluded with the sarcophagi. After the funerary ceremonies had been completed, the raised roof-slab of the burial-chamber weighing about forty-five tons was lowered and the trench in the antechamber filled and covered with a pavement, so that no outward sign of its existence remained. In spite of all the pre-cautions taken, however, this Pyramid suffered the same fate as all its predecessors, and Petrie, when at length he succeeded in reaching the burial-chamber, found that all the movable objects had been plundered and the bodies, together with the wooden inner coffins, had been burnt.

Nothing is known about the circumstances which prompted Amenemhat III to build two Pyramids. Since only one Pyra-mid could have been his tomb, the second—presumably that of Dahshur—must have been left empty. Senusret III may also have constructed, besides his Pyramid at Dahshur, a cenotaph of Mastaba form at Abydos, thus providing his soul with a second tomb, which it could occupy when so inclined, near the traditional tomb of Osiris. Religious motives could hardly have governed the choice of either Dahshur or Hawara, and therefore it can only be assumed that Amenemhat decided to replace his first tomb at Dahshur by the more elaborate Pyramid and Mortuary Temple at Hawara.

With the death of Amenemhat III, the Middle Kingdom virtually came to an end. A fourth Amenemhat and a queen named Sebekneferu figure at the end of the XIIth Dynasty in the later historical records, but the evidence of contemporary inscriptions suggests that Amenemhat IV never reigned independently; he was probably co-regent with Amenemhat III—an office sometimes held by the heir apparent when the reigning king became advanced in years—and was deprived of his succession to the full title by premature death. Sebekneferu was subsequently appointed co-regent, and she may well have continued as the sole occupant of the throne for a short time after the demise of Amenemhat III. Neither Amenemhat IV nor Sebekneferu has left a Pyramid which can be identified with certainty, but E. Mackay, when working under Petrie in 1910-11, found at Mazghuna—about three miles south of Dahshur—the remains of two ruined Pyramids which so closely resembled in plan the Hawara Pyramid of Amenemhat III that it must be supposed that all three Pyramids were approximately contemporaneous. Some small improvements embodied in the design of the two Pyramids at Mazghuna indicate that their builders had profited from the experience gained at Hawara; it seems highly probable therefore that the Mazghuna Pyramids belonged to Amenemhat IV and Queen Sebekneferu, but which of these Pyramids was built for the king and which for the queen cannot be determined from the existing evidence.

During the two centuries occupied by the XIIIth–XVIIth Dynasties, Egypt passed through the second dark period in her dynastic history. Ruled by a succession of weak and ephemeral kings, the country lapsed into a state of anarchy only comparable with the disorder which followed the end of the Old Kingdom. By an unfortunate chance, this period of chaos coincided with a vast ethnic movement which affected the whole of Western Asia and ultimately reached Egypt. At about the end of the XIIIth Dynasty or the beginning of the XIVth Dynasty, a host of Asiatics, the majority of whom were probably Semites, invaded the country, bringing with them a weapon of which the Egyptians had previously had no experience. These invaders were known as the Hyksos—a name which Manetho explained as meaning "Shepherd Kings," but which probably means "Rulers of Foreign Countries"— and their new weapon was the horse-drawn chariot. With the help of this weapon, their army gained not only in quality of arms but also in power of manœuvre. Having overcome whatever resistance they may have encountered, the Hyksos established their capital at Avaris, the site of which has not yet been located with absolute certainty; it appears, however, to have been in the north-east of the Delta and may have been identical with the city later known as Tanis—the Zoan of the Old Testament. From there they governed the whole of the Delta and Middle Egypt at least as far as Cusae, which lay about thirty miles north of Asyut. Further south, a native Egyptian dynasty continued to rule at Thebes, but probably only as vassals rendering tribute to their Hyksos overlords. At length, however, one of these vassals named Kamose, possibly the last king of the XVIIth Dynasty, revolted and drove the Hyksos out of Middle Egypt, and may even have recovered Memphis. The complete expulsion of these foreign oppressors followed in the beginning of the sixteenth century B.C. when Ahmose I, the founder of the XVIIIth Dynasty, captured Avaris and pursued the invader back into Southern Palestine.

Royal funerary monuments dating from the so-called Second Intermediate Period (i.e. the XIIIth–XVIIth Dynasties) are rare—a fact which is no doubt partly to be explained by the unsettled political conditions of that time. Nevertheless, the ruined remains of two Pyramids belonging to kings of the XIIIth Dynasty were discovered by Jéquier in the neighbourhood of Shepseskaf's *Mastabat Fara'un* at Sakkara. One of these Pyramids was built by a king named Khenjer, but the owner of the second, which appears never to have been finished, is unknown. Both Pyramids resemble, in general plan, the Pyramid of Amenemhat III at Hawara, and in each tomb the burial-chamber consists of a single block of quartzite roofed with beams of the same material. In the unfinished Pyramid, Jéquier estimated that the burial-chamber weighed as much as 150 tons. One new feature was introduced into the fashioning of this monolith, namely that the lower portions of both the sarcophagus and the Canopic chest were carved in one piece with the floor of the chamber; the two lids were composed of separate pieces. Not a single tomb of the Hyksos kings has yet come to light, and, in consequence, it is impossible to know whether they adopted the Egyptian practice of building Pyramids or whether they were buried in some other kind of tomb. References to the Pyramids of the XVIIth Dynasty kings occur in the Abbott Papyrus, now in the British Museum. This papyrus reports the findings of a committee appointed by a vizier of the XXth Dynasty to investigate certain allegations of neglect of duty, resulting in tomb robbery, laid by the Mayor of Thebes against the Mayor of the Necropolis on the west bank, where these Pyramids were situated. Although material evidence is scant, it seems clear that the superstructures, built of crude brick, covered an area of only about 25 feet square; the four faces sloped inwards at an angle of about 65°, which gave the buildings the appearance of being tall and slender. At the apex was a capstone made, at least in some instances, of limestone and engraved with the name and titles of the king. The burial-chamber was carved out of the rock foundation of the Pyramid chapel.

Perhaps the last Egyptian king to build a Pyramid was Ahmose I. His real tomb lay at Thebes, the capital, but a cenotaph which he built at Abydos was in the shape of a Pyramid. He also constructed at Abydos a dummy Pyramid for his grandmother, Tetisheri, whose actual tomb, although not yet found, is stated in an inscription discovered at Abydos to have been situated at Thebes. These two Pyramids were, however, exceptional; the remaining kings of the XVIIIth Dynasty and their successors for many generations built neither tombs nor cenotaphs of pyramidal form. Experience must by that time have shown that the Pyramid gave unnecessary prominence to the location of the tomb and that, even after the adoption of every stratagem which human ingenuity could devise, plunderers were ultimately able to force their way into the burial-chamber, and not only to despoil the contents, but also to violate the body. A different method of countering these evils was now attempted. Instead of constructing their Mortuary Temples and tombs together in one place, the Pharaohs of the New Kingdom built their temples in the Nile valley and hollowed out deep caverns in the western cliffs for tombs. By this method it was hoped that the knowledge of the actual location of the tomb would be shared only by those who had assisted in its construction, by a small number of officials and by members of the royal household. The architect of the first tomb of this kind to be constructed in the famous "Valley of the Kings"—a valley running parallel with the Nile behind Deir el-Bahri—describes the secrecy with which the work was carried out in the following words: "I supervised the excavation of the cliff-tomb of His Majesty [Thutmose I] alone, no one seeing and no one hearing." Neither Thutmose I nor his architect, however, could possibly have known that the lonely valley which they had chosen was destined to become the regular burial-place of the Pharaohs for many generations to come; inevitably the secret of the whereabouts of the royal tombs became common knowledge. Robbery was bound to follow sooner or later, and Tutankhamen alone of the sixty or more royal persons buried in this valley was left virtually undisturbed until modern times. His tomb was only spared by the fortunate chance which guided Rameses VI to excavate his own tomb in the cliff immediately above the tomb of Tutankhamen, with the result that the entrance to the latter became deeply buried under rubble thrown out from the upper tomb, and must early have been forgotten. Fifty-three mummies from the other tombs in the valley, including those of such famous Pharaohs as Thutmose III, Seti I and Rameses II, were ultimately transferred to an unfinished tomb at Deir el-Bahri, and to the tomb of Amenhetep II, where they remained without further disturbance until their discovery at the end of the last century.

Although scarcely meriting comparison with the royal Pyramids, private tombs of pyramidal form or incorporating a Pyramid in their architectural design were built from the Middle Kingdom until Roman times. The earliest examples at present known—found by Mariette at Abydos—consisted of a small brick Pyramid mounted on a rectangular podium, both parts being covered with a coat of mud-plaster and whitewashed. Within the Pyramid lay a burial-chamber, conical in shape and corbelled in construction. A second chamber was sometimes built in the podium to serve as a Serdab. Most of these tombs had no external chapels, but some were provided with a two-storeyed chapel projecting from the side. Each storey consisted of one chamber only, the upper containing a niche for the stela and the lower affording the only means of access to the Serdab.

During the New Kingdom, a more elaborate type of private tomb, outwardly resembling the upper-class dwelling-house of the time, came into fashion. Some of the best examples were found by the excavators of the French Institute of Archæology when digging at Deir el-Medina, a little to the south of the Valley of the Kings (fig. 29). Each tomb consisted of two parts, a superstructure and a substructure. Above

FIG. 29.—*Private tombs at Deir el-Medina.*

ground lay a court enclosed on three sides by a wall of brick or stone. On the fourth side of the court stood a chapel, usually masked by a colonnade. Internally, the chapel consisted of a single room decorated with painted scenes and having a stela recessed in the back wall. Mounted on the roof was a hollow brick Pyramid, capped with a block of limestone. Figures of the owner adoring the Sun-god, together with short inscriptions, were carved on all four sides of the capstone. A niche in the side of the Pyramid facing the court contained a statuette of the owner, who was sometimes represented kneeling and holding a miniature stela. The burial-chamber, which lay deep in the rock beneath the chapel, was a barrel-vaulted room connected by a sloping shaft with the court above.

More than eight hundred years after the last royal Pyramid had been constructed in Egypt, pyramidal tombs suddenly made their appearance in the Sudan. The builders were a line of kings whose capital—known in ancient times as Napata—was situated on the banks of the Nile in the province of Dongola, a short distance downstream from the Fourth Cataract (fig. 30). Concerning the racial origin of these kings, very little information has yet come to light, but an inscription found by Reisner during his excavation of their tombs suggests that they were of South Libyan stock. Napata offered no rich pasturage to attract the settler; on the contrary, it lay in one of the most barren parts of the Nile Valley, and its importance was principally due to its geographical position on the main trade route between Central Africa and Egypt, which enabled its rulers to control the passage of slaves and supplies of ivory, ebony, myrrh, resin, incense and other products required by the Egyptians. The rich gold-fields of the eastern desert were also included in their domain. To ensure an uninterrupted flow of these commodities, the kings of Egypt during the Middle Kingdom and again during the XVIIIth–XXth Dynasties had incorporated the Northern Sudan into their empire. In the latter period in particular, temples were built in honour of the Egyptian gods at many places between the First Cataract and the Fourth Cataract. The largest of these temples stood at Napata where a high table mountain, now called Gebel Barkal, acquired the reputation of being the dwelling of the

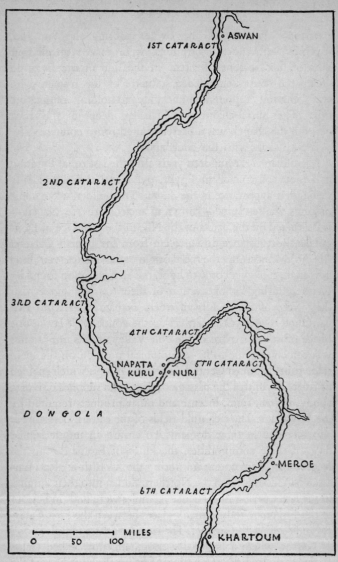

FIG. 30.—*The Nile from Aswan to Khartoum.*

god Amen. At the end of the XXth Dynasty (*c.* 1090 B.C.), internal weakness forced Egypt to relax her grip on the Northern Sudan and, little more than a century later, the ancestors of the kings who were to build the Pyramids gained possession of the country, without, however, causing its people to discard the Egyptian religion or to abandon the fund of technical knowledge which they had learned from the Egyptians.

Nothing is known concerning the relations between the early rulers of Napata and the Libyan kings who formed the XXIInd and XXIIIrd Dynasties of Egypt. The XXIVth Egyptian Dynasty consisted of one king only, Bocchoris by name, whose reign did not exceed six years in length and whose authority over the country was at best extremely tenuous and may have been purely nominal, for Egypt had disintegrated politically into a number of independent districts, each governed by a petty despot. At that time Kashta, king of Napata, and his Ethiopian army advanced northwards beyond the First Cataract and conquered Egypt as far as Thebes. His successor, Piankhy, completed the conquest, to establish himself in about 721 B.C. as the first king of the XXVth Dynasty —a dynasty consisting, apart from Piankhy, of four kings named Shabaka, Shabataka, Tirhaqa and Tanutamen, one of whom, Tirhaqa, is mentioned in the Bible as helping Hezekiah[1] to resist the Assyrians. These kings, although of foreign blood, were not true aliens like the Hyksos invaders; they were already thoroughly Egyptianised, and Piankhy, at least, regarded his conquest of Egypt as a crusade to restore to the god Amen some of that pre-eminence of which he had been deprived by years of political dissension.

Perhaps as a result of seeing the Pyramids of the early Egyptian kings at Sakkara, Giza and elsewhere, Piankhy abandoned the Mastaba type of tomb built by the kings of Napata who preceded him and erected a Pyramid. The site

[1] II Kings xix. 9.

which he chose was at Kuru, about five miles downstream from Napata, in the midst of a large cemetery already containing the tombs of his ancestors. Scarcely a stone of the superstructure of this Pyramid still remains in position, but it is evident that it occupied an area of only about 40 feet square.

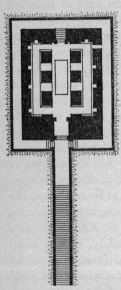

Subsequent Pyramids in a better state of preservation suggest that its four sides inclined inwards at an angle of about 68°. Beneath this structure lay a pit, roofed with a corbel vault, which served as a burial-chamber. To enable the chamber to be entered after the Pyramid had been built, an open stairway was cut from a point east of the superstructure to a door in the east wall of the chamber. After the funeral, this stairway was filled with rubble, and a mortuary chapel, consisting of a single room decorated with reliefs, was erected on top. Shabaka, when constructing his Pyramid, added a short tunnel to the end of the stairway and cut his burial-chamber out of the rock. The mortuary chapel was built against the east side of the Pyramid, directly above the tunnel, and the stairway—filled after the funeral like the trench of Piankhy— lay outside the east wall. In this way, the chapel stood on a rock foundation, and its construction could be completed during the lifetime of the king. Tirhaqa, in his Pyramid at Nuri some five miles distant from Napata, developed the tunnel into a small antechamber and enlarged the burial-chamber into a hall divided by rock pillars into three aisles;

he also cut a corridor which surrounded both apartments and gave access to the hall by a staircase at its eastern end (fig. 31). Some of his successors increased the number of underground chambers in their Pyramids to three by interposing between the antechamber and the burial-chamber a room inscribed on its walls with the so-called "Negative Confession" from the Book of the Dead. In spite of these modifications in matters of detail, however, the general pattern of the tomb as first developed by Shabaka was never radically changed.

In addition to the kings' Pyramids, Reisner found in the cemetery of Kuru a row of five Pyramids built for the queens. Close to this row lay twenty-four graves of horses, four of which belonged to the horses of Piankhy and four to those of Tanutamen, while the remainder were equally divided between the horses of Shabaka and Shabataka. Each horse was richly caparisoned with silver trappings and strings of beads. They were, without doubt, sacrificed at the time of the king's death, in order that they might accompany him to the Next World. Only one instance of a horse-burial is known from Egypt, although chariots were included in the tombs of royalty and some nobility during the New Kingdom. The sacrifice of the royal steeds was therefore probably an innovation by Piankhy, whose affection for horses is witnessed by a passage in his famous Victory Stela. In this graphic account of his conquest of Egypt, he describes his indignation at the discovery that Namlat, the despot of Eshmunein, had allowed his horses to starve during the siege which he himself had laid to the city. Namlat was ultimately pardoned, but he came near to paying with his life for his neglect of the horses.

In about the year 661 B.C., the Assyrian king Ashurbanipal brought to an end a number of inconclusive encounters between Assyria and the kings of the XXVth Dynasty by defeating Tanutamen and conquering the whole of Egypt as far as Thebes. Tanutamen retreated to Napata, where he and his successors continued to rule without serious interference for about 350 years. Their kingdom was bounded on the north by the First Cataract and on the south by the swamps of the White Nile. With only two exceptions, these kings, of whom there were twenty-one including Tanutamen, were buried at Nuri in Pyramids of the standard size and shape; the two exceptions were Tanutamen himself and a later king, both of whom erected their Pyramids at Kuru. In addition to the kings' Pyramids, the Nuri cemetery contained fifty-three smaller Pyramids belonging to queens and princesses.

From about 300 B.C. until 350 A.D., when the kingdom was finally overwhelmed by the Abyssinians, the capital was situated at Meroe, a hundred and thirty miles north of Khartoum. Twice during this period rival claimants to the throne endeavoured, with some measure of success, to re-establish the capital at Napata, but on each occasion the dissident faction ultimately succumbed and the authority of Meroe remained unchallenged. Both the kings of Meroe and their rivals at Napata continued to be buried in Pyramids, nearly fifty in Meroe and eighteen in Napata (Plate 14A); all these Pyramids, like their predecessors, were of stone except those built at Meroe after 200 A.D., when brick coated with plaster was employed.

A barbarous custom, already practised during the Middle Kingdom in the Northern Sudan, was revived by the kings of Meroe. This custom was the burial of his servants with the king in his tomb, so that their spirits might continue to serve him in the Next World. Whether they were actually buried alive or were put to death before burial is still open to conjecture. The queens were not subjected to this treatment, but were buried, also in Pyramids, in a separate cemetery on the west side of the city. In this connection, Strabo makes the following statement: "It is still the custom in Ethiopia that when the king, by accident or otherwise, has lost the use of a member, or a member itself, all his usual followers (those who are destined to die at the same time as himself) inflict on themselves a similar mutilation, and that explains the extreme care with which they watch over the person of the king."[1] Strabo may have been misled in matters of detail, but the excavations of Reisner at Meroe suggest that the general accuracy of his assertion need not be doubted.

[1] Strabo, *Geographica*, Bk. XVII, II, 3.

CHAPTER VII

CONSTRUCTION AND PURPOSE

EXTANT Egyptian records, whether written or pictorial, throw no light on the methods employed by the builders of the Pyramids either in planning or in constructing their monumental works. Close study of the buildings, combined with an ever-increasing knowledge of the implements available to the builders, has, however, made it possible to determine many details of construction with certainty and the likely limits of possibility can often be surmised where positive evidence is lacking. Nevertheless, several problems remain to be solved, and in such cases it is only possible to suggest an answer without any pretence of support other than the belief that the means proposed would achieve the results which can be observed.

When choosing the site for a Pyramid, it was necessary that certain overriding considerations should be borne in mind: it must be situated west of the river—the side of the setting sun; it must stand well above the level of the river, but not be too remote from its west bank; the rock substratum must be free from any defect or tendency to crack; it should be situated not far from the capital and possibly even closer to a palace which the king may have built as a residence outside the capital. Of the sites chosen by the kings of the Old Kingdom, Sakkara and Abu Sir lay in sight of Memphis, Abu Roash about seventeen miles distant to the north and Dahshur only five miles away to the south. Thirty-three miles separated Memphis from Meidum, where one Pyramid alone was built. Proximity to the river was an important factor, because much of the stone used for the Pyramid and its adjacent buildings must be conveyed from the quarries by ship. Thus, during the season of the inundation an expanse of desert only 250 yards in width lay between the river and the Pyramid at Meidum, while at Giza the interval was about a quarter of a mile; at Dahshur and Abu Roash, however, the most practical routes for hauling the building materials measured about a mile.

A suitable site having been found, the first task of the builders was to remove the thick surface layer of sand and gravel so that the buildings might stand on a firm foundation of rock. Levelling and smoothing of the rock were then begun, the pieces removed being either used to fill up depressions or placed on one side for subsequent employment. How accurately this operation could be performed is demonstrated by the Great Pyramid, in which the perimeter of the bed deviates from a truly level plane by only a little more than half an inch —the almost imperceptible amount by which the south-east corner stands higher than the north-west corner. Such a high degree of accuracy in the technique of levelling was undoubtedly the outcome of accumulated experience gained by generations of Egyptians, dating back to the pre-Pyramid Age, when preparing their lands for irrigation by means of water conducted through channels and canals from the river. To level an area like the base of a Pyramid it would only be necessary to surround it on all four sides with low banks of Nile mud, fill the enclosure so formed with water and cut a network of trenches in the rock in such a manner that the floor of each trench lay at the same depth beneath the surface of the water; the intervening spaces could be levelled individually after the water had been released. In actual practice the whole area to be covered by the Pyramid was not always reduced to the same level as the perimeter, but, as the Great Pyramid shows, a mound of rock might be left in the centre to be used at a later stage in the work of construction.

The last of the preliminaries to be accomplished on the site was the execution of an accurate survey in order to ensure that the base of the Pyramid should form as nearly as possible a perfect square, each side of which would be so oriented as to face directly one of the four cardinal points. Wooden rods laid end to end or long cords were used for the performance of this operation. The unit of measurement was the Royal Cubit (20·62 inches in length) consisting of seven *palms* or twenty-eight *digits*, one *palm* being equal to four *digits*. If cords were used, they were probably composed of palm-fibre or flax-fibre, and would certainly have stretched when used; it is therefore hardly surprising that there should be a difference of 7·9 inches in length between the longest and shortest sides of the Great Pyramid—indeed, it seems remarkable that on sides exceeding 9,000 inches in length so small an error should have occurred, especially when it is remembered that the central mound of rock would have rendered impracticable any measurement of the diagonals to check the accuracy of the square.

An exact orientation of the Pyramid on the four cardinal points could only have been achieved with the aid of one or more of the celestial bodies, since the magnetic compass was certainly unknown to the ancient Egyptians. The results of the method, as exemplified by the Great Pyramid and the Pyramid of Chephren, left little to be desired, the errors in the four sides of the former being the following fractions of one degree:

North side .	.	.	2′ 28″ south of west
South side .	.	.	1′ 57″ south of west
East side .	.	.	5′ 30″ west of north
West side .	.	.	2′ 30″ west of north

According to Petrie's survey, the mean error of the east and west sides of Chephren's Pyramid was about 5′ 26″ west of north.[1] Which or how many of the celestial bodies were employed to attain these results cannot be deduced with certainty, but it was clearly only necessary to fix one cardinal point exactly and the remaining three could be determined by the use of simple instruments well within the competence of the Pyramid builders. East and west could have been discovered approximately by the rising and setting of the sun on the two equinoctial days every year and north by an observation of the Pole Star, but in each case the resultant error (even after allowance has been made for a change in the position of the Pole in relation to the Pole Star in the course of about 4,500 years) would have been greater than the amount revealed by at least the two main Pyramids of Giza.

A simple method of determining true north, and one which may therefore have been employed, was by sighting on a star in the northern heavens and bisecting the angle formed by its rising position, the position from which the observation was made and its setting position. To achieve the degree of accuracy needed, it would have been necessary either to be able to see the true horizon at the points where the star rose and set or to create an artificial horizon at a uniform height above those two points. Since an observation of the true horizon would be precluded anywhere on land by irregularities, however slight, in the ground, an artificial horizon would be required. This end could have been secured by building a circular wall with a diameter of a few feet on the already levelled rock-bed of the Pyramid. The height of the wall must be sufficient to prevent a person standing within the circle from seeing anything outside other than the sky, but, subject to this single reservation, it should not be higher than such a person could

[1] Among other Pyramids surveyed by Petrie were three in the orientation of the east and west sides of which he observed the following errors:

Bent Pyramid: 9′ 12″ west of north.
Meidum Pyramid: 24′ 25″ west of north.
Pyramid of Mycerinus: 14′ 3″ east of north.

reach. For the whole of its circumference, the top of the wall must be on an absolutely even plane—a requirement which again could easily have been attained by means of water, temporary mud-banks on the inner and outer peripheries of the top surface providing the support necessary to prevent

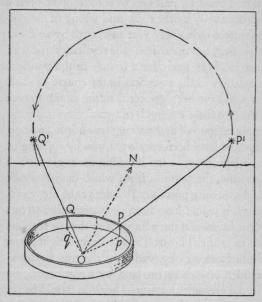

FIG. 32.—*A method of discovering true north.*

the water from flowing away. The observation would be made by one person sighting over a short perpendicular rod driven into the ground at the radius of the circle (fig. 32, O); a second person standing within the circle would receive directions from the first and, at the moment when the star (fig. 32, P¹) appeared above the wall, would place a mark on the wall directly in line between the observer and the star. This operation would first be performed towards the east (fig. 32, P) and subsequently, some hours later, towards the west (fig. 32, Q¹ and Q), the same star being sighted on both occasions. A plumb-line (which the Egyptians of the Pyramid Age are known to have possessed) would then be suspended from the two marks on the wall and corresponding marks made on the ground at points perpendicularly below (fig. 32, *p* and *q*). By bisecting the angle *pOq*, true north would be obtained and the bisecting line N-O would run due north and south. As a check, the operation could be repeated by sighting several different stars in the same way before dismantling the wall. East and west would lie at angles of 90° to the line obtained, but an actual specimen of the set-square or other instrument used to measure such an angle has not yet been found; contemporary buildings with corners forming a perfect right angle prove, however, that an accurate instrument for this purpose must have been available.

At the same time as the preliminary work was being conducted on the Pyramid site, other preparations for building were being made elsewhere. The foundation of the Causeway, composed of stone quarried in the locality, was being laid so that it could be used for the passage of material when constructional work on the Pyramid began. Fine limestone blocks for the outer casing of the buildings were being quarried on the east bank of the Nile at Tura in the Mukattam hills. The men employed on this work painted the names of their gangs in red ochre on the blocks before they were taken from the quarry; although these names were very often erased in the course of subsequent operations, enough remains to perpetuate many of the gangs. As examples, the following names, found by Alan Rowe, occur on casing-blocks of the Meidum Pyramid[1]: "Stepped Pyramid Gang," "Boat Gang," "Vigorous Gang," "Sceptre Gang," "Enduring Gang," "North

---

[1] Alan Rowe, *The Museum Journal*, Philadelphia, Vol. XXII (1931), p. 21 (Pl. VI)

Gang" and "South Gang." A block in the Great Pyramid bears the name: "The Craftsmen-gang, How powerful is the White Crown of Khnum Khufu!" Why these names were placed on the stones is not evident, unless it was with the intention of facilitating the task of keeping a tally of the work done by each gang. Far away to the south, at Aswan, another group of men was quarrying granite for columns, architraves, door-jambs, lintels, casing-blocks and sometimes the outer sarcophagus. That this undertaking was not without its hazards is testified by an inscription in a tomb at Aswan belonging to a Governor of the South, named Uni, who lived in the reigns of Pepi I and Merenra. In this inscription Uni states with pride that as a result of the control which he had exercised over the more unruly elements in the vicinity it had been possible for the first time in history to send a quarrying expedition under him to Aswan protected by only one warship.

Limestone, whether obtained from the surface of the rock, as at Giza, or extracted by tunnelling, as at Tura, presented the Pyramid builders with no serious difficulties in its quarrying. A recent discovery by W. B. Emery in the archaic cemetery of Sakkara has shown that even in the Ist Dynasty the Egyptians possessed excellent copper tools, including saws and chisels, which were capable of cutting any kind of limestone (Plate 14B). As an aid to sawing, a wet abrasive material such as moistened quartz sand, which is plentiful in Egypt, may have been employed, but there is no positive evidence either of the material used or of the practice. Chisels and wedges were, however, the tools most favoured for quarrying limestone, the former for cutting the blocks away from the rock on every side except the bottom and the latter for detaching the blocks at the base. In a tunnel-quarry, for instance, a deep hollow resembling a shelf and extending across the whole breadth of the passage was first cut between the roof and the block to be detached. The purpose of this hollow was to allow a quarryman to crawl across the top of the block and separate it from the rock behind by chipping vertically downwards with a chisel struck by a wooden mallet. At the same time other quarrymen made similar vertical cuttings down the two sides. Finally, wedges were inserted into holes cut at the bottom in order to make a horizontal split in the rock, which freed the block entirely. Sometimes the wedges were composed of wood, and the split was achieved by wetting the wood and so causing it to expand. The process was afterwards repeated on the rock below, without the necessity of cutting the initial hollow, until floor level had been reached; a new series of cuttings, starting at roof level, was then begun deeper in the tunnel.[1] Surface-quarrying was carried out by exactly the same method. It possessed a great advantage over tunnel-quarrying, in so far as the space for working was not so confined and a greater number of men could therefore be employed at one time. On the other hand, the finest limestone often lay in strata buried deeply beneath the surface, and tunnelling offered the only practical means of access.

The methods employed in the Pyramid Age for quarrying granite and other hard stones are still a subject of controversy. One authority has even expressed the opinion that hard stone quarrying was not attempted until the Middle Kingdom; before that time, he maintains, the amount needed could have been obtained from large boulders lying loose on the surface of the ground.[2] It seems difficult, however, to believe that a people who possessed the degree of skill necessary for shaping the colossal monoliths built into the granite Valley Building

[1] Many soft-stone quarries in the United Kingdom are worked at the present time in the way described above, the only important difference being the substitution of steel tools and the greater use made of the saw. The mason's pick, now used instead of chisels, may also have been known to the ancient Egyptians, but no specimen has yet been found.

[2] A. Lucas, *Ancient Egyptian Materials and Industries* (1934), pp. 62–3.

of Chephren were not also able to hew rough blocks of this stone out of the quarry, particularly since tunnelling was never adopted. Furthermore, on the backs of the slabs roofing Mycerinus' burial-chamber marks made by the insertion of wedges may still be seen, and the natural inference appears to be that the operation denoted by these wedge-marks was the splitting of the slabs from the rock in the quarry. This method of quarrying was certainly practised in later times, as is demonstrated by the countless rows of wedge-slots still visible to-day in the Aswan quarries (Plate 14c); there is nothing to suggest that quarrymen were not detaching blocks by the same device in the Old Kingdom. The slots may either have been made by rubbing an abrasive powder with stone or by means of a metal tool. Since copper is the only metal known to have been available in Egypt before the Middle Kingdom, it has been supposed that the Egyptians had mastered a process, now lost, of giving copper a very high temper, but this surmise has not yet been proved.

An alternative and more laborious method of quarrying granite was by pounding the rock around the block to be detached with balls of dolerite—a hard greenish stone found over a wide area of the eastern desert near the Red Sea. An unfinished obelisk dating from the New Kingdom, which still lies at Aswan, was undoubtedly quarried by this method, and there is no inherent improbability in the supposition that quarrymen were already acquainted with the technique in Pyramid times.

By whatever method of quarrying the granite blocks were obtained, the procedure for reaching stone of the quality required, if it were not available in the uppermost stratum, would have been similar. Granite, like many another stone, if heated to a high temperature and then suddenly cooled, will develop superficial cracks, and the face, when subjected to the slightest friction, will immediately crumble away. A fire lit on the rock to be pared down would soon raise its temperature to the requisite degree, and the application of cold water would cause the disintegration of the surface, which could then be rubbed away with the aid of a small stone scraper. If necessary, the process could be repeated many times until stone of the desired hardness had been reached.

By no means the least remarkable achievement of the Pyramid builders was the transport of the blocks from their quarries to the site of the Pyramid. Some of the heaviest pieces of local limestone embodied in the Mortuary Temple of Mycerinus, according to Reisner's estimate,[1] weigh about 200 tons. In comparison with this amount, the casing-blocks of the Great Pyramid, which average only about $2\frac{1}{2}$ tons, and the 50-ton granite roof-slabs of the King's Chamber may seem trivial, but it must be remembered that the latter required not only to be loaded on barges and subsequently unloaded, but also, for the most part, to be raised at the end of their journey to a very considerable height above ground-level. The navigation of these megaliths, probably undertaken in the main during the inundation season, may well have been the least formidable part of the whole task, though the control of heavily laden barges on a fast-flowing river must always have been a hazardous operation requiring great skill. For transport over land, the method employed was probably the same whether the weight to be moved was 200 tons or $2\frac{1}{2}$ tons, the number of men being regulated by the amount of the weight. What was this method? It is highly improbable that wheeled vehicles were used, because, although some of the carrying possibilities of the wheel had been realised at least as early as the Vth Dynasty,[2] scenes in tombs of the XVIIIth Dynasty demonstrate that, even after a lapse of a thousand years, statues and heavy

[1] Reisner, *Mycerinus*, p. 70.
[2] A relief in the Vth Dynasty tomb of Kaemheset at Sakkara shows a scaling-ladder mounted on wheels. (See Somers Clarke and R. Engelbach, *Egyptian Masonry*, Fig. 83.)

blocks of stone were not moved by wheeled transport. Instead, sledges were employed, and there can be little doubt that the Pyramid builders also used this method. Each block was probably levered on the sledge either directly from the ground or by way of a low ramp composed of brick or stone. Both sledge and block, lashed together by ropes, may then have been raised again by means of levers, in order that wooden rollers might be placed underneath. The loaded sledge would subsequently be dragged over a way paved with baulks of timber by men pulling on ropes attached to the sledge. An illustration of the actual process of transport was included by Jehutihetep, a nobleman of the XIIth Dynasty, in his tomb at El-Bersheh (fig. 33). In this scene an alabaster statue of Jehutihetep, which probably weighed about 60 tons, is mounted on a sledge pulled by 172 men.[1] Water or some other liquid is poured on the ground to lessen the friction and thus facilitate haulage.

With his material close at hand and the site prepared, two difficult problems still confronted the Pyramid builder: he must raise the stones to the height required and must lay them so that the monument gained internal cohesion and regularity of outward form. Before attempting to explain how these problems were overcome, it may be worth while to stop and consider the main internal and external features of the structures to be built, without, for the present, having any regard to the chambers and corridors.

When describing the Pyramid of Meidum it was stated that its core consisted of several layers of masonry diminishing in height from the centre outwards and leaning on a central nucleus at an angle of about 75° (fig. 12). Each layer was cased from top to bottom with Tura limestone, and its outer surface

---

[1] Reliefs from the Palace of Sennacherib at Nineveh, now in the British Museum, show that the Assyrians of the seventh century B.C. transported their sculptures by a very similar method.

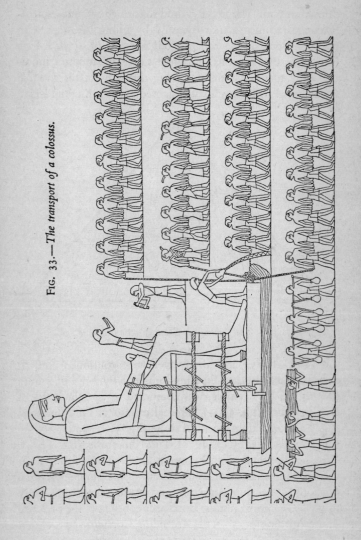

FIG. 33.—*The transport of a colossus.*

dressed smooth. The step Pyramid so formed was subsequently converted into a true Pyramid by filling the steps with packing-blocks and adding an outer casing of dressed Tura limestone. Borchardt has shown that the same method, modified only to the extent of leaving the faces of the internal casing-stones rough, was still practised by Pyramid builders in

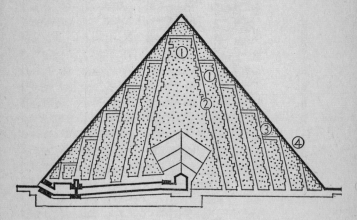

FIG. 34.—*The Pyramid of Sahura, section looking east.*

the Vth Dynasty,[1] and it may well have continued until an even later date in the Old Kingdom. The Pyramid of Sahura at Abu Sir, for example, was composed of upright layers of core masonry (fig. 34, 1), internal casings of fine limestone (fig. 34, 2), packing-blocks of stone (fig. 34, 3) and lastly the usual smooth outer casing of Tura limestone (fig. 34, 4). Whether the three main Pyramids at Giza were also built in this fashion is uncertain and, without dismantling substantial portions of their superstructures, no examination seems likely to yield conclusive results. Borchardt considered the presence of the "girdle-stones" in the Ascending Corridor as proof that

[1] L. Borchardt, *Das Grabdenkmal des Königs Sahure*, Vol. I, p. 29.

the Great Pyramid followed the standard pattern, each "girdle-stone" being part of an internal casing,[1] but two equally eminent authorities, Somers Clarke and R. Engelbach, refused to accept Borchardt's arguments[2]; even if the "girdle-stones" are not internal casings, however, it need not follow that such casings do not exist elsewhere in the Pyramid. It is, moreover, irrefutable that all the surviving subsidiary Pyramids at Giza were built with internal casings, and it would be strange if the main Pyramids were composed in a different way. Externally, all Pyramids built after the Bent Pyramid at Dahshur were alike, except in size and in such small details as the angle of incline and the kind of stone used for the lower courses of the outer casing. The normal angle of incline was about 52°—a slope which, in the Pyramid of Meidum and in the Great Pyramid, would have resulted if the height had been made to correspond with the radius of a circle the circumference of which was equal to the perimeter of the Pyramid at ground-level. The northern stone Pyramid at Dahshur, with its gradient of 43° 36', provides the only striking exception to this rule.

Herodotus, who was presumably quoting the tradition current in Egypt during his time, makes the following assertions with regard to the building of the Great Pyramid: "The Pyramid was built in tiers, battlementwise, as it is called, or, according to others, stepwise. When the Pyramid was completed in this form, they raised the remaining stones to their places by means of machines formed of short beams of wood. The first machine raised them from the ground to the top of the first step. On this there was another machine, which received the stone upon its arrival, and conveyed it to the second step, whence a third machine advanced it still higher.

[1] L. Borchardt, *Einiges zur dritten Bauperiode der grossen Pyramide bei Gise* (Cairo, 1932).
[2] Somers Clarke and R. Engelbach, *Ancient Egyptian Masonry*, pp. 123-4.

Either they had as many machines as there were steps in the pyramid, or possibly they had but a single machine, which, being easily moved, was transferred from tier to tier as the stone rose—both accounts are given and therefore I mention both. The upper portion of the pyramid was finished first, then the middle, and finally the part which was lowest and nearest the ground."[1] Archæological discovery, while tending to confirm the concluding sentence, has so far revealed little evidence in support of Herodotus' statements as a whole, but it must be admitted that Pyramid construction is a subject on which the last word has certainly not yet been written.

In the absence of the pulley—a device which does not seem to have been known in Egypt before Roman times—only one method of raising heavy weights was open to the ancient Egyptians, namely by means of ramps composed of brick and earth which sloped upwards from the level of the ground to whatever height was desired. If, for instance, a short wall were to be built, the stones for each course after the lowest would be taken to the required level on a ramp constructed against the wall for the whole of its length and projecting outwards at right angles to the line of the wall. With the addition of each successive course of masonry, the ramp would be raised and also extended so that the gradient remained unchanged. Finally, when the wall had been built to its full height, the ramp would be dismantled and the outer faces of the stones, which had not previously been made smooth, dressed course by course downwards as the level of the ramp was reduced. A late example of such a ramp could, until very recently, be seen against the unfinished First Pylon of the Temple of Karnak,[2] and proof that the method was already practised in earlier times has been furnished by the discovery

---

[1] *Herodotus*, II, 125 (Rawlinson's translation).
[2] Somers Clarke and R. Engelbach, *op. cit.*, Fig. 87.

of the remains of ramps at the Pyramid of Amenemhat I at Lisht and at the Pyramid of Meidum. Aerial photographs strongly suggest that substantial remains of ramps lie buried under the sand at Dahshur, but a practical demonstration must await further excavation.

If it be conceded, as the evidence would appear to demand, that ramps were employed by the builders of the Pyramids, how were these ramps set out? The most plausible answer seems to be that a single supply-ramp was constructed to cover the whole of one side of the Pyramid. As the Pyramid rose in height, so the ramp was increased both in height and in length; simultaneously the top surface would become progressively narrower to correspond with the constantly diminishing breadth of the Pyramid face. If the angle of incline of the Pyramid were 52°, the two side faces of the ramp would also slope at an angle of 52°, so that any risk of "land-slides" would be eliminated. The three sides of the Pyramid which were not covered by the supply-ramp would have foot-hold embankments of sufficient width at the top to allow for the passage of men and building material, but, since they were not required for raising the stones from the ground, their gradient on the exposed outer surface could be as steep as would be compatible with firmness. Wooden baulks, some of which were actually found *in situ* by the American excavators at Lisht, would be placed on the top surface of both the supply-ramp and the foot-hold embankments in order to provide a firm roadway for the passage of sledges bearing the stone blocks.

As an illustration of the practical application of the method suggested, let it be imagined that a Pyramid has been built to half its final height.[1] Nothing of the stonework already laid

---

[1] In the following description, as elsewhere in this chapter, liberal use has been made of the conclusions contained in *Ancient Egyptian Masonry* by Somers Clarke and R. Engelbach (Oxford, 1930).

would be visible from the ground, because three of the outer faces would be entirely covered by the foot-hold embankments and the fourth face would be screened by the supply-ramp. The top surface of the Pyramid would resemble a square platform and would be ready to receive the next course of masonry. The first stones to be hauled up to the platform would be core-blocks from the local quarries; their sides and top surfaces would be left rough, but the bottom surfaces—the so-called bedding joints—would be smooth. These stones would be taken to the centre of the platform and laid against each other, the gaps caused by the irregularities in their sides being often left unfilled. Care was taken to extend the new course evenly in all four directions, so that it always remained approximately in the form of a square, and at regular intervals its sides would be made absolutely equal in length by the addition of an internal casing composed of Tura limestone laid directly above the corresponding casing in the floor of the platform; the outer face of the casing would be cut so as to incline inwards at an angle of about 75°, but it would not be dressed smooth. At length, the area of the course being laid would have been enlarged until only a narrow margin at the outer edges of the original platform remained uncovered. At that stage the packing-blocks of local limestone would be added and considerably greater attention would be given to securing close joints. In the Great Pyramid the packing-blocks were laid in such a way that they sloped slightly inwards towards the centre of each course, with the result that a noticeable depression runs down the middle of each face—a peculiarity shared, as far as is known, by no other Pyramid.

The core having been completed, only the outer casing of Tura limestone remained to be added. It was a delicate operation and imperfections in the setting of the stones would not only mar the outward appearance of the monument, but, unless counteracted, would lead to irregularity in the pyramidal form. The joints, moreover, must be as close as possible. In order to save time and to achieve the highest possible degree of accuracy, the fitting of the rising joints—those between neighbouring blocks on the same course—was probably carried out by highly skilled masons working on ground-level. Only by such a method could the results to be observed in the so-called oblique rising joints—those cut either not at right angles to the bedding joint or not parallel with the central axes of the Pyramid—have been attained. Possibly the joints between the backs of the casing-stones and the front faces of the packing-blocks were also fitted on the ground so that, when each block finally reached the men who were to lay it, only the upper surface and the front—already cut to the Pyramid angle but not dressed—needed further attention from the masons.

Even after making such careful preparations, the laying of a casing-block was still a difficult task, especially if it were a large block weighing perhaps more than ten tons. Doubtless it would be carried on its sledge to the furthest possible point, namely on the embankment directly opposite the place in the structure which it was ultimately destined to occupy. The block would then be levered sideways off the sledge until it rested on battens placed ready to receive it on top of the casing-stone in the course below; in order to enable levers to be used, bosses were left by the masons on the outer face of every casing-block. While it stood in that position, a thin layer of mortar would be spread over both the bedding joint and the rising joint about to be formed. The main purpose of the mortar was to provide a kind of lubricant so that the casing-block, after being lowered to its bed, might be slid first into contact with the block of casing previously laid and then back against the packing-blocks. How this last operation was performed is not quite clear, but it is possible that it could have been achieved by pulling on ropes attached to a baulk of timber laid across the free outer corner of the casing-block and then pressing it back into line by levering from in front. The few remaining casing-blocks at the foot of the Great Pyramid offer the best examples of such jointing hitherto discovered; the credit for being the first to bring their excellence to the notice of the modern world belongs to Petrie, who wrote of them: "Several measures were taken of the thickness of the joints in the casing-stones. The mean thickness of the joints of the north-eastern casing-stones is 0.02 inches, and therefore the mean variation of the cutting of the stone from the straight line and from a true square is but 0.01 on a length of 75 inches up the face, an amount of accuracy equal to the most modern optician's straight-edges of such a length. . . . Though the stones were brought as close as $\frac{1}{50}$ inch, or, in fact, in contact, the mean opening of the joint was but $\frac{1}{100}$ inch."

When the casing-stones on all four sides of the course had been placed in position, it would be necessary to make a survey in order to ascertain whether the correct form had been retained. Small deviations were almost inevitable and, if detected in time, could be counteracted in the laying of the next course. While this work was in progress, the main supply-ramp and the foot-hold embankments would be raised to the new level of the Pyramid, and masons would be employed on the task of dressing the tops of the stones just laid—the bedding joints of the course about to be added. So the building would continue to grow course by course until lastly the capstone, generally made of granite, would be placed on the apex. As a means of securing the stone firmly to its bed, a projection resembling a disk would be carved in the centre of the base to fit like a tenon into a mortise cut to receive it in the middle of the top course of masonry. It may therefore be deduced that the capstone, already shaped but still in the rough, was taken to the top of the Pyramid on its sledge, and then supported on levers while the sledge was being removed. Battens would be

inserted underneath and a thin layer of mortar be spread ove
the bed; finally, after the removal of the battens, it would b
lowered by means of levers placed under the side-bosses. A
inscription found by Jéquier at the Pyramid of Queen Ujebte
refers to the gilded capstone on her Pyramid, which sugges
that these stones were, at least sometimes, overlaid with gol
No early example has yet come to light, but the Cair
Museum possesses a fine specimen from the Pyramid of Amen
emhat III at Dahshur; it is made of grey granite, and on i
four faces are carved inscriptions containing invocation
addressed to the Sun-god and to three other deities.

The laborious process of assembling the Pyramid was nov
finished, and work could be started on dressing the four oute
faces, beginning with the capstone. As the work proceede
the supply-ramp and the foot-hold embankments would b
lowered, thus making fresh courses of casing-stones accessibl
for dressing. In order to complete the task more quickly, it
possible that the reduction of the ramp and embankments wa
not carried out gradually, but in layers of several feet; woode
scaffolding would then be erected in their place so that a larg
number of men could be employed on different levels at th
same time. Scaffolding was certainly known to the Egyptian
and the time saved by its use when dressing the five acres
casing on each face of the Great Pyramid, for example, wou
have been very considerable. When at length the who
operation had been completed, the builders would be free a
the ground clear for erecting the Mortuary Temple, the co
ridor of the Causeway and the Valley Building, some
which had certainly had their foundations laid before
construction of the Pyramid had been begun.

No mention has yet been made of the method where
corridors and chambers would be incorporated into Pyram
In one respect, the task resembled that of building the inte
casings; both operations necessitated the introduction

closely fitting stones into a core otherwise composed of rough masonry. Since, however, the corridors and chambers occupied so small a portion of the whole Pyramid, they may have been built almost independently of the rest of the work. Subsidiary ramps, capable of being dismantled in a few hours, could have been erected at any stage convenient, so that blocks could be taken to a considerably greater height than the level of the course under construction. In this way, the men employed would have time to complete their work on the interior of the Pyramid before the surrounding courses of core-masonry had risen to such a height that it would become necessary to roof the corridor and chambers; afterwards, access to the interior would not be possible until the foot-hold embankment or supply-ramp covering the northern face of the Pyramid had been lowered to the level of the entrance. As a further aid, the stones would be carefully prepared before they were required by the builders; the roofing slabs of the King's Chamber in the Great Pyramid, for instance, were fitted together on the ground and numbered so that, when they were taken to their final position, they could be reassembled with the minimum delay. The sarcophagus, portcullises and, in the Great Pyramid only, the plug-blocks would be introduced before the walls of the chamber, slots or gallery in which they were to rest had been fully built.

It must be emphasised that the foregoing attempt to reconstruct the methods used by the Pyramid builders differs in many important respects from the views expressed by some authorities.[1] The main divergence of opinion arises in connection with the number and arrangement of the ramps—a problem on which archæological investigation has not yet revealed sufficiently clear evidence to enable positive deduc-

---

[1] Petrie, "The Building of a Pyramid" in *Ancient Egypt*, 1930, Pt. II, pp. 33-9; N. F. Wheeler, "Pyramids and their Purpose" in *Antiquity*, Vol. IX (1935), p. 172-4.

tions to be made. Petrie, in one of his last essays on this subject, stated his belief that the casing-stones of the Great Pyramid had been taken to their respective courses with their outer faces already dressed, and that they were laid in position from the inside. The casing would thus have been laid first in every course, and the core have been filled in afterwards. By such a method, as Petrie pointed out, only one ramp would have been required and three faces of the Pyramid would have been finished as soon as their casing stones had been laid. In support of his views Petrie wrote: "There is a small difference of angle between the [casing-] blocks at their junction, proving that the faces have not been even smoothed since being built together."[1] There is certainly no good reason for doubting the accuracy of Petrie's observations or his deductions in so far as they apply to the method adopted for laying the few casing-stones of the Great Pyramid which have survived to the present day, but his general conclusion that the same procedure would have been followed when laying all the casing-stones of the building is open to grave objections. All the stones in question stand on the lowest course; beneath them lies a smooth pavement of Tura limestone which also projects outwards beyond the Pyramid to a width of about two feet. It would have been impossible to lay these stones from the outer side without damaging the fringe of the pavement which was to remain exposed. Likewise, it would have been undesirable to dress the lower edge of stones after they had been placed in position: the surface of the pavement would inevitably have been chipped and scratched. Moreover, these particular casing-stones may well have been laid before the core in order to define the size and orientation of the Pyramid base. Slight adjustments in the setting of the stones could so much more easily be made if they were free at both back and front; any error at the base would result in the faulty orienta-

[1] Petrie, *op. cit.*, p. 34.

tion of the whole monument, and might destroy its regularity
of form. If Petrie could have shown that casing-blocks on a
higher level than the bottom course in any Pyramid were laid
at an angle to each other, his argument would have carried
greater weight. Furthermore, the evidence in favour of the
method of laying casing-stones from the front is very considerable. Several unfinished works testify that it was the
technique employed by Egyptian builders from the inception
of megalithic masonry until the latest times. An example
exists even in a Pyramid, namely the Pyramid of Mycerinus,
where the limestone which cased the upper portion was
completely dressed, but the granite casing lower down was
left partly in the rough, thus marking the point where work
on the monument came to a premature end. Laying masonry
from the front, however, necessitated both leaving the outer
faces of the stones in the rough until they had been placed in
position and the erection of embankments against the outer
face of the course previously laid, which would have involved,
in the case of a Pyramid, building embankments against all
four faces.

A suggestion regarding the construction of Pyramids which
owes its origin to Richard Lepsius was that their size was
determined by the length of their owner's reign—the so-
called accretion theory. Undoubtedly some Pyramids, notably
the Step Pyramid of Zoser and the Meidum Pyramid, underwent successive enlargements and some, probably including
the Great Pyramid and the Pyramid of Mycerinus, were
altered internally while under construction, but changes in the
original design were, on the whole, exceptional. If length of
reign had possessed any direct bearing on the dimensions of
a Pyramid, it might have been expected that Pepi II, who
occupied the throne for about ninety-four years, would have
built a Pyramid several times larger than that of Mycerinus,
who reigned only about eighteen years, or that Cheops in a

reign of about twenty-three years would have failed to build a Pyramid equal to that of Unas, who is believed to have ruled for thirty years. Clearly, therefore, the length of a king's reign did not necessarily affect the size of his Pyramid; the determining considerations seem rather to have been his personal inclinations, his power and the religious beliefs current in his time.

In the face of so many unknown or unconfirmed factors, speculations regarding the number of men required for building one of the larger Pyramids and the time needed for the work may perhaps appear vain. Certainly, any estimate based on the evidence now available must lack precision and can only serve to convey an approximate idea. Herodotus claims to have been informed that the Great Pyramid was built in twenty years. Levies numbering one hundred thousand men, he says, were employed for "periods of three months" on transporting the stones from the quarry to the Pyramid.[1] Herodotus seems to have intended his readers to understand that the aggregate of men engaged annually was 400,000—four separate groups of 100,000, each group being employed for three months in the year. Such a number would, however, have been unnecessarily large, as a simple mathematical calculation will demonstrate. If the estimated total of 2,300,000 separate blocks in the Pyramid is approximately correct, the average number of blocks to be transported annually for twenty years would have been 115,000. The mean weight of the blocks is about $2\frac{1}{2}$ tons, a weight which Petrie believed could have been handled by a gang of eight men.[2] Assuming that Petrie was right and that only 100,000 men were employed in a year, each gang would have been required to move ten blocks in twelve weeks. Such a task would almost certainly have been within the ability of a gang, bearing in mind

[1] Herodotus, II, 124.
[2] Petrie, The Pyramids and Temples of Gizeh, p. 210.

that the distance to be traversed, especially by the core blocks, was not very great. Moreover, as Petrie pointed out, the work could have been done during the inundation season, between the end of July and the end of October, when the land could not be cultivated and the majority of the population would have been idle.

There can be little doubt but that, in addition to the 100,000 men levied annually for the special purpose of transporting the blocks of the Great Pyramid, other workers were engaged in building the Pyramid. These men, consisting of skilled masons and an attendant body of labourers, were continuously employed during the whole year preparing and laying the blocks and erecting or dismantling the ramps and foothold embankments. They lived, it must be presumed, in the buildings found by Petrie lying west of the Pyramid of Chephren. About 4,000 men, according to Petrie's estimate, could have been housed in these barracks, and that figure would therefore represent the total number of permanent workers. The chips of stone cast away by the masons were dumped over the side of the cliffs both north and south of the Pyramid. Commenting on the size of the dumps, Petrie wrote: "They are probably equal in bulk to more than half of the Pyramid."[1]

But for an unfortunate chance which renders its value problematical, a significant clue might have been forthcoming from the Pyramid of Meidum, where some blocks marked with royal dates were discovered. The highest of these dates was "year 17," which, it must be supposed, refers to the reign of Seneferu. In the course of that reign, however, the method of counting regnal years appears to have been changed from the older system, whereby the kings computed their reigns in terms of the biennial census of their property, to an annual unit of reckoning. Thus "year 17" may have been composed of some census years (each of two calendrical years) and some

[1] Petrie, *op. cit.*, p. 213.

single years; the number of each kind being unspecified. Even
if the exact composition of the date could be determined, it
would still be necessary to discover in which year of the king's
reign work was begun before deductions concerning the time
taken to build the Pyramid could be drawn.

A complete solution to such problems as the methods used
by the Pyramid builders, the number of men employed and
the time required for the task would undoubtedly shed a very
valuable sidelight on technical development in ancient times,
but it would hardly be likely to provide an answer to an even
more interesting question, namely why the early Egyptian
kings should have chosen to construct their tombs in the
pyramidal form. Before this question is considered, however,
the derivation of the name is worth examining. In Egyptian,
this type of tomb was called *m(e)r*, a name which has never
yet been suspected of concealing any descriptive significance.
The word "Pyramid" owes its origin to the Greek *pyramis*,
plural *pyramides*, for which a satisfactory Egyptian derivation
has often been sought, but in vain. A geometrical term *per-em-
us* (literally "what goes [straight] up from the *us*"—a word of
uncertain meaning), which embodies the requisite consonants,
is used to indicate the vertical height of a Pyramid in an
Egyptian mathematical treatise.[1] To suppose, however, that
pyramis was derived from *per-em-us* would imply that the
Greeks either mistook the meaning of the Egyptian term or,
for reasons unknown, deliberately named the whole structure
after a part, by the linguistic process known as synecdoche.
In the absence of any more convincing explanation, it seems
better to regard *pyramis* as a purely Greek word which had no
etymological connection with the Egyptian language. An
exactly similar word exists with the meaning "wheaten cake,"
and the suggestion has been made that the early Greeks used
this word humorously as a name for the Egyptian monu-

[1] The Rhind Mathematical Papyrus in the British Museum.

ments,[1] possibly because, when seen from a distance, they resembled large cakes. The word *obeliskos*, which in addition to meaning an obelisk also means a "little spit" or "skewer," furnishes another example of the same kind of process of thought whereby the Greeks, instead of borrowing a foreign word, jocularly adapted a descriptive word of their own to name an object which had no exact parallel in their own country.

Ludwig Borchardt believed that the true Pyramid had evolved from the step type of Pyramid as a simple architectural development, in the same way as the latter, in its turn, had grown out of the earlier Mastaba.[2] Visible evidence of the transformations appeared to him to be provided, in one instance, by the Step Pyramid of Zoser, where the outline of one end of the original Mastaba could still be seen on the southern face, and, in the other instance, by the Pyramid of Meidum, where a stepped structure had been converted into a true Pyramid by filling the steps with masonry so that the sides sloped at one continuous angle from top to bottom. The two monuments in question seem undoubtedly to have undergone the transformations ascribed to them, but before it could be claimed that the later form was merely a development inspired by artistic motives, it would be necessary to show that the monument in its final form was the first known example of its kind. Such a claim cannot now be advanced for the Step Pyramid because a brick tomb of a step pattern dating from the Ist Dynasty has recently been found by W. B. Emery at Sakkara.[3] It is highly improbable that the claim for the Meidum Pyramid is based on any more secure foundation.

[1] W. G. Waddell, *Herodotus*, II, p. 139.

[2] L. Borchardt, *Die Entstehung der Pyramide* (Berlin, 1928).

[3] W. B. Emery, "A Preliminary Report on the Architecture of the Tomb of Nebetka," in *Annales du Service des Antiquités*, Vol. XXXVIII (1938), pp. 455-9. Reisner (*Tomb Development*, p. 123) tentatively ascribed the Layer Pyramid of Zawiyet el-Aryan to the IInd Dynasty, but the evidence is not conclusive.

The Bent Pyramid, although rhomboidal in its finished form, was almost certainly designed as a true Pyramid, but was slightly modified when half built, either in order to hasten its completion or because its inexperienced builders feared lest the steep slope intended for its sides should jeopardise the solidity of the whole structure.[1] Its owner is not known with certainty, but there are good reasons for believing that this tomb was built before the Meidum Pyramid, at least in its final form, had been erected. The inward incline of its casing-stones, for instance, is paralleled by a similar slant in the casing-stones of the Step Pyramid; the outermost casing-stones of the Meidum Pyramid, on the other hand, are laid flat, and in that respect agree with subsequent Pyramids. Possibly the Meidum Pyramid marks the transition from the earlier to the later method of building, for its inner layers of casing-stones are laid in slanting courses.

If it be admitted that the Bent Pyramid was originally designed as a true Pyramid and that it was built before the Meidum Pyramid, an explanation of the pyramidal shape must be sought elsewhere than in the sphere of architectural evolution; a further problem also arises, for a reason is required to account for the reversion to a step Pyramid design in the Meidum Pyramid, as it was first constructed, after the builders of the Bent Pyramid had introduced the true pyramidal form. A possible solution to the second problem will be offered at a later stage in the present discussion.

J. H. Breasted, writing about the importance of the Pyramid, stated: "The pyramidal form of the king's tomb was of the most sacred significance. The king was buried under the very symbol of the Sun-god which stood in the holy of holies in the Sun-temple at Heliopolis, a symbol upon which, from the

[1] It may not be without significance that its companion at Dahshur—possibly the next true Pyramid to be built—was set at the same angle as the upper part of the Bent Pyramid.

day when he created the gods, he was accustomed to manifest himself in the form of a Phœnix; and when in mountainous proportions the Pyramid rose above the king's sepulchre, dominating the royal city below and the valley beyond for many miles, it was the loftiest object which greeted the Sungod in all the land and his morning rays glittered on its shining summit long before he scattered the shadows in the dwellings of humbler mortals below."[1] If, as Breasted believed, the Pyramid was an enlarged copy of the solar symbol kept in the temple of Heliopolis, it follows that the symbol, probably a stone object, was pyramidal in shape, but what did it represent? Only one answer suggests itself: the rays of the sun shining down on earth. A remarkable spectacle may sometimes be seen in the late afternoon of a cloudy winter day at Giza. When standing on the road to Sakkara and gazing westwards at the Pyramid plateau, it is possible to see the sun's rays striking downwards through a gap in the clouds at about the same angle as the slope of the Great Pyramid. The impression made on the mind by the scene is that the immaterial prototype and the material replica are here ranged side by side.[2]

Is it necessary to suppose with Breasted that the Pyramid was merely intended as a copy of the solar symbol in the temple of Heliopolis? Could it not also have possessed an independent significance? The Pyramid texts often describe the king as mounting to heaven on the rays of the sun. Spell 508 of these texts, for instance, reads: "I have trodden those thy rays as a ramp under my feet whereon I mount up to that my mother, the living Uræus on the brow of Ra." Again, Spell 523 reads: "Heaven hath strengthened for thee the rays

[1] J. H. Breasted, *The Development of Religion and Thought in Ancient Egypt*, p. 72.
[2] Alexandre Moret, *Le Nil*, p. 203, makes the following observation: "These great triangles forming the sides of the Pyramids seem to fall from the sky like the beams of the sun when its disk, though veiled by storm, pierces the clouds and lets down to earth a ladder of rays."

of the sun in order that thou mayest lift thyself to heaven as the eye of Ra." The temptation to regard the Pyramid as the means whereby the dead king could ascend to heaven seems irresistible. Such an explanation would give the Pyramid a practical purpose entirely in keeping with the other elements in the royal mortuary complex. Moreover, the Pyramid would not be the only material representation of an intangible object included in the king's funerary equipment; the wooden boats placed near the Pyramid in pits lined with Tura limestone were representations of the immaterial boat in which the dead king would traverse the sky in company with the Sun-god. The underlying conception in each case was the principle of substitution: a model, whether it be a stone statue of a person or a scene carved in relief, was thought to possess all the virtues of the actual object which it represented. Size was not a matter of primary importance to the efficacy of the substitute, and herein may be one reason for the rapid decline in the dimensions of the Pyramid after the time of Cheops and Chephren.

In the light of the foregoing hypothesis, it may be worth while to glance again at the Egyptian word for a Pyramid; perhaps it may yet be shown to possess a significance which has so far not been noticed. The Egyptians frequently designated the constituent parts of their temples and sacred enclosures by names which were indicative of their particular functions. In the temple of Heliopolis, for example, the building which housed the solar symbol, called in Egyptian *benben*, was named the "House of the Benben." The tomb, it has already been remarked, was called the "Castle of Eternity." A number of different elements within the Pyramid complex also possessed descriptive names: the Causeway was called the "Entrance of the Haul" (*ra-sta*), meaning the way along which the sledges bearing the body of the dead king and his personal possessions would be hauled; the false door in the sanctuary was named the "Entrance of the House" (*ra-per*) and the sacred boat the "Divine Barque." *M(e)r*, a Pyramid, could belong to the same class of name if it could be established that it was a compound consisting of the prefix *m*, found in Egyptian to convey the meaning "place," and a known root composed of the two consonants *ʿr*, which means "to ascend," "to go up": *m(e)r* would then mean the "Place of Ascension." The disappearance of the *ʿ* (which corresponds with the *ayin* of the Semitic languages), particularly when it occurs in connection with the consonant *m* in the formation of a word, would not be without parallel, but the case cannot be considered as proved while it is only possible to offer a negative argument. Until, therefore, more positive evidence for the derivation is forthcoming, the most that can be claimed for the interpretation "Place of Ascension" is that it does not run counter to known philological laws and its appositeness is such as to create a predisposition in its favour.

A further point of interest is suggested by the hieroglyphic spelling of the word *ʿr*. It was the regular practice of the Egyptians when writing to add a sign, the so-called determinative of sense sign, to the consonantal spelling of a word; vowels were never written. The sense sign attached to *ʿr* is ⌂, which has generally been regarded as a double stairway, but it could equally well have been a representation of a step Pyramid, for the Egyptians, when depicting an object, always gave a full view, either from the front or from the side. The technique of drawing a three-quarter view was unknown to them. Thus, the determinative of *m(e)r* is always △, which represents the front view of a true Pyramid surrounded by a rectangular enclosure wall. If ⌂ does represent a step Pyramid, then it must have been chosen as the determinative of the word *ʿr*, because step Pyramids were particularly associated with the idea of ascending. Again the Pyramid texts seem to offer the explanation. Spell 267 reads; "A staircase to heaven is laid for him (i.e. the king) so that he may climb up to heaven thereby." The same conception is repeated almost literally in Spell 619. Both types of Pyramid would therefore admit, essentially, of a single explanation, and the variation in their form would have resulted from their possessing different prototypes.

The Egyptians were not the only ancient people of the Middle East who believed that heaven and the gods might be reached by ascending a high building; a kindred trend of thought prevailed in Mesopotamia. At the centre of any city in Assyria or Babylonia lay a sacred area occupied by the temple complex and a royal palace. Within the temple complex was a high brick tower known as the Ziggurat. Describing the Ziggurat of Babylon—the supposed origin of the Biblical Tower of Babel—Herodotus states:

"In the middle of the precinct there was a tower of solid masonry, a furlong in length and breadth, upon which was raised a second tower, and on that a third, and so on up to eight. The ascent to the upper towers is made on the outside, round all the towers. . . . On the topmost tower there is a spacious temple, and inside the temple stands a great bed covered with fine bed-clothes, with a golden table by its side. There is no statue of any kind set up in the place, nor is the chamber occupied of nights by any one but a single native woman who, as the Chaldeans, the priests of this god, affirm, is chosen for himself by the deity out of all the women of the land. They also declare—but I for my part do not credit it— that the god comes down in person into this chamber, and sleeps upon the couch."[1]

Ziggurats, like the Pyramids, were given individual names[2]; the Ziggurat of Sippar, for example, was called the "House of the Staircase of the bright Heaven"—a name which itself

---

[1] *Herodotus*, I, 181-2 (Rawlinson's translation).
[2] See pp. 243-4.

emphasises that the building was considered as a link between heaven and earth. The resemblance between the two edifices does not, however, extend to sepulchral realms, for the Ziggurat was certainly not a tomb, whereas every Pyramid fulfilled that purpose.

Owing to the paucity of written evidence, any attempt to reconstruct the historical and religious background of the Pyramids is fraught with hazards and, at best, can yield only inconclusive results. Nevertheless, the problem is one which has to be faced all too often when endeavouring to compose from archæological remains a mental picture of the course of events in the remote past. In many ways, it is a task which is closely analogous to that of solving a jig-saw puzzle: many pieces from diverse sections of the puzzle may be joined into separate little units long before the links can be discovered, and how often it occurs that some unexpected turn in the pattern results in the necessity for a readjustment in the solver's preconceived idea of the relationship between the various units! In archæological interpretation, the framework of the puzzle is generally provided by certain events which can be dated within narrow limits, but large interstices remain to be filled, partly with concrete facts and partly with conjecture; as fresh information becomes available either from excavation or from a reconsideration of the material already accessible more of the interstices will be filled, but also some of those which had formerly been completed will be found to have been arranged in an incorrect order and suitable adjustments will require to be made.

If the simile be applied to the early Egyptian royal tombs, the three main pieces of the puzzle are the Mastaba, the step Pyramid and the true Pyramid; the problem is to try to fill up the gaps which separate these three pieces. Between the Mastaba and the two kinds of Pyramid lay a wide gulf; the former, as a representation of the king's residence, carried no implication that the After-life would be spent anywhere else than in the tomb and the latter signified that access to the celestial regions was anticipated. The precise point in history when the change in style of tomb occurred cannot yet be determined, but the extreme limits seem to be the middle of the Ist Dynasty and the beginning of the IIIrd Dynasty; Aha and Jer, assuming that they occupied the tombs at Sakkara ascribed to them, were buried in Mastabas, but Zoser built a step Pyramid. Did this alteration in the pattern of the tomb result from some change in religious creed? If so a fusion of the two creeds seems to have been achieved by the time of Zoser, because, in addition to his Pyramid, he provided himself with a Mastaba (the South Mastaba), presumably as a cenotaph. Whether this fusion had been preceded by a bitter sacerdotal struggle or whether it was a peaceful development is not known; once the fusion had taken place both creeds continued to exist in harmony, and the kings must have intended to divide their After-life between the tomb and the celestial regions.

Unfortunately the Layer Pyramid and the Unfinished Pyramid, both at Zawiyet el-Aryan, are too badly destroyed or too incomplete to provide any evidence beyond the bare fact that other kings of the IInd-IIIrd Dynasties, besides Zoser, built step Pyramids. There is nothing, however, to show that they also built, or ever intended to build, supplementary Mastabas. The Bent Pyramid at Dahshur, until its ownership has been proved, can hardly be taken into consideration, but none of its architectural features would suggest that it belonged to a later date than the Pyramid of Meidum. Seneferu built two Pyramids, one at Meidum and the other at Dahshur, the former being completed as a step Pyramid before it was transformed into a true Pyramid, and the latter being designed from the start as a true Pyramid; it seems clear therefore that Seneferu's original intention was to have one Pyramid of each type, and thus provide himself with both the older and the newer fashions of tomb. Again the question arises whether the transition to the newer kind of tomb was effected without friction; subsequent events suggest that the passage was not entirely smooth. Meidum lay twenty-eight miles from Dahshur, and some reason may well have existed for placing the two tombs so far apart. Can this reason have been that Seneferu entertained fears lest friction should occur between the priesthood of the step Pyramid and the priesthood of the true Pyramid? The ultimate transformation of the Meidum Pyramid into a true Pyramid may have been rendered necessary by the king's realisation that the two factions would never become reconciled, and his knowledge of the dangers to his own fortunes in the After-life which might result from rivalry between two priestly organisations, only one of which could become the custodian of his body. By his conversion of the Meidum Pyramid into a true Pyramid instead of demolishing it, Seneferu not only provided himself with a cenotaph, in case some harm should befall his tomb at Dahshur, but also gave visible proof of the eclipse of the step Pyramid cult.

With the supremacy of the new cult well established, Cheops proceeded to build the greatest and most geometrically true of all Pyramids, a monument which would probably have gained a place in an even shorter list of "Wonders" than the chosen seven. Its companion, the Pyramid of Chephren, was but little inferior in size, and royal support for the new cult might therefore appear to have passed unbroken from father to son. Between these two rulers, however, the throne was occupied by Dedefra, a son of Cheops by a secondary wife. Two points about his tomb attract notice: first, it was not built at Giza, where ample space would have been available, but at Abu Roash, five miles away, and secondly its substructure was entirely different from that of any Pyramid built after the Unfinished Pyramid at Zawiyet el-Aryan and the Step Pyramid of Zoser. Can it be that Dedefra originally intended to build a step Pyramid, possibly in return for assistance given to him by the priesthood of that cult when he secured the throne? This question must remain unanswered, for scarcely a stone of the superstructure lies in position and the possibility that the pattern of the substructure was dictated by the nature of the rock cannot be overlooked.

After Dedefra, the only ruler of the Old Kingdom to abandon the true Pyramid was Shepseskaf. The simplest explanation for this retrogression is that he was prompted by a desire to break away from the oppressive influence of the priests of the Sun-god at Heliopolis, and the Mastaba would supply all the needs of a non-celestial After-life. His wife, Khentikaues, followed his example, erecting her Mastaba near the Valley Building of her father Mycerinus, but the Heliopolitan cult was again in the ascendant before her death and, with the foundation of the Vth Dynasty, its triumph was complete. Years of struggle may, however, have led to the adoption of a more compromising attitude on the part of its priests, for the Pyramid texts prove that, by the end of the Vth Dynasty at least, all the earlier doctrines of the After-life had been preserved regardless of their many contradictions. No marked change in Pyramid construction occurred during the VIth Dynasty. Thenceforth, although the Pyramid was retained, it is doubtful whether it possessed any significance except that of being the conventional pattern of the royal tomb.

POSTSCRIPT

While this book was in proof, a report appeared in the Press [1] that Abdessalam Hussein Effendi, excavating at Dahshur for the Service des Antiquités, had discovered in the Bent Pyramid some blocks bearing the name of Seneferu. A full appreciation of the significance of the discovery must await the publication of the excavator's own report, but it now seems evident that this Pyramid belonged to Seneferu and not to Huni, his predecessor. If the Meidum Pyramid was Seneferu's second Pyramid, as appears likely, the northern stone Pyramid at Dahshur must have belonged to another king, whose identity future excavation may be expected to reveal.

[1] *Illustrated London News,* 22nd March and 5th April, 1947:

MAJOR PYRAMIDS OF THE OLD AND MIDDLE KINGDOMS

Name of King	Dynasty	Location	Approximate Dimensions of Base	Name of Pyramid
Zoser (Step Pyramid)	III (c.2815 B.C.)	Sakkara	411 ft. E.-W. by 358 ft. N.-S.	—
Kha-bau (?) (Layer Pyramid)	III (?)	Zawiyet el-Aryan	276 ft. sq.	—
Neb-ka (?) (Unfinished Pyramid)	III (?)	Zawiyet el-Aryan	—	The Pyramid: "Neb-ka (?) is a star"
Huni (?) [1] (Bent Pyramid)	III	Dahshur	620 ft. sq.	—
Seneferu	IV (c.2690 B.C.)	Meidum	473 ft. sq.	The Southern Pyramid: "Seneferu gleams"
Seneferu (?) [1]	IV	Dahshur	719 ft. sq.	The Pyramid: "Seneferu gleams"
Cheops (Great Pyramid)	IV	Giza	756 ft. sq.	The Pyramid: "Cheops is one belonging to the horizon"
Dedefra .	IV	Abu Roash	320 ft. sq.	—
Chephren .	IV	Giza	708 ft. sq.	The Pyramid: "Great is Chephren"
Mycerinus	IV	Giza	356 ft. sq.	The Pyramid: "Mycerinus is divine"
Userkaf .	V (c.2560 B.C.)	Sakkara	231 ft. sq.	The Pyramid: "Pure are the places of Userkaf"
Sahura	V	Abu Sir	257 ft. sq.	The Pyramid: "The Ba of Sahura gleams"
Neferirkara	V	Abu Sir	360 ft. sq.	The Pyramid: "Neferirkara has become a Ba"
Neferefra .	V	Abu Sir (?)	—	The Pyramid: "The Bas of Neferefra are divine"
Niuserra .	V	Abu Sir	274 ft. sq.	The Pyramid: "The Places of Niuserra are enduring"
Isesi .	V	Sakkara	270 ft. sq.	The Pyramid: "Isesi is beautiful"
Unas .	V	Sakkara	220 ft. sq.	The Pyramid: "Beautiful are the places of Unas"

See, however, Postscript opposite.

Name of King	Dynasty	Location	Approximate Dimensions of Base	Name of Pyramid
Teti .	VI (c.2420 B.C.)	Sakkara	210 ft. sq.	The Pyramid: "Lasting are the places of Teti"
Pepi I .	VI	Sakkara	250 ft. sq.	The Pyramid: "Pepi is established and beautiful"
Merenra .	VI	Sakkara	263 ft. sq.	The Pyramid: "Merenra gleams and is beautiful"
Pepi II .	VI	Sakkara	245 ft. sq.	The Pyramid: "Pepi is established and alive"
Ibi . .	VII (c.2294 B.C.)	Sakkara	102 ft. sq.	—
Neb-hepet-Ra Menthu-hetep	XI (c.2132 B.C.)	Deir el-Bahri	70 ft. sq.	The Pyramid: "Glorious are the places of Neb-hepet-Ra"
Seankh-ka-Ra Menthu-hetep	XI	Western Thebes	Unfinished	—
Amenemhat I	XII (c.1990 B.C.)	Lisht	296 ft. sq.	The Pyramid: "Amenemhat is high and beautiful"
Senusret I	XII	Lisht	352 ft. sq.	The Pyramid: "The one who is associated with the places of Senusret"
Amenemhat II	XII	Dahshur	263 ft. sq.	—
Senusret II	XII	Illahun	347 ft. sq.	The Pyramid: "Senusret is strong"
Senusret III	XII	Dahshur	350 ft. sq.	The Pyramid: "Senusret is at rest"
Amenemhat III (?)	XII	Dahshur	342 ft. sq.	—
Amenemhat III	XII	Hawara	334 ft. sq.	The Pyramid: "Amenemhat has become a Ba"(?).
Queen Sebekneferu (?)	XII	Mazghuna	—	—
Amenemhat IV (?)	XII	Mazghuna	—	—
Khenjer .	XIII (c.1777 B.C.)	Sakkara		

BIBLIOGRAPHY

Introduction

J. H. Breasted, *The Development of Religion and Thought in Ancient Egypt*. New York, 1912.

É. Drioton and J. Vandier, *Les Peuples de l'Orient Méditerranéen* (*L'Égypte*). Paris, 1938.

W. B. Emery, *The Tomb of Hemaka*. Cairo, 1938.

A. Erman, *A Handbook of Egyptian Religion* (English translation by A. S. Griffith). London, 1907.

A. Erman, *Die Religion der Ägypter*. Berlin, 1934.

A. H. Gardiner, *The Attitude of the Ancient Egyptians to Death and the Dead*. Cambridge, 1935.

A. H. Gardiner, *The Contendings of Horus and Seth* (The Chester Beatty Papyri, No. I). Oxford, 1931.

H. Kees, *Totenglauben und Jenseits-Vorstellungen der alten Ägypter*. Leipzig, 1926.

M. Meunier, *Plutarque, Isis et Osiris*. Paris, 1924.

K. Sethe, *Übersetzung und Kommentar zu den altägyptischen Pyramiden-texten*. Glückstadt.

K. Sethe, *Urgeschichte und älteste Religion der Ägypter*. Leipzig, 1930.

J. W. S. Sewell, *The Calendars and Chronology*, in S. R. K. Glanville, *The Legacy of Egypt*. Oxford, 1942.

G. Steindorff in K. Baedeker, *Guide to Egypt and the Sudan* (8th edition). Leipzig, 1929.

J. Vandier, *La Religion égyptienne*. Paris, 1944.

Chapter I

N. de G. Davies, *The Mastaba of Ptahhetep and Akhethetep*. London, 1900-01.

P. Duell, *The Mastaba of Mereruka*. Chicago, 1938.

W. B. Emery, *The Tomb of Hor-Aha*. Cairo, 1939.

H. Junker, *Giza, Grabungen auf dem Friedhof des Alten Reiches bei den Pyramiden von Giza*, Vols. I-V. Vienna, 1929-41.

J. E. Quibell, *The Tomb of Hesy*. Cairo, 1913.

G. A. Reisner, *The Development of the Egyptian Tomb down to the Accession of Cheops*. Cambridge, Massachusetts, 1935.

G. Steindorff, *Das Grab des Ti*. Leipzig, 1913.

CHAPTER II

E. Drioton and J.-P. Lauer, *Sakkarah, The Monuments of Zoser*. Cairo, 1939.

C. M. Firth, J. E. Quibell and J.-P. Lauer, *The Step Pyramid*. Cairo, 1935.

A. Hermann, *Führer durch die Altertümer von Memphis und Sakkara*. Berlin, 1938.

J. B. Hurry, *Imhotep*. Oxford, 1926.

J.-P. Lauer, *La Pyramide à degrés*. Cairo, 1936–39.

G. A. Wainwright, *The Sky Religion in Egypt*. Cambridge, 1938.

CHAPTER III

A. Barsanti, *Fouilles de Zaouiét el-Aryān* (1904–06), in *Annales du Service des Antiquités*, Vol. VIII, pp. 201–10. Cairo, 1907.

A. Barsanti, *Ouverture de la pyramide de Zaouiét el-Aryān*, in *Annales du Service des Antiquités*, Vol. II, pp. 92–4. Cairo, 1901.

L. Borchardt, *Die Entstehung der Pyramide an der Baugeschichte der Pyramide bei Mejdum nachgewiesen*. Berlin, 1928.

L. Borchardt, *Ein Königserlass aus Dahschur*, in *Zeitschrift für ägyptische Sprache*, Vol. XLII, pp. 1–11. Leipzig, 1905.

F. Ll. Griffith, *The Inscriptions of the Pyramid of Medum*, in W. M. F. Petrie, *Medum*. London, 1892.

G. Jéquier, *Douze ans de fouilles dans la nécropole memphite*. Neuchâtel, 1940.

G. Jéquier, *Rapport préliminaire sur les fouilles exécutées en 1924–5 dans la partie méridionale de la nécropole memphite*, in *Annales du Service des Antiquités*, Vol. XXV, pp. 71–5. Cairo, 1925.

G. Maspero and A. Barsanti, *Fouilles de Zaouiét el-Aryān* (1904–05), in *Annales du Service des Antiquités*, Vol. VII, pp. 257–86. Cairo, 1906.

Ch. Maystre, *Les Dates des pyramides de Snefrou*, in *Bulletin de l'Institut français d'archéologie orientale du Caire*, Vol. XXXV, pp. 89–98. Cairo, 1935.

W. M. F. Petrie, *A Season in Egypt*, 1887.   London, 1888.

W. M. F. Petrie, *The Pyramids and Temples of Gizeh*.   London, 1883.

W. M. F. Petrie, E. Mackay and G. A. Wainwright, *Meydum and Memphis (III)*.   London, 1910.

G. A. Reisner, *op. cit.*

G. A. Reisner and C. S. Fisher, *The Work of the Harvard University Museum*, in the *Bulletin of the Museum of Fine Arts*, No. 54. Boston, 1911.

A. Rowe, *Excavations of the Eckley B. Coxe, Jr., Expedition at Meydum, Egypt*, 1929–30, in the *Museum Journal*, Pennsylvania, March 1931.

H. Vyse and J. S. Perring, *Operations carried on at the Pyramid of Gizeh*.   London, 1840–42.

Chapter IV

J. Baikie, *The Sphinx*, in J. H. Hastings, *Encyclopædia of Religion and Ethics*, Vol. XI, pp. 767–8.   Edinburgh, 1920.

T. J. C. Baly, *Notes on the Ritual of Opening the Mouth*, in the *Journal of Egyptian Archæology*, Vol. 16, pp. 173–86.   London, 1930.

E. v. Bergmann, *Die Sphinx*, in *Zeitschrift für ägyptische Sprache*, Vol. XVIII, pp. 50–1.   Leipzig, 1880.

A. M. Blackman, *Some Notes on the Ancient Egyptian Practice of Washing the Dead*, in the *Journal of Egyptian Archæology*, Vol. V, pp. 117–24.   London, 1918.

A. M. Blackman, *The Rite of Opening the Mouth in Ancient Egypt and Babylonia*, in the *Journal of Egyptian Archæology*, Vol. X, pp. 47–59.   London, 1924.

L. Borchardt, *Einiges zur dritten Bauperiode der grossen Pyramide bei Gise*.   Berlin, 1932.

L. Borchardt, *Gegen die Zahlenmystik an der grossen Pyramide bei Gise*. Berlin, 1922.

L. Borchardt, *Längen und Richtungen der vier Grundkanten der grossen Pyramide bei Gise*.   Berlin, 1926.

BIBLIOGRAPHY

L. Borchardt and K. Sethe, *Zur Geschichte der Pyramiden*, in *Zeitschrift für ägyptische Sprache*, Vol. 30, pp. 83–106. Leipzig, 1892.

J. Capart and Marcelle Werbrouck, *Memphis à l'ombre des pyramides*. Brussels, 1930.

S. Clarke and R. Engelbach, *Ancient Egyptian Masonry*. Oxford, 1930.

J. H. Cole, *The Determination of the Exact Size and Orientation of the Great Pyramid of Giza* (*Survey of Egypt, Paper No. 39*). Cairo, 1925.

D. E. Derry, *Mummification*, in *Annales du Service des Antiquités*, Vol. XLII, pp. 235–65. Cairo, 1942.

É. Drioton, review of B. Grdseloff, *Das Reinigungszelt*, in *Annales du Service des Antiquités*, Vol. XL, pp. 1007–14. Cairo, 1940.

B. Grdseloff, *Das ägyptische Reinigungszelt*. Cairo, 1941.

U. Hölscher, *Das Grabdenkmal des Königs Chephren*. Leipzig, 1912.

G. Jéquier, *Manuel d'archéologie égyptienne*. Paris, 1924.

G. Jéquier, *Le Mastabat Faraoun*. Cairo, 1928.

H. Junker, *op. cit.*

H. Junker, *Von der ägyptischen Baukunst des Alten Reiches*, in *Zeitschrift für ägyptische Sprache*, Vol. 63, pp. 1–14. Leipzig, 1928.

W. M. F. Petrie, *The Pyramids and Temples of Gizeh*. London, 1883.

G. Rawlinson, *History of Herodotus* (Everyman's Library, edited by E. H. Blakeney). London, 1912.

G. A. Reisner, *op. cit.*

G. A. Reisner, *Hetep-Heres, Mother of Cheops*, in the *Bulletin of the Museum of Fine Arts*, Vols. XXV (Special Supplement), XXVI and XXX. Boston, 1927–32.

G. A. Reisner, *A History of the Giza Necropolis*, Vol. I. Cambridge, Massachusetts, 1942.

G. A. Reisner, *Mycerinus, The Temples of the Third Pyramid at Giza*. Cambridge, Massachusetts, 1931.

Selim Bey Hassan, *Excavations at Giza*. Oxford and Cairo, 1932–1943.

E. Baldwin Smith, *Egyptian Architecture as a Cultural Expression*. New York, 1938.

W. Stevenson Smith, *A History of Egyptian Sculpture and Painting in the Old Kingdom*. Oxford, 1946.

W. Stevenson Smith, *Old Kingdom Sculpture*, in the *American Journal of Archæology*, Vol. XLV, pp. 514–28. Concord, New Hampshire, 1941.

H. Vyse and J. S. Perring, *op. cit.*

W. G. Waddell, *An Account of Egypt by Diodorus Siculus*, in the *Bulletin of the Faculty of Arts, University of Egypt*, Vol. I, Parts 1 and 2. Cairo, 1933.

CHAPTER V

L. Borchardt, *Das Grabdenkmal des Königs Nefer-ir-ke-Re*. Leipzig, 1909.

L. Borchardt, *Das Grabdenkmal des Königs Ne-user-Re*. Leipzig, 1907.

L. Borchardt, *Das Grabdenkmal des Königs Sahu-Re*. Leipzig, 1910–13.

L. Borchardt, *Die Pyramiden, ihre Entstehung und Entwicklung*. Berlin, 1911.

F. W. von Bissing, *Das Rē-Heiligtum des Königs Ne-woser-Re*. Berlin, 1905.

É. Drioton, *Une représentation de la famine sur un bas-relief égyptien de la Vᵉ Dynastie*, in *Bulletin de l'Institut d'Égypte*, Vol. XXV, pp. 45–54. Cairo, 1942–43.

A. Erman, *The Literature of the Egyptians* (translated by A. M. Blackman). London, 1927.

C. M. Firth, *Excavations of the Department of Antiquities at Sakkara (1928–29)*, in *Annales du Service des Antiquités*, Vol. XXIX, pp. 64–70. Cairo, 1929.

C. M. Firth and B. Gunn, *The Teti Pyramid Cemeteries*. Cairo, 1926.

B. Grdseloff, *Deux inscriptions juridiques de l'Ancien Empire*, in *Annales du Service des Antiquités*, Vol. XLII, pp. 25–70. Cairo, 1942.

G. Jéquier, *La Pyramide d'Aba*. Cairo, 1935.

G. Jéquier, *La Pyramide d'Oudjebten*. Cairo, 1928.

G. Jéquier, *Le Monument funéraire de Pepi II*. Cairo, 1936–41.

G. Jéquier, *Les Pyramides des reines Neit et Apouit*. Cairo, 1933.

P. Lacau, *Suppressions des noms divins dans les textes de la chambre funéraire*, in *Annales du Service des Antiquités*, Vol. XXVI, pp. 69–81. Cairo, 1926.

P. Lacau, *Suppressions et modifications de signes dans les textes funéraires*, in *Zeitschrift für ägyptische Sprache*, Vol. 51, pp. 1–64. Leipzig, 1914.

E. Meyer, *Geschichte des Altertums*. Berlin, 1921.

Selim Bey Hassan, *Excavations at Sakkara* (1937–38), in *Annales du Service des Antiquités*, Vol. XXXVIII, pp. 519–20. Cairo, 1938.

K. Sethe, *Die altägyptischen Pyramidentexte*. Leipzig, 1908–22.

K. Sethe, *Übersetzung und Kommentar zu den altägyptischen Pyramiden-texten*. Glückstadt.

CHAPTER VI

E. R. Ayrton, C. T. Currelly and A. E. P. Weigall, *Abydos III*. London, 1904.

G. Brunton, *Lahun I, The Treasure*. London, 1920.

B. Bruyère, *Fouilles de l'Institut français du Caire,* Vol. VIII. Cairo, 1933.

H. Carter, *Report on the Tomb of Menthuhotep I* in the *Annales du Service des Antiquités*, Vol. II, pp. 201–5. Cairo, 1901.

Nina M. Davies, *Some Representations of Tombs from the Theban Necropolis*, in the *Journal of Egyptian Archæology*, Vol. 24, pp. 25–40. London, 1938.

W. F. Edgerton, *Chronology of the Twelfth Dynasty*, in the *Journal of Near Eastern Studies*, Vol. I, pp. 307–14. Chicago, 1942.

A. H. Gardiner and H. I. Bell, *The Name of Lake Moeris*, in the *Journal of Egyptian Archæology*, Vol. 29, pp. 37–50. London, 1943.

J. E. Gautier and G. Jéquier, *Fouilles de Licht*. Cairo, 1902.

B. Gunn, *The Name of the Pyramid-Town of Sesostris II*, in the *Journal of Egyptian Archæology*, Vol. 31, pp. 106–7. London, 1945.

B. Gunn and A. H. Gardiner, *The Expulsion of the Hyksos,* in the *Journal of Egyptian Archæology*, Vol. V, pp. 36–56. London, 1918.

H. R. Hall, *The Ancient History of the Near East*. London, 1913.

W. C. Hayes, *The Entrance Chapel of the Pyramid of Sen-Wosret I*, in the *Bulletin of the Metropolitan Museum of Art*, New York, 1934, Section 2, pp. 9–26.

BIBLIOGRAPHY

A. Lansing, *The Museum's Excavations at Lisht*, in the *Bulletin of the Metropolitan Museum of Art*, New York, Vol. XV (1920), pp. 3–11 ; Vol. XXI (1926), Section 2, pp. 33–40 ; Vol. XXIX (1934), Section 2, pp. 4–9.

A. M. Lythgoe, *The Treasure of Lahun*, in the *Bulletin of the Metropolitan Museum of Art*, December 1919 (Part II). New York, 1919.

A. C. Mace, *Excavations at Lisht*, in the *Bulletin of the Metropolitan Museum of Art*, November 1921, Part 2, pp. 5–19 ; December 1922, Part 2, pp. 4–18.

J. de Morgan, *Fouilles à Dahchour*. Vienna, 1895–1903.

E. Naville and H. R. Hall, *The XIth Dynasty Temple of Deir el-Bahari*. London, 1907–13.

P. E. Newberry, *The Co-regencies of Ammenemes III, IV and Sebeknofru*, in the *Journal of Egyptian Archæology*, Vol. 29, pp. 74–5. London, 1943.

W. M. F. Petrie, *Hawara, Biahmu and Arsinoe*. London, 1889.

W. M. F. Petrie, *Illahun, Kahun and Gurob*. London, 1890.

W. M. F. Petrie, *Kahun, Gurob and Hawara*. London, 1890.

W. M. F. Petrie, G. Brunton and M. A. Murray, *Lahun II*. London, 1923.

W. M. F. Petrie, G. A. Wainwright and E. Mackay, *The Labyrinth, Gerzeh and Mazghuneh*. London, 1912.

D. Randall-MacIver and A. C. Mace, *El-Amrah and Abydos*. London, 1902.

M. Raphael, *Nouveau nom d'une Pyramide d'un Amenemhēt*, in *Annales du Service des Antiquités*, Vol. XXXVII, pp. 79–80. Cairo, 1937.

G. A. Reisner, *Excavations at Napata, the Capital of Ethiopia*, in the *Bulletin of the Museum of Fine Arts*, Vol. XV, No. 89, pp. 25–34. Boston, 1917.

G. A. Reisner, *Known and Unknown Kings of Ethiopia*, in the *Bulletin of the Museum of Fine Arts*, Vol. XVI, No. 97, pp. 67–81. Boston) 1918.

G. A. Reisner, *The Royal Family of Ethiopia*, in the *Bulletin of the Museum of Fine Arts*, Vol. XXI, No. 124, pp. 12–27. Boston, 1923.

J. Vandier, *La Tombe de Nefer-Abou*. Cairo, 1935.

H. E. Winlock, *The Eleventh Egyptian Dynasty*, in the *Journal of Near Eastern Studies*, Vol. 2, No. 4, pp. 249–83. Chicago, 1943.

H. E. Winlock, *Excavations at Deir el-Bahri, 1911–1931*. New York, 1942.

H. E. Winlock, *Neb-hepet-Re Mentu-hotpe of the Eleventh Dynasty*, in the *Journal of Egyptian Archæology*, Vol. 26, pp. 116–19. London, 1940.

H. E. Winlock, *The Theban Necropolis in the Middle Kingdom*, in the *American Journal of Semitic Languages*, Vol. XXXII, pp. 1–37. Chicago, 1915.

H. E. Winlock, *The Tombs of the Kings of the Seventeenth Dynasty at Thebes*, in the *Journal of Egyptian Archæology*, Vol. X, pp. 217–77. London, 1924.

H. E. Winlock, *The Treasure of El-Lahun*. New York, 1934.

Chapter VII

L. Borchardt, *Die Entstehung der Pyramide an der Baugeschichte der Pyramide bei Mejdum nachgewiesen*. Berlin, 1928.

J. H. Breasted, *op. cit.*

S. Clarke and R. Engelbach, *op. cit.*

J. H. Cole, *op. cit.*

W. B. Emery, *A Preliminary Report on the First Dynasty Copper Treasure from North Saqqara*, in *Annales du Service des Antiquités*, Vol. XXXIX, pp. 427–37. Cairo, 1939.

B. Gunn, review of T. E. Peet, *The Rhind Mathematical Papyrus*, in the *Journal of Egyptian Archæology*, Vol. XII, pp. 123–37. London, 1926.

A. Lucas, *Ancient Egyptian Materials and Industries* (2nd Edition). London, 1934.

A. C. Mace, *Excavations at the North Pyramid of Lisht*, in the *Bulletin of the Metropolitan Museum of Art*, Vol. IX, p. 220. New York, 1914.

G. Maspero, *Note sur le pyramidion d'Amenemhait III à Dahchour*, in *Annales du Service des Antiquités*, Vol. III, pp. 206–8. Cairo, 1902.

BIBLIOGRAPHY

W. M. F. Petrie, *The Building of a Pyramid*, in *Ancient Egypt*, 1930 Part II, pp. 33–9. London.

W. M. F. Petrie, *The Pyramids and Temples of Gizeh*. London, 1883.

G. Rawlinson, *op. cit.*

A. Rowe, *op. cit.*

K. Sethe, *Übersetzung und Kommentar zu den altägyptischen Pyramiden-texten*. Glückstadt.

S. Smith, *A Babylonian Fertility Cult*, in the *Journal of the Royal Asiatic Society*, October 1928, pp. 849–75.

W. G. Waddell, *Herodotus*, Book II. London, 1939.

N. F. Wheeler, *Pyramids and their Purpose*, in *Antiquity*, Vol. IX, 172–85. Gloucester, 1935.

INDEX

INDEX